Praise for *Code Name Blue Wren*

"An entertaining story of cunning espionage."

us Reviews

"A must-read for espionage fans."

T0283911

hers Weekly

"*Code Name Blue Wren* might be the most mesmerizing spy story I've ever read. It shows how a brilliant manipulator secretly working for the Cubans finagled her way deep into the US military—and the anguish of the friends and family she so easily conned. Jim Popkin captures the brutal realities of modern espionage. I couldn't stop reading this."

—Mark Leibovich, author of *This Town* and *Thank You for Your Servitude*

"For espionage devotees, Jim Popkin's *Code Name Blue Wren* is a critical read. In great detail, Popkin explores the case of Ana Montes, who became a mole in the Defense Intelligence Agency for Cuban intelligence. A mole who was almost never caught thanks to years of incompetence by the FBI's counterspies. But thanks to the dogged persistence of a dedicated NSA analyst, who bypassed the FBI at great risk to her career, Montes was arrested shortly after the 9/11 attacks. Left in her wake was the likely death of an American Green Beret killed in action in El Salvador and the pro-American troops fighting alongside him."

—James Bamford, bestselling author of *The Puzzle Palace* and *Spyfail: Foreign Spies, Moles, Saboteurs, and the Collapse of America's Counterintelligence*

"Jim Popkin uncovers riveting details about one of the most damaging spy cases in US history, revealing new insights into the highly sensitive secrets that Ana Montes gave to her Cuban handlers. Through remarkably extensive interviews with her relatives and coworkers, he exposes not only what she did but why. This is the definitive history of how one of America's most highly regarded intelligence analysts betrayed her country, and how she almost got away with it."

—Pete Williams, former NBC News justice correspondent

"This spy tale reads like a new season of *Homeland*—except this Ice Queen's traitorous double-life was entirely real. Jim Popkin takes us deep into a long-ignored story of an intel officer who went rogue, spilling US secrets to Cuba, endangering US operatives, and tricking presidents and her own sister at the FBI in the process."

—Carol Leonnig, Pulitzer Prize–winning reporter at the *Washington Post* and author of *Zero Fail: The Rise and Fall of the Secret Service*

CODE NAME BLUE WREN

The True Story of America's
Most Dangerous Female Spy—
and the Sister She Betrayed

JIM POPKIN

HANOVER
SQUARE
PRESS

HANOVER
SQUARE
PRESS™

Recycling programs
for this product may
not exist in your area.

ISBN-13: 978-1-335-01755-0

Code Name Blue Wren

First published in 2023. This edition published in 2024 with revised text.

Copyright © 2023 by Jim Popkin

Copyright © 2024 by Jim Popkin, revised text edition.

Hanover Square Press
22 Adelaide St. West, 41st Floor
Toronto, Ontario M5H 4E3, Canada
HanoverSqPress.com
BookClubbish.com

Printed in U.S.A.

To Zach, Phoebe, and Ben

CODE NAME BLUE WREN

Table of Contents

INTRODUCTION

On a foggy Friday morning in Washington, DC, Ana Montes began her morning routine with precision. She washed, neatly made her bed, and slipped on a sensible sleeveless top in cornflower blue. The single forty-four-year-old government employee had carefully saved to buy her two-bedroom co-op apartment in DC's well-to-do Cleveland Park neighborhood, thanks in part to a last-minute cash gift from her father, and her tidy home was decorated with mementos from her extensive travels abroad. The bookshelves were crammed with hundreds of books—grad-school classics on Che Guevara and Karl Marx, paperback travel guides on the Caribbean, and nonfiction titles including *Spy Versus Spy: Stalking Soviet Spies in America* and *Your Memory: How It Works and How to Improve It*. Ana took one last look in the mirror at her no-fuss hair, short with bangs and a part, and locked the door behind her.

As she eased her red Toyota Echo into traffic, Ana had no idea it would be her last day of freedom for more than two decades. And no clue that she was being followed. On the half-hour drive to the headquarters of the Defense Intelligence Agency (DIA), where she worked as a top analyst for the intelligence arm of the US Department of Defense, unmarked cars tracked her every turn. Drivers operating in undercover teams from an FBI surveillance unit were keeping a close eye on Ana this momentous day, but always from a respectable distance.

DIA headquarters at Bolling Air Force Base was alive with activity. Privately, Ana had always called her employer the "war machine," and the moniker never fit more aptly. In the ten days since Bin Laden's terrorists had taken down the World Trade Center and dive-bombed the Pentagon with commercial planes, the entire US military was girding for battle. The DIA was in overdrive, getting set to help launch Operation Enduring Freedom to destroy Al Qaeda training camps and hammer the Taliban regime in Afghanistan. For DIA's war planners, the task couldn't be more personal. Saudi-born terrorist Hani Hanjour had deliberately piloted American Airlines Flight 77 into the west wall of the Pentagon on September 11, slamming into offices occupied by DIA staffers going about their morning routines. The resulting explosion killed seven DIA employees, all of whom worked for the agency's Office of the Comptroller. They were husbands and wives, mothers and fathers, all working as military accountants and budget managers. The 9/11 attacks marked the first time that DIA employees were killed in the line of duty in the United States, and was the largest single loss of life in the history of the DIA.

Amid the bustle that Friday morning, September 21, 2001, Ana eased through security and past the armed military officers in the lobby. She settled into her sixth-floor cubicle, #C6-146A. But she wouldn't be there long. A veritable squadron of FBI agents and twitchy DIA officers was hiding in nearby offices. They had even prepositioned a nurse, with an oxygen tank and CPR equipment, as a precaution. For this was the day that Ana Montes—the Pentagon's superstar analyst who had just won a prestigious fellowship at the CIA—was to be arrested and publicly exposed as a secret agent for Cuba.

The FBI had worried for years that the Cubans had placed a mole deep inside the upper echelons of the US Intelligence Community. But the special agent leading the case didn't have a name or even a government agency where the spy worked. The Bureau had, at first, clumsily hunted for an Unknown Subject, or UNSUB. Now, after years of digging on a case that the FBI had code-named "Blue Wren," the evidence was irrefutable that the Blue Wren UNSUB was, in fact, Ana Montes. In court-authorized break-ins of her apartment, the FBI had found secret communications with the Cubans on Ana's laptop, making it clear that Montes had revealed the true names of at least four covert US intelligence officers who had been operating in the shadows in Cuba. The Cubans had thanked Ana, noting ominously of one American spy she had outed, "We were waiting here for him with open arms."

Ana Montes briefed generals and a president, won national intelligence awards, and helped craft US government policy on Cuba. An acerbic personality known somewhat derisively in the halls of Washington as the "Queen of Cuba" for her mastery of Cuban military and political affairs, she led a dangerous double life. Montes leaked information that likely led to the death of an American Green Beret killed in action in El Salvador and the pro-American troops fighting alongside him. She freely shared the identities of hundreds of Americans working on Cuban intelligence matters around the globe. She revealed the existence of a stealth satellite so costly and highly classified that US government officials still won't utter its name more than two decades later. Montes's betrayal was considered so grave that Defense Department hard-liners wanted her to pay with her life.

But it wasn't just those treasonous acts that convinced America's top counterintelligence executive to go before Congress and label Montes "one of the most damaging spies in U.S. history." It was that she performed her duties so efficiently for so long, and in the process "compromised all Cuban-focused collection programs." That's a bureaucrat's way of saying that Montes trashed practically every scheme the US devised to eavesdrop on the Castro regime from the mid-1980s until 2001. What's more, Montes may have had access to as many top-secret files as the two worst traitors in modern American history—Aldrich "Rick" Ames at the CIA and Robert Hanssen at the FBI. She not only poisoned nearly every secret plan that American intelligence officials hatched in Cuba, but she also helped author some of the US government's own policies on the region. Montes was playing multiple hands of the deck at once, divulging highly classified information to an adversary with a long history of selling state secrets to our sworn enemies, and then turning around and influencing the way the US understood and countered the Cuban threat. As one despondent victim described it years after Ana's arrest, "my life's work went up like a bonfire set from within."

Ana Belén Montes is sometimes called the most important spy you've never heard of. Her relative obscurity is mostly a fluke of timing. When the FBI finally arrested her, the nation was still shell-shocked from the 9/11 terrorist attacks. That very week, President George W. Bush threatened an imminent attack on Afghanistan, the stock market ended its worst week in sixty-eight years, and fresh details emerged on the flight training the 9/11 hijackers received while living among us. In that environment, news that a senior Pentagon analyst had been charged as a Cuban spy mostly elicited a shrug. The *New York Times* played the story the following day on Page A7. *NBC Nightly News* and *The TODAY Show* didn't assign stories at all. For most Americans, the headlines came and went.

But now that Montes has pleaded guilty, completed her sentence, and is scheduled to be freed from federal prison in January 2023, her astounding story raises fresh questions. How did a well-educated daughter of a US military officer betray her country and pull off her magician's act for so long? What white lies did investigators tell, to protect sources, as they brought Ana to justice? What classified secrets did Montes divulge? Why has no one ever dared reveal the story of the stubborn National Security Agency analyst who risked her career to find the spy she knew was passing secrets to the enemy? The unsung federal worker, who escaped Cuba with her family when she was just a girl, later was humiliated and threatened with arrest for her actions to expose Castro's top spy.

Finally, why did Ana spy?

Yes, she suffered years of abuse at the hands of her domineering and violent father—a Freudian psychoanalyst of all things—leading the CIA in a "Secret" psychological profile to conclude that Ana's childhood "solidified her desire to retaliate against authoritarian figures." But motivations are rarely that clean, that trite. What cocktail of resentment, narcissism, and insecurity would convince someone to deliberately choose a life of endless betrayal and double-dealing?

Spying, it turns out, is a lot more Bourne than Bond. It's a lonely, tortured mess of a life. Yes, Ana donned wigs and used fake passports to travel to exotic locations, had affairs, learned to defeat polygraphs, and talked to Havana through ciphers and cutouts and high-frequency radio blasts. She even kept distress codes on water-soluble disappearing paper. It all sounds exciting, even romantic, until you learn that her handlers would go completely dark when they sensed danger. Ana often had no one to talk to, and the Cubans were not too keen on letting her ditch the spy game to start a family. No wonder Montes experienced crying spells and panic attacks, began showering compulsively, and eating only boiled potatoes. A lifetime of deceit took its toll.

Montes didn't just deceive her colleagues and country. Her betrayal was intensely personal. Her mercurial father was a former US Army colonel. The boyfriend she hoped to marry was, of all people, an American who ran a Cuban intelligence program for the Pentagon's US Southern Command. Two of Ana's siblings were active FBI employees; their spouses were true-blue FBI, too.

In fact, Ana's only sister, Lucy, worked her entire career for the Bureau. The highlight of her distinguished thirty-one-year career: helping the FBI flush Cuban spies out of the United States. As Ana was blithely disclosing the true names of CIA officers operating undercover in Havana, her sister, Lucy, joined a top-secret task force run by the FBI and NSA to rid Miami of Cuban spies. The arrest of Florida's "Wasp Network" of Cuban operatives would have a direct impact on Ana in Washington, limiting her lifeline to her handlers and triggering bouts of depression and anxiety.

Little did Lucy Montes know that the most notorious Cuban spy of all was sitting right next to her at baptisms, weddings, and funerals. This book is Lucy's story, too, and reflects her attempt to reclaim the name of an American family that once was known solely for its achievements in medicine, law enforcement, and academia. "We all grew up in the same household, we all had the same parents," Lucy said. "It never even entered my mind that my sister would be capable of such a thing, because we weren't raised that way." Ana Belén Montes, the ultimate target of operation Blue Wren, kept them all guessing for nearly seventeen years.

Chapter 1.

THE WORLD'S WORST SORORITY

"The place is a combat zone tucked inside of a madhouse."

—ANA MONTES LETTER FROM PRISON, 2013

Seventy-four-year-old Lynette Fromme lives in a dark-green Quonset hut in upstate New York. Her once-famous auburn hair has long since turned white. When the weather kicks up, the rain seeps through the domed roof of her converted shed and the wind batters its steel walls. Living in a drafty World War II outbuilding is far from perfect, but, candidly, neither is Lynette.[1]

More commonly known as "Squeaky" Fromme, Lynette is a living flashback of America's dark past. She will be forever remembered as the most loyal groupie of Charles Manson, the ex-con turned cult leader whose followers murdered actress Sharon Tate and at least eight others in Los Angeles in 1969. In a gesture of solidarity with "Charlie," Squeaky gouged a bloody X in her forehead and camped outside the LA courthouse where her leader and his flock were on trial for their lives. The Manson Family den mother kept vigil at Temple and Broadway for months.

Six years later, still under Charlie's spell, Squeaky attempted to assassinate President Gerald Ford. Dressed in a bloodred robe, she hid among the crowd as Ford walked through Capitol Park in Sacramento. She pulled a loaded Colt .45 on the president as he shook hands with supporters just two feet away. A Secret Service agent grabbed the semiautomatic and arrested Fromme, then twenty-six, before she could finish the job. "Can you believe it? It didn't go off," she shouted.[2]

Fromme received a life sentence and, over the next thirty-four years, shuffled between federal prisons from California to Florida to Kentucky. She was hardly the model inmate. In 1979 in Pleasanton, California, she bashed a fellow prisoner in the head with the claw end of a hammer. In 1987, she escaped from the lockup in Alderson, West Virginia. She spent a day and a half on the run in the frigid mountains of southern West Virginia before being captured on Christmas Day. At trial, she admitted she had broken out to see Manson, "my husband, my brother, my father, my son."[3]

By the summer of 1998, the Bureau of Prisons had had enough. They transferred Fromme to an intimate new prison-within-a-prison reserved for the nation's most dangerous women. Its antiseptic name doesn't reveal much, but the "Admin Unit" just outside Fort Worth, Texas, has become the Supermax for female offenders in the United States. A self-contained fortress on the grounds of the Carswell Federal Medical Center, the Admin Unit houses Al Qaeda terrorists, serial murderers, drug lords, and everyday psychotics. The ladies live together, typically just about twenty at a time, in the world's worst sorority house.

Lynette "Squeaky" Fromme still reveres Charles Manson and may not be a reliable witness for most things. But more than three decades behind bars has made her an expert on prison life. She was released from Carswell in 2009 and offered up her hard-earned observations reluctantly, and with precision.

Lynette recalls when Ana Montes first arrived at the Admin

Unit in late 2002.[4] She waited for the new girl to reveal herself. "She didn't kowtow to anybody," Lynette said in a series of on-the-record phone interviews. "And I've seen plenty of women come in and the scariest people in there, they picked to try to make friends with. And it's disastrous because these people know what they're doing and eventually a lot of these girls ended up getting beat up because it was artificial."

In her two-decade confinement at the Admin Unit, including seven years bunking near Squeaky, Montes tried to disassociate herself with her grim surroundings. "Nothing ever happens to me personally because I have neither friends nor enemies. I act like I'm neutral like Sweden or a rock in the corner," she once wrote to a friend. Lynette concurs. "She is the least talkative person that I probably ever met. She is the most taciturn person… She wasn't trying to ingratiate herself nor was she trying to be tough." Trying to blend in at Carswell was a sound plan. At various points, Ana's neighbors included a homemaker who strangled a pregnant woman and then used a kitchen knife to remove her unborn baby, a nurse who murdered four hospital patients by injecting them with massive amounts of adrenaline, and, more recently, the cocaine-smuggling wife of Mexican drug kingpin Joaquin "El Chapo" Guzmán.

With her grad-school books, yoga routine, and refined manners, Ana wouldn't seem to be much of a threat inside the Lizzie Borden ward of federal penitentiaries. And yet her jailers kept her on a tight leash. "Ana had a lot of rules on her," Squeaky Fromme said. "She had more restrictions than I did."

Let that sink in. Ana Montes, doctor's daughter and demure US government insider, lived under tighter prison restrictions than the gun-toting former lover of Charles Manson. Ana had morphed, seemingly overnight, from dutiful oldest child to dangerous American traitor.

Chapter 2.

TOPEKA

"Ana Belén Montes's childhood experiences, family relationships, and arrested psychological development contributed to her ideological and moral development and increased her vulnerability to recruitment by a foreign intelligence service."

—FROM A CLASSIFIED PROFILE OF MONTES WRITTEN BY THE CIA'S COUNTERINTELLIGENCE CENTER ANALYSIS GROUP

For newlyweds Alberto and Emilia Montes, February 28, 1957, was a day of joy and promise. Their first child, Ana Belén Montes, had just been born at the US Army Hospital in Nuremberg, West Germany, and was named for her two grandmothers. Ana had big brown eyes and gold curly hair and her parents couldn't stop posing with her. And smiling.

Understandably, Alberto was flying high. The son of a grocer who had only gotten as far as the sixth-grade[5], Alberto had beaten the odds by graduating Magna Cum Laude from a four-year college in Puerto Rico and then earning a government scholarship to attend Albany Medical College, one of the oldest medical schools in the nation. True, he had to borrow cash from a distant relative just to afford the plane ticket to upstate New York—the first airplane flight of his life. And in the summers, when his classmates were off relaxing, he had to hustle factory jobs at a Philadelphia dye mill to keep up with med-school bills.

But now here he was, a fresh-faced captain working in the dispensary for the United States Army at the sprawling Grafenwöhr Army Base in West Germany, with a baby, Ana, and a feisty, whip-smart twenty-one-year-old wife, Emilia, at his side.

Sixteen months later, at the same Army hospital, the good Lord smiled again. This time, Al and Emilia welcomed baby Luz to the world, nicknamed Lucy. Just as a US Army private named Elvis Presley showed up in Germany as part of his tank battalion training, Captain Montes and his growing family headed in the opposite direction. Alberto completed his three-year military hitch and flew with his wife and baby girls to the States, landing in New York on August 26, 1958. Bright days, and a new job with better pay in the American heartland, lay ahead.

None of this good fortune was preordained. Ana's parents, Emilia and Alberto, were from families of modest means, and it was only through smarts and sacrifice that they had so quickly left the farms and barrios of Puerto Rico behind. Alberto's father was one of eleven children in his family and had started his working life as a boy. Alberto's mother, who was orphaned at age nine after her policeman father was killed by machete-wielding locals in the Dominican Republic, left school after third grade. Alberto's parents were literate but never learned English. Young Alberto grew up in the Depression in a house without electricity or indoor toilets. But Alberto's parents had a fierce work ethic that they passed down to their four children. Alberto's dad, Ana and Lucy's grandfather, worked 6½ days a week in his grocery store in Manatí, on Puerto Rico's northern coast, selling on credit to farmers who often could not afford to pay him back. "Though he was very enthusiastic about having a business, [my father] made very little money because he was soft-hearted," Alberto wrote in an autobiography he presented to his children one Christmas in 1995. "He could not bear the thought that their families would go hungry, unless he sold on credit." The next Montes generation fared better. Alberto became a doctor, his sister a teacher, his younger brother a Jesuit priest, and his baby brother a college sociology professor.

Ana and Lucy's mother, Emilia, was from a higher social standing. Her father, Carlos Badillo y Vadi, worked as a book-keeper at the San Vicente sugar mill near Vega Baja, the town right next to Manatí. It was a steady job at one of the region's top employers. The sugar company built and owned the Badillo family's four-bedroom home and picked up the rent and utilities, and Emilia and her little brother never went hungry. "I had a lovely childhood. We had what we need[ed] and more," Emilia said.[6] "I spent my first 18 years in an apparently happy and healthy family, without even thinking about the future."[7] Carlos and his wife, whose first name was Belén, encouraged their daughter's studies. They bought Emilia a set of encyclopedias and the de-termined schoolgirl devoured them cover to cover. She was ex-pected to follow in the footsteps of her aunts, who had gone to college and become teachers, pharmacists, professionals. "Her father told her that her future was going to be in the United States, and she needed to learn to speak English," remembered daughter Lucy Montes. Emilia did just that and went to Mount Saint Agnes, a Catholic women's college in Baltimore.

By fall 1958, Ana Montes's young family was on its way. Ad-ventures awaited in the American plains. From the age of five, Alberto had dreamed of working as a physician. He had watched his little brother, Carlos, nearly die as a baby when he devel-oped diphtheria in Puerto Rico and could no longer breastfeed. When a local doctor diagnosed Carlos and gave him "diphtheria antitoxin shots," Carlos recovered in two days. Young Alberto stood in awe of Dr. Lopez's heroics and "I decided that one day I would become a physician." And now it was a reality.

Alberto had secured a job as a general physician at the Win-ter VA Hospital in Topeka, Kansas. Now called the Colmery-O'Neil Veterans' Administration Medical Center, it was named in honor of the World War I pilot who is considered the main architect of the G.I. Bill. Ana's father began seeing patients at the hospital, treating veterans of the Korean War and World War II.

Topeka in the 1950s could not have been more different from the tropical homeland Emilia and Alberto had left behind. The capital city of Kansas had less than one hundred thousand residents at the time, and about 92 percent of them were White. Census takers back then didn't even record the Latino population, which in Topeka would have been negligible.[8] In the early 1950s, famously, the Board of Education of Topeka operated under the doctrine of "separate but equal" at its public schools, relegating area Black children to poorly performing schools. The policy led the Supreme Court to rule in the landmark *Brown v. Board of Education of Topeka* case that segregation in the elementary schools of Topeka, and all other public schools in the nation, was unconstitutional. "Separate educational facilities are inherently unequal," the Court declared in 1954, in a case championed by the Topeka chapter of the NAACP.

Racial strife was still apparent when the Montes family flew to Topeka in 1958. Just days after their arrival, an openly racist op-ed ran in the *Wichita Eagle*, a leading newspaper. "The United States has had trouble for years with Puerto Ricans who have flocked into New York City and area to find a better way of life than in their homeland… The crime wave attributed to the Puerto Ricans in and around New York City is terrific," the *Eagle* stated. "Undoubtedly the West needs a better policy. It can't be done, however, based on unlimited immigration of colored people."[9] Not surprisingly, Mexican Americans who lived in Topeka at the same time were "publicly ridiculed and called cruel derogatory names," Thomas Rodriguez writes in his Topeka memoir, *Americano: My Journey to the Dream*. Rodriguez recalls that "Mexicans were not allowed to eat in many of Topeka's restaurants" and banned from certain swimming pools in the city. Around the time when the Montes family arrived in Topeka in the late '50s, he writes, White parents began complaining to officials at Topeka High School to "do something to stop interracial dating between Mexican-American boys and White girls."[10]

Alberto and Emilia were light-skinned and classified as "White" in US government records. As a doctor's family, they were treated with kindness in the Kansas suburbs. They settled in at a comfortable house in southwest Topeka, an easy drive from the veterans hospital and walking distance to McEachron Elementary School. Their new home was on a dirt road with a pretty backyard and a party line, or shared telephone line, for a phone. Alberto began refining his skills as a doctor at the hospital, while dressing in his Army fatigues for Army Reserve training during the weekend. As was traditional then, Emilia cooked and took care of the girls. She recalls that Ana would often become jealous when Emilia nursed baby Lucy. Ana would warn her mother that "a big dog outside was going to take Lucy" away.[11]

In June of 1959, Ana and Lucy were joined by a new playmate. Baby Alberto was born and thereafter called "Tito," to distinguish him from his father, Alberto, and grandfather Alberto before him. Dr. and Mrs. Emilia Montes now had three babies, all less than two and half years old, under the roof of their suddenly chaotic three-bedroom, one-and-a-half-bath home on Topeka's W. 29th Street.

Manatí and the San Vicente sugar mill might as well have been a million miles away. There was no family to lean on in Topeka, and few friends yet to be found. Emilia was loving and patient with her babies and Alberto was attentive. "Dad was a very good father when we were very young. He would change our diapers and help feed us and do all kinds of things," Lucy said. Alberto ruled the roost as many men did in that era, doling out a weekly allowance to Emilia and making most decisions for the household. He was clearly "el jefe," as his father had been before him, and expected quasi military-level deference at home.

Alberto's days were packed. He had decided to specialize in psychiatry, and had won admittance in 1958 to the prestigious Menninger School of Psychiatry. Colocated at Winter Veterans Administration Hospital, the school was one of the best in the nation at educating post-WWII professionals in the booming new field. General Omar Bradley, who had commanded US Army troops during the Invasion of Normandy, had helped start Winter Hospital's training program for young psychiatrists after the end of World War II.[12]

Improbably, tiny Topeka had become the epicenter of Freudian theory and the understanding of the human mind. In the 1920s, Harvard-trained Dr. Karl Menninger, with his father and brother, established a clinic in Topeka in an old farmhouse. It had beds for thirteen patients. An early ad for their private sanitarium promised "treatment of the nervously and mentally sick" with showers, Sitz baths, and hydrotherapy that is "preferable to drug sedation."[13] As the Menninger clinic expanded, the mind-body treatment offered in Topeka was revolutionary for its time. "Previously, psychiatric treatment had been conducted one-on-one over a long period—perhaps five to seven years. The Menninger idea was to provide a 'total environment' for its clinic patients in which there would be a family atmosphere, physical exercise and medical doctors from various disciplines who could give patients comprehensive care," the *New York Times*[14] recounted in a 2,000-word obituary when Dr. Menninger died in 1990 at age ninety-six.

Karl Menninger became the toast of Topeka. He helped to popularize psychiatry with publication of his first book, *The Human Mind*, in 1930, and with a regularly appearing advice column in the *Ladies' Home Journal*. Although Sigmund Freud, the founder of psychoanalysis, had been publishing for decades when Menninger came on the scene, most Americans remained in the dark about the advances in understanding of human emotion and mental illness. "To the general public, the mentally ill or emotionally disturbed were often 'lunatics' to be confined in insane asylums," the *Times* reported. "Dr. Menninger had a hand in changing those conceptions through his papers, articles and books, some of which became bestsellers." The Menninger family would go on to create an empire in Topeka for treating mental disorders. At its height, it mushroomed into two sprawling campuses in Topeka, a workforce of more than a thousand people, and a multimillion-dollar budget.

At its core, the success of the Menninger Foundation was based on Karl Menninger's deep understanding of the human psyche and the enduring influence of parents on their children. "In childhood parents represent omnipotent gods,"[15] Menninger wrote in his bestseller, *The Human Mind*. As a disciple of Freud, Menninger knew that the loving role of parents was one of the basic precepts of emotional well-being. "It is much easier, more logical and more efficacious to help a child grow up with love and courage than it is to instill hope in a despondent soul," he said. "What mother and father mean to them is more than psychiatrists can ever mean."[16]

And yet, over his long career as one of the nation's top psychiatrists, Dr. Menninger had witnessed "almost unbelievable cruelties systematically practiced by parents upon children."[17] In an essay for *The Atlantic Monthly* in 1939 called "Women, Men, and Hate," Menninger expounded. "The secret cruelties that parents visit upon their children are past belief…in my capacity as a psychiatrist I shudder at the tales of brutality I am obliged to hear."

If psychiatrist-in-training Alberto Montes ever read Dr. Menninger's well-known and now-obvious observations on love and parenting, he had a funny way of showing it. As the Montes children would later bear witness, they grew terrified of their father's hair-trigger temper and unpredictable mood swings. In a twisted irony for the ages, Dr. Alberto Montes became a successful and noted Freudian analyst. A Freudian psychotherapist armed with a leather belt.

Chapter 3.

THE HOTHOUSE

"Parents who whip their children should not be surprised if these children, once they attain the power and authority for doing so, take revenge upon the next generation."

—DR. KARL A. MENNINGER, THE HUMAN MIND

By the 1960s, Alberto Montes had established himself as a respected figure in Topeka. In his crisp suits doing rounds at the Winter VA Hospital or at the world-famous Menninger School of Psychiatry, he had earned the admiration of colleagues and administrators alike. The Army reservist was humble, compassionate, and generous. Years before in medical school, his family recalls, a small group of displaced Puerto Ricans had heard that one of their countrymen was studying nearby. They were poor and freezing in the Albany cold. The desperate laborers sought out Alberto and asked if he had any money to buy a coat. Alberto didn't have much but literally gave them the coat on his back.

Even the Menninger family itself believed in Alberto's promise. "I remember him as a nice guy," said Dr. Walter Menninger, now ninety years old, who was Alberto's classmate at the Menninger School in Topeka.[18] The son of one of the founders of the family empire and a nephew to the world-famous Karl Men-

ninger, "Dr. Walt" would later become dean of the Karl Menninger School of Psychiatry and CEO of the Menninger Clinic.
But back as eager students in the three-year training program at
his family's psychiatry school, Dr. Walt recalls "Al" Montes as
diligent and hardworking. Montes was one of five Latino doctors in the thirty-two-member class of 1958 at the Menninger
School of Psychiatry, all of whom were men. It was Alberto's
competence and inner drive that attracted the attention of one
of Menninger's senior psychiatrists.

Dr. Herbert C. Modlin came to Topeka in 1946 and was appointed chief of psychiatric services at Winter Hospital. In 1949,
he joined the staff of the Menninger Clinic, where he remained
for forty-five years and became head of the Department of Psychiatry and Law.[19] In the early 1960s, Dr. Modlin asked his junior
colleague, Alberto Montes, to join him in an ongoing, fifteen-
year study of drug-addicted physicians who had been admitted
to the C. F. Menninger Memorial Hospital for treatment. The
resulting publication was one of the crowning achievements of
Alberto's burgeoning career. The paper was read at the annual
meeting of the American Psychiatric Association in Los Angeles
in 1964 and was published months later in the *American Journal
of Psychiatry*.[20]

Drs. Modlin and Montes spent years studying twenty-five
physicians who had become hooked on morphine, Demerol,
Dexedrine, and other drug cocktails. Their influential report,
Narcotics Addiction in Physicians, has been cited in the medical
literature for years. It opens a window into the Freudian methodology Dr. Montes learned in Topeka, and later perfected at
hospitals in Baltimore. When Dr. Montes put these drug-addled
doctors on his couch in Topeka, he went deep to learn why these
disciples of Hippocrates "trained to preserve human life and
minister to human pain" had become so hell-bent on destroying
their marriages and careers. As any self-respecting practitioner
of Freud knows, it all starts with the parents.

Dr. Montes learned that the physician-addicts "generally described their fathers as stern and depriving, or passive and indifferent, or volatile and flamboyant." About 85 percent of the doctors criticized their mothers as "demanding, dominating, depressive," or worse. Put it all together and these self-destructing doctors with doomed relationships were living proof of the need for immersive Freudian discovery, Dr. Montes wrote. He noted that the doctors in his control group had gone "searching for a parental surrogate in a spouse" and routinely showed signs of "unresolved oedipal strivings."

One might think that a physician who had become expert in wounded healers, Freudian theory, and the dark side of the "psychophysiological imbalance in childhood" would be especially kind to his own children back home. But it was not to be.

By the time Alberto published his landmark paper, baby Juan Carlos had joined the Montes family, bringing their number to six. Alberto and Emilia had made good friends in Topeka, particularly with the Latin American doctors who had been hired at Menninger. The doctors and their wives were frequent dinner guests on W. 29th Street, with the lively and opinionated Emilia holding court in the kitchen.

Ana's mother, Emilia, took advantage of her proximity to the Menninger facilities, after a series of tragedies. In 1962, her father Carlos died of a heart attack in Puerto Rico, at age fifty-seven. Just two years later, Emilia's brother Carlos, nicknamed Coco, died in an automobile accident on the island.[21] He was in his late twenties. Her only sibling had been out campaigning in the countryside on behalf of a political party, Vanguardia Popular, that the history books describe as a "radical" nationalist youth group opposed to US intervention in the region and the draft of Puerto Ricans into the US Army.[22] At Coco's funeral, Emilia visited her father's grave for the first time. "That was the most painful day of my life. I stood at the cemetery watching the family and my mother's awful sorrow and felt that I was looking at a picture on a wall. I was not present," Emilia wrote. Suddenly all alone, Emilia's mother, Belén, grew despondent. She died within months of her son's tragic accident.

Back in Topeka, Ana's mother, Emilia, sought relief from a Menninger therapist. Her entire family had perished in just a few short years and "I was the only one left alive from that happy home in San Vicente." The guilt was overwhelming. "I could not attend my father's funeral because my last baby was due within a week; I was not at my mother's side when she died; I did not enjoy my brother's last years of his young life," she would write in an unpublished autobiography. "For the next ten years I went through life as if my mind, my soul and my heart had been locked in a box or maybe I placed them on a shelf and closed the door."

As their mother grieved, Ana, Lucy, and Tito coped, making friends from the neighborhood and nearby school. Ana easily managed As in first grade in McEachron Elementary School, with a single B+ in math. But trouble awaited. The outside world was largely unaware of the man their father, Alberto, had become behind closed doors and the "secret cruelties" he visited upon his children at 4004 W. 29th Street.

Lucy Montes lives in southern Florida now and is retired from the FBI. She loves her father, who died in 2000 at age seventy-one, and goes to pains to recount his good and gentle side when they were young—countless visits to local libraries to teach the importance of reading, weekend hikes with his brood to the top of nearby Burnett's Mound in Topeka, and sunny family vacations in Puerto Rico. The compliments trip off Lucy's tongue. Compassionate. Sensitive. Warm. Affectionate. She's even hung her father's medical diplomas on the wall of her ranch-style home. But even now, more than two decades after his death, she can't forget that her father began beating her and her siblings when they each turned five or six years old, for the slightest of childhood infractions. "Yes, he was a very stern man. He had a violent temper. That's true. My father had a violent temper," Lucy said. "Oh yeah, with the belt, we got it with the belt. When he got angry."

Disobedience and disrespect led to the belt. Spills at the table and a lost possession might trigger Alberto, too. But the truly frightening part was the unpredictability of it all, especially for a child. "Nobody ever knew what was going to set him off," Lucy said.

Like many strict disciplinarians, Alberto had been raised in similar fashion. His father, Alberto the grocer, was known as a gruff man who also beat his children. While he could be forgiving to customers who couldn't pay for their groceries at his Manatí store, he was less tolerant with his own kin. Alberto's dad, the grocer, was physically and psychologically abusive, Lucy's father once told her. In the Montes home in Puerto Rico, the fear of a severe beating was used to encourage compliant behavior. When Alberto and his young siblings acted out, their mother would warn them that once Dad came home "he would really fix us." As Ana's father, Alberto, recalled of his childhood in Manatí, "That threat really froze us in our tracks! I was not sure what [my father] would do, but I feared it was something terrible, unspeakable."

Dr. Montes and his father had always had a difficult relationship, especially once it became known that the elder Alberto had a mistress in Puerto Rico. She was a cook who worked for a local dentist. Alberto's father rubbed the relationship in his son's face, taking the young boy to meet his lover's parents. Once, the mistress even cooked for the entire Montes family in Manatí, forcing Alberto to hide his father's secret from his unsuspecting mother. "It was so humiliating, and I was so angry at both Father and Mother," Alberto wrote in 1995. What's more, the cycle of violence had started even earlier. Dr. Montes's grandfather used to beat his children with a bat, including Alberto the grocer. By the time Ana, Lucy, and Tito reached grade school, they were on the short end of a family tradition of corporal punishment and cruelty stretching back more than a half century.

Plenty of fathers in the 1960s believed in the "spare the rod, spoil the child" school of parenting. The beatings alone could never explain Ana's rationale for becoming a Cuban agent. But it's clear that Alberto's brutish behavior had a deep impact on the entire family. In Topeka and in Des Moines, Iowa, where the family briefly moved, and then later in the suburbs of Baltimore, Alberto became a five-foot-seven-inch terror to his children—and wife. "He had a bad temper and a bad marriage with my mother. So, yeah, he was a violent man. It affected her enormously, all of us," Lucy said. "My mother was afraid of him too... There wasn't much she could do for us."

Dr. Walter Menninger, Alberto's former classmate and once one of the foremost psychiatrists in the nation, says he had no clue what was happening behind the closed doors at the home of his old friend, Al. "This business of kind of the double life, of the professional image and what colleagues are aware of and then what happens when you go home at night, that's a puzzlement," he said. But he added that childhood scars rarely heal completely. "How we are treated in our earliest years can somehow partially be compensated, but bad roots in the beginning do leave their scars," he said. "It's just a reality that early-life experiences do have persisting impacts and get replicated." And even psychiatrists who study childhood trauma are not immune, he said. "Unfortunately, understanding does not necessarily modify behavior... when the front door or back door is closed and you are in the privacy of your home, the earliest lessons get repeated."

As Alberto's eldest child, Ana Montes learned that cruel lesson well. Alberto expected a lot from his overachieving daughter and treated her harshly when she disappointed.

When she was about eight, Ana developed a severe allergy to the family's cats. In fact, almost anything could trigger her allergies, from a Christmas tree to dust mites to nuts. Her condition morphed into allergy-induced asthma, restricting her breathing. Most families would run off to the pediatrician for medical relief. But Ana's father, the doctor, had other treatments in mind.

One day, as Ana struggled to breathe, Alberto grew annoyed. He led Ana into the family's living room in their Topeka home. There, he guided his eight-year-old daughter into a chair and probed whether her asthma had an emotional cause. Alberto, by now deep into training as a psychiatrist, was testing out a theory on his gasping child. Lucy recalls watching in horror as her father tried to cure Ana's diminished breathing through therapy alone. Ana refused to cry and sat, stoically, until she nearly passed out. "We were all afraid of him. That was his flaw," Lucy said.

Decades later, after pleading guilty to espionage and being debriefed by psychologists from the CIA and US Navy, Ana unloaded on her father. She recounted that her dad had been verbally and physically abusive and "happened to believe that he had the right to beat his kids." At home, Ana said, "he felt he was entitled. He was the king of the castle and demanded complete and total obedience." The CIA profilers agreed. "She vilifies her father, Alberto, whom she believed had two personas: a public, 'well educated, conservative, honest, well intentioned, and empathetic' man and a private brutal ruler."

Lucy and Ana are only sixteen months apart and shared a bedroom as sisters for seventeen years. They were very close when they were little, and Ana took on a motherly role with her baby sister. "She was my little helper and the big sister," Emilia said. Ana would walk Lucy to school, bathe with her, and patiently read Lucy books at night. On the first day of school, it often was Ana—not their mother—who escorted Lucy to her classroom and introduced her to her new teachers.

One night after yet another beating by her father with the dreaded strap, Lucy recalls crying for hours and telling Ana, "I hate my father." But Ana learned at an early age to shield her emotions, even from her adoring little sister, when it was her turn for a whipping. "My sister didn't cry. She must have been seven years old," Lucy said. "She didn't say anything."

Chapter 4.

STEVIE WONDER AND
CHOCOLATE CHIP COOKIES

"Summer, beaches, soccer, Stevie W., P.R., chocolate chip cookies, having a good time with fun people."

—ANA MONTES'S FAVORITE THINGS, AS LISTED IN HER SENIOR YEARBOOK FROM LOCH RAVEN HIGH SCHOOL IN TOWSON, MARYLAND

In 1967, Alberto Montes moved his family again. His VA days and Army Reserve commitment behind him, he had landed a position as a staff psychiatrist at another of the nation's most respected psychiatric hospitals, the Sheppard and Enoch Pratt Hospital in Towson, Maryland. Ana was ten, Lucy nine, Tito eight, and baby Carlos about five when they traded the Midwest for the comfortable upper-middle-class suburbs of Baltimore.

Leaving friends behind was intimidating, but the family began looking forward to a change of place. "It seemed exciting. Mom was real happy to be moving. It was a big city," Lucy said. The kids began school at Oakleigh Elementary, part of the Baltimore County Public School system, and explored the region. There were occasional family trips to Washington, DC. Alberto, a big fan of the hit TV show *The F.B.I*, starring Efrem Zimbalist Jr., insisted that he take his children on a tour of FBI Headquarters in DC. Today, Ana's mug shot peers down from the walls of the same fortresslike structure that the Montes children visited long ago, part of an exhibit on Ana's 2001 arrest for espionage.

In Maryland, Alberto had less time—and patience—for his family. As he would acknowledge to his children years later, five years before his death, "I had to work to support you, and I had to work extra hours to support my training... This took a toll on me, which affected Emilia and you. I was less available emotionally to you, and I became more irritable and intolerant." Working as a psychiatrist at Sheppard Pratt only added to that toll.

Opened in 1891 on a lush 340-acre campus just north of Baltimore, what was then known as the Sheppard Asylum was funded by a successful Baltimore merchant and Quaker. Moses Sheppard had wanted to create a facility that would feel more like a home than a prison. Upon his death he donated nearly $600,000 to the asylum, the largest bequest ever made to mental health at that time, and left clear instructions for what he expected. His will gives clues to how inhumanely mental patients had once been treated in America. Sheppard stipulated that no patient was to be confined belowground; all were to have privacy, sunlight, and fresh air. And all patients were to receive courteous treatment in a "curative environment."[23]

By the 1960s, though, Sheppard Pratt had fallen on hard times. It was flirting with bankruptcy and had become known for the warehousing of longtime patients. When Dr. Robert W. Gibson became medical director in 1963, he established an outpatient department, opened the gates to the public, desegregated the staff, and created an adolescent unit. The *Baltimore Sun* would later credit him with transforming Sheppard Pratt "from a 19th century-style asylum" into a modern psychiatric hospital, "nationally known and locally appreciated."

Just a year after Alberto Montes came on board, Dr. Gibson established Sheppard's first Department of Research. Alberto became part of a group of young psychiatrists putting Sheppard Pratt back on the map and improving standards of hospital care, transitioning from the warehousing of troubled souls to actual therapeutic intervention. At the same time, Alberto began taking on private patients and advancing his study of Freudian psychoanalysis. He would train for eight years at the Baltimore-District of Columbia Institute for Psychoanalysis, earning a degree in 1975.

Treating mental disease had been an early passion. As a boy growing up in Manatí, Alberto recounts being mesmerized by a young woman, Teresa, who often experienced psychotic episodes that were public and embarrassing. Teresa would walk the streets of Manatí naked, shouting obscenities and throwing stones at the neighbors' houses. After her husband abandoned her, she was placed in a Puerto Rican psychiatric hospital where she received insulin shock therapy, a once-popular treatment in which patients were injected with large doses of insulin to induce daily comas. Weeks later, Teresa "came back home as normal as any of us," Dr. Montes wrote. "That stuck in my mind."

Closer to home, Alberto also was on hand when his mother battled her own demons. In the summer after his second year of medical school, Alberto was visiting Manatí on a rare vacation. He had been reading Freud and his classic, *Interpretation of Dreams*, when his mother, Ana, had a total breakdown. "She was very agitated, upset, talked 'nonsense,' began screaming, wanting to run out of the house," Alberto recalled. Mom became Alberto's first psychiatric patient, by necessity. "I interpreted her upsets like one interprets a dream." He listened patiently for hours as his mother described her fear of being abandoned by her husband, the death of her mother when she was just six, and the brutal murder of her father when she was nine and left orphaned. Alberto and his family took mother to an area psychiatrist who prescribed sleeping pills and administered three electroshock treatments. After a few weeks, Mom began to recover. "It took me a long time to realize how much this emotional release of painful (some forgotten) feelings had had a *healing* effect on her, and how Freud's method worked!" Alberto wrote. His mother had two relapses later in life.

At Ana's new suburban home in Parkville, Maryland, outside Baltimore, the move from Kansas didn't prompt a change in behavior. Alberto continued to whip and slap his children and began openly feuding with Emilia. Alberto hurt Emilia once, badly twisting her arm and making her cry, Lucy admits. "My parents had a very bad marriage. Completely mismatched," Lucy said. "They fought a lot, they screamed a lot, it affected all of us."

When the couple argued, they resorted to Spanish. As a child, Lucy couldn't follow along and said her father would remind her of TV actor Desi Arnaz from the *I Love Lucy* series, when his character "Ricky Ricardo" would lose his head and start screaming double-time at his wife in Spanish. But Ana was always watching and took it all in. "I think it affected Ana more, without a doubt. Ana was the oldest, she understood more Spanish than the rest of us," Lucy said. "So she would've been acutely aware of what was going on between my parents. I think it affected her more than it did us."

Emilia felt trapped, and powerless to control her powder keg husband. "He was a very strict disciplinarian," Emilia once said of Al. He and his eldest child often fought. "They clashed. He was strong-willed, very much like [Ana.]"[24] Emilia acknowledged that when the children were little, Al "was very loving toward them and helped to care for them when he was home." But as his career advanced, "Al behaved like an Army man and sometimes gave orders like a sergeant. He could not accept any challenges from his children or me." She added that he "was hard on my kids *after* they reached adolescence; maybe he had no adolescence himself." Years later, Emilia was still in dismay. "How could he forget his psychiatric training?" she pleaded.

Towson and Parkville may have been less than fifteen miles from Baltimore, but it was a suburban bubble. During the 1968 riots in Baltimore following the death of the Reverend Martin Luther King Jr., six people were killed and more than seven hundred injured. The looting and arson were so extensive that President Lyndon Johnson sent some five thousand US Army soldiers to restore the peace.[25] But that was in Baltimore. In predominantly White Towson, garden clubs and church community meetings went on as planned. While Towson residents lived for a few days under a county-wide curfew, the blinders were on. The same week as the riots, the Towson Afternoon Newcomers' Club held a "Life Is Funny" talk at its regular luncheon, and the Towson YMCA announced plans for a fun kids' trip to Washington, DC—scene of some of the worst rioting and arsons in the nation—complete with scavenger hunts and a pet show. And Hutzler's Budget Store in Towson kicked off its "Get a Head Start on Spring" sale, with full page ads hawking $3.99 bonnets and $2.99 plastic clutch bags.

The Montes kids eased into life in suburbia, and escaped any racial animosity. Ana and Lucy began to grow apart. Once inseparable, Ana started to crave independence and her own friends. Ana began to find her little sister annoying and "kind of kept me at arm's length," Lucy said. By junior high at Parkville Middle School, Ana continued as an A student, diligent and organized. Lucy, Tito, and Carlos easily made friends on Haverhill Road, riding bikes on their dead-end street and sledding in the winter. Tito joined a church group, and later studied to become a minister.

Sometimes the children of abusive fathers find communion in resisting a common enemy. The Montes children tried not to dwell on their father's rage and baffling duality. "That wasn't discussed. It was just accepted," Lucy said. "We didn't have a choice. We had no say."

Emilia had had enough. Willful, charismatic, and blunt by nature, she began to assert herself in her deteriorating marriage. With the dawn of the 1970s and the nascent women's movement, she could begin to see a life for herself as someone other than a mother and compliant doctor's wife. Emilia and Al separated in 1972, and she convinced her tyrannical husband to move out. Ana was fifteen years old, Lucy fourteen. "He spoke to each child before he left, he invited them to live with them," Emilia recalled. "They declined." That first night, Alberto came back to the house to see his kids, almost as if nothing had happened. For a few months, he would stop by the house every evening on the way home from the hospital. But then the visits slowed and Alberto would only drop by on Sundays, pick up the kids for dinner, and return them back home. "We were relieved when he moved out," Lucy said. "There was too much tension and we were afraid of my dad."

With Alberto living in a nearby apartment, there was room to breathe. Ana became a star student at Towson's newly built Loch Raven High School, home of the Raiders, where she was one of only a handful of students with Hispanic surnames. She graduated with a 3.9 grade-point average and found it hard to be academically challenged. She chafed at the rules in high school, which she found "so controlling." On the surface, she had it all. In her senior yearbook portrait from 1975, Ana is all smiles, with light brown hair draped across her shoulders and a delicate crucifix on her neck. She could be a 1950s sorority sister. Next to her class photo, she lists her favorite things as summer, singer Stevie Wonder, Puerto Rico, chocolate chip cookies and "having a good time with fun people."

But the bubble-gum sentimentality was a mask. Ana was changing. In her basement, she hung a poster of Che Guevara, the Marxist revolutionary who had helped to overthrow Cuba. Ana idolized her mother and was deeply disturbed by Alberto's volcanic temper and the contemptuous way he had treated Emilia. And even when her father moved out, Ana continued to resist his ham-handed attempts to control her. "He didn't seem to be able to handle our teenage years. He didn't seem to be able to handle any defiance or rebellion or disobedience," Lucy said. Ana began to openly rebel. "She would challenge him and confront him, and he would lash out," Lucy said. Emilia agreed: "Ana resented her dad's disciplinary ways and stood up against his commands," she added.

Ana grew openly defiant. One summer when Emilia was home recuperating from minor surgery, Ana wanted to go with high school friends for a few nights to Ocean City, Maryland, a beach town and popular kids' hangout. Al insisted that parents had to go as chaperones and tried to cancel the trip. Ana refused. "Al was home and [Ana] said she was leaving for the beach," Emilia recalled. "He was furious and slapped her in front of her friends. She said nothing but cried and left mortified and hurt." Emilia could only stand by and watch. "I truly felt helpless that I could not prevent this from happening."

Ana and her mother grew incredibly close, with one friend observing that Emilia shared details of her failed marriage with her teenaged daughter. "I thought that Ana seemed to be her mother's therapist. It's almost like she talked to Ana like a friend, not a child," the friend said, concerned that Ana was carrying around a lot of emotional baggage at such a young age.

Lucy did well in school but suffered her own indignities. Her father slapped her once when she went for an innocent walk with a boy on the boardwalk. She was fifteen. "That pretty much ended my relationship with my Dad after that. That was it. I just shut myself off from him completely" until after college.

Alberto just couldn't seem to progress with the times. When he was courting Emilia in 1955, he was never allowed to be alone with her until after they married. Dating back then, he would try to explain to his children, "was done under the watchful eye of the girl's father or mother." Alberto seemed to long for those rigid days of his youth. "You may think this was ridiculous, but it certainly ensured the virginity of the brides... and a test of the man's intentions. This is how we protected our young people who could not control their strong sexual drives," he once wrote. "We have forgotten that, to the detriment of our youth."[26]

Emilia finally stepped out of Alberto's shadow for good. She went back to college in Baltimore and finished her undergraduate work, earning a degree in international relations. She took a job as a receptionist for the IRS, making her own income for the first time. Later, Emilia went to work as a translator for the Social Security Administration in Woodlawn, Maryland, taking advantage of the federal government's new priority recruitment of minorities. Her hard work for the federal government paid off, and the US Equal Employment Opportunity Commission (EEOC) hired her to investigate cases of workplace discrimination. She would stay with the EEOC for more than a decade, one of many Montes family members to work for the federal government.

Five years after their separation, Emilia and Alberto formally divorced. They had agreed to wait until 1976 to officially split, to hit the twenty-year marriage threshold that the Social Security Administration required at the time for a spouse to collect benefits. Alberto, who was dating by this time, filed divorce papers first stating that their separation had been "mutually voluntary" and that there was no hope of reconciliation. Emilia's lawyer aggressively countered a month later, denying that the split-up had been voluntary, alleging that Alberto had abandoned Emilia, and informing the Court that the doctor was capable of earning $100,000 a year, a fat salary for 1976.

By June 1977, the lawyer games were over and a settlement had been reached. Alberto gave Emilia the family's four-bedroom rancher at 1902 Haverhill Road in Parkville, alimony of $300 per month for three years, plus the couple's 1974 Plymouth. Emilia was awarded custody of Carlos, fifteen, and Tito, seventeen, with Dr. Montes getting visitation rights. He agreed to pay child support until both boys turned eighteen; Ana and Lucy had already left for college.

Just one month after his divorce, Alberto remarried.[27] His second wife was Nancy Winton, a pretty Sheppard Pratt psychiatric nurse with two children. Nancy is deceased, but her daughter Michelle lives in Colorado now and recalls Dr. Montes vividly. Michelle was nine when her mother remarried, and she and her eleven-year-old brother briefly lived with their mom and new stepfather in a house on the grounds of Sheppard Pratt. Michelle got to know Ana and all the Montes children and enjoyed having older stepbrothers and stepsisters. But she still trembles when discussing Alberto.

One day at the Sheppard Pratt home, in the shadow of the great psychiatric hospital, Michelle and her brother experienced their stepfather's terrifying initiation rite. "We did something that he didn't like. I don't know whether we were being too loud or what, and so he came up with a belt," Michelle said. "I don't want to talk about the actual hitting," she said emphatically. "We had never even imagined that kind of punishment, so for us, it was incredibly upsetting and frightening."

Michelle's biological father lived nearby and learned about the severe beating. He threatened Alberto and said that if he ever touched his children again, he would call the police. "And after that, we were never touched again," Michelle said.

After a year or so, Al and Nancy and her two kids moved to a spacious home in an affluent North Baltimore neighborhood called Roland Park, a streetcar suburb developed in the 1890s. The emotional abuse continued. Alberto would yell and intimidate his stepchildren one day, and could be caring the next. "He had a temper. Yeah. I mean, he was a classic abuser," Michelle said.

Michelle remembers once when the Montes boys were visiting, and everyone was goofing off while watching TV. Alberto was always a stickler for noise and came downstairs in a rage. He lined up the suspects and demanded to know who had caused the commotion. "We immediately knew we were in trouble, and everybody got dead quiet," Michelle said. "And it just kind of dawned on me: Everybody's afraid of him. Nobody outside this house has any clue what's going on in this house."

Another time, Michelle says that her mother had to work late at the hospital and asked her to prepare Alberto's dinner. "We had been doing dive rolls in gymnastics that day, and I had a horrible headache," Michelle recalls. She came home and fell asleep on the family's couch. When Alberto finished work at 6:00 p.m., Michelle was still napping. "He came home and was furious that his dinner wasn't ready. I was pretty out of it and tried to explain. I just remember him yelling at me, which did wonders for my headache. Not just yelling at me—screaming at me. Just completely ballistic over the fact that his dinner wasn't ready."

Michelle says that her mother couldn't escape Alberto's wrath, either. Once, she recalls, Alberto hurt Nancy so badly that she passed out. "We were downstairs. And they were upstairs fighting, which they often were. And we heard her scream and I remember hearing a thump. And so we came running upstairs and we were banging on the bedroom door, yelling for our Mom. And then a few minutes later they came out. It was really quiet in there. And they came out and she was obviously hurt." Nancy's arm was badly injured and Alberto took his wife to the hospital, Michelle says, and Alberto immediately "felt really bad." Michelle believes her mother covered for Alberto and never reported the assault.

Lucy can confirm some aspects of the frightening story. She was living with her dad in the Roland Park house at that time, after college, and heard about the fight when she got home that evening. She asked her father what had happened with Nancy. "He said they had gotten into an argument. She ran out of the room, walked down the stairs, slipped, and fell. And he thought that her arm was dislocated." Alberto, the doctor, tried to pop his wife's arm back into its socket, but it was clearly broken. "I knew that something really, really bad had happened that night. And I wasn't sure my dad was telling me the truth," Lucy said.

Michelle is in her midfifties now, but the memories feel fresh. "Even if he didn't touch any of us, it was just the constant walking around on tiptoes and eggshells." She and her brother worried what would happen if Alberto got angry at them, but couldn't act out for fear their biological father would learn. "If we make him angry and he can't take it out on us, then is he going to do something to Mom?" she says she wondered. And yet she points out that Alberto could also be kind and considerate. "There were times, little times where, way down deep inside things, this nice man would peek out." Nancy and Alberto stayed married for nearly two decades, divorcing in 1995.[28]

Meanwhile, Emilia was embracing her newfound independence. Left to her own devices, she found her voice. In 1975, she was the organizer of Baltimore's Showcase of Nations, a twenty-nation "Spanish fiesta" designed to show off the Spanish-speaking community to Baltimore residents. Emilia, who now included her maiden name, Badillo, when talking to reporters, was described by the *Baltimore Sun* as "a gregarious Puerto Rican."[29] In an article on the Showcase of Nations, she went out of her way to knock down then-prevalent tropes of Latinos as poor, uneducated, and unmotivated. Even though "other Baltimoreans are not aware of us," she told the press, local Latinos "are doctors, professors, retired diplomats, tailors, butchers, and so on."

While running the festival, Emilia had a run-in with the local Cuban community. Well-connected Cuban exiles lobbied her for top billing at the Showcase. Emilia would have none of it.

"Emilia Montes said, 'This is not true. The Cubans don't represent everybody,'" recalled Javier Bustamante, a fellow community leader from Spain. "They had a knockdown, drag-out fight," he said.[30] To reporters at the time, however, Emilia was diplomatic and didn't reveal the whole story. "We have some little jealousies and rivalries, but I see people working together and helping each other. Latins are always jealous of one another but I think the fair will bring us together," she told the *Baltimore Sun* in 1975.[31] Years later, after Ana's arrest, she was more forthcoming about her dustup with the Baltimore-based Cubans. In an interview with the *Miami Herald*, she said, candidly: "The Cubans and I had our encounters. They don't fight clean."

By the mid-1970s, Emilia was doing more than just organizing food festivals and sharing her favorite guanime recipes with the media. She began to express her progressive political beliefs, in articles and frequent letters to the editor, offering withering critiques of wrongheaded American policies, dimwitted writers, and anyone deemed disrespectful of her community. Emilia was a DJ playing classic Latin hits on a Baltimore radio channel and joined Puerto Rican clubs in the region. She wasn't active with any political party, Lucy says, but became a vocal liberal in her own right. When the *Baltimore Sun* wrote a profile of local Hispanics in 1976,[32] Emilia and some friends shared that they had had encountered "barriers of prejudice and ignorance" at the hands of longtime Americans who "tend to believe the stereotype of the Latin as a lazy, backward primitive." Emilia added: "Some of our people have had to apply for welfare and have gone through a humiliating ordeal at the hands of some social service agency workers."

When the *Evening Sun* of Baltimore wrote an op-ed mocking the notion that a woman might become a US Supreme Court Justice, Emilia rose to the challenge. The writer is "one of your best nitwits," Emilia fumed. "We have many capable women lawyers and judges in the United States. Are they to be considered for this post that ought to go to a woman (we are 51 percent of the population)," she asked, or will the next Justice be "another Nixon-style mediocrity?" Emilia was equally outraged that the *Evening Sun* had derided as "government hat-tipping to minorities" the prospect of placing another African

American on the high court. "Positions like these ought to go to the most intelligent, best prepared person, regardless of sex, racial or ethnic relationship," Emilia wrote. "In the meantime, we welcome 'government hat-tipping.'"[33]

Later, when Argentina invaded the Falkland Islands and Great Britain dispatched a naval task force to take back control of the British territory, Emilia spoke out again. In letters to the *Baltimore Evening Sun*, she pleaded with the Reagan Administration to side with Latin America or at least remain neutral during the Falklands War. "The Latin American nations desire to be aligned with the U.S. but we seldom behave like a leader of nations; instead we bully them," she wrote. "What we did in Nicaragua 50 years ago comes now to haunt us." It was a sentiment, with near-identical language, that Emilia's precious Ana would parrot in a different context years later.

After her arrest, Ana confided to CIA psychologists that her mother "grew up" during her tortured marriage and "created a life for herself." Emilia became a role model for Ana and a "stable influence" in her formative years. One friend described Emilia as "feisty, brilliant, ambitious, idealist, a dreamer, a writer... This woman could have been governor, another [Supreme Court Justice Sonia] Sotomayor or whatever."

The CIA concluded that Ana "wanted to emulate her mother's ability to fight for causes that helped people and affected positive change." Ana would soon discover her own cause to fight for in the most unlikely venue—on a junior-year abroad program while chasing boys in Spain.

Chapter 5.

THE CAULDRON

In 1975, Ana eagerly left home and began college at the University of Virginia in Charlottesville. UVa was an unlikely choice for a young feminist and budding leftist. Founded by Thomas Jefferson, the storied university had only accepted its first female undergraduates five years earlier and had struggled to embrace the social changes emblematic of the 1970s. When the *Cavalier Daily* school newspaper reported in Ana's freshman year that University President Frank Hereford was a member in the Whites-only Farmington Country Club near campus, student reaction was tepid at first. But when Hereford dug in his heels and the club declined to admit Blacks, hundreds of UVa students marched to the president's home. He was forced to end his club membership[34] and, as a peace offering, the university opened its first-ever "Minority Affairs Office."[35] A year later, the *Cavalier Daily* reported that many Black students "still see the University as a bastion of upper class whites" and feel a "somewhat hostile" attitude from faculty and students.[36]

Ana lived in a dorm across from the football field her freshman year and quickly formed a tight group of friends. The bonds were so strong that, even after her arrest for espionage, the husband of Ana's UVa roommate wrote a newspaper column suggesting Ana must be innocent. "There must be a terrible mistake. Ana couldn't be a spy—at least not for the Cubans," he wrote, noting that Ana and her UVa friends had attended his wedding. He went on: "The FBI, after all, falsely accused Wen Ho Lee, a Los Alamos scientist, of giving nuclear secrets to the Chinese. The government jailed him and ruined his life—then released him when its case fell apart."[37] Ana "is no radical leftist," the friend, journalist Gideon Gil, wrote in a 2001 column that has not aged well. "The only secret she gave us was her mother's luscious flan recipe…" The article reveals Ana's superb acting skills and the near blind faith that Ana's friends placed in her.

The University of Virginia didn't have a sorority on Sorority Row until Ana's sophomore year,[38] and UVa's preppy fraternities dominated campus social life. Ana and her friends would go to frat parties and generally stick together in a pack. In 1976, Ana had a few counseling sessions to deal with feeling physically threatened by an ex-boyfriend at college "whom she perceived as stalking her."[39]

No longer under her father's thumb, Ana flourished at UVa. "College gave her much more 'independence,' which she strongly desired," the CIA wrote. Ana began wearing bright colors, openly embracing her Puerto Rican roots, and amusing friends by belting out George Thorogood and the Destroyers tunes. Jimmy Carter, the Georgia governor who had helped manage his family's peanut farm in Plains, Georgia, was in the White House, having run as an honest outsider ready to heal the nation in the aftermath of the scandals of the Nixon Watergate era. Ana felt comfortable expressing her liberal worldview at college with like-minded friends. She smoked weed occasionally, we know from government background investigations revealed years later.[40] But there was always a serious and reserved side. She supported herself by waitressing at faculty dinners for the university's catering office, and studied hard, maintaining a 3.4 GPA. Alberto had volunteered to pay for her college tuition but threatened to renege once when Ana told him she was going to New Orleans to party with friends for a few days. Her father couldn't give up control. Ana headed off to Bourbon Street, anyhow.

After two years at UVa, Ana switched her major from history to foreign affairs. She had discovered her life's work. She signed up to study in Spain for her junior year abroad with the Institute of European Studies.[41] She took classes in Madrid and made some extra cash by translating and typing up interviews with Spanish political leaders (her Spanish had improved greatly since childhood), under the direction of an Ohio State University professor.[42] For the stereotypical college coed, a year of study abroad in Europe often is an excuse to travel, drink good wine, and look for love. Ana checked all those boxes, for sure. But Spain became so much more.

Madrid in 1977 was electric with possibilities. Generalissimo Francisco Franco, Spain's dictatorial ruler for thirty-six years and a former Nazi collaborator, was finally gone. As his authoritarian regime dissolved, everyday Spaniards relished their newfound liberties. New political parties sprang to life; even the Communist Party became legal. Criticism of the government was accepted, no longer resulting in a prison sentence. But not everyone embraced the transition to constitutional democracy. In January 1977, right-wing extremists assassinated five labor activists from the Communist Party of Spain in a brazen attack in the center of Madrid, in what became known as the Atocha Massacre. As Spain was recovering and preparing to hold its first free election in forty years, Ana and a new class of eager college transplants was just coming to town.

Ana "Mimi" Colon was one of them. Born in Puerto Rico

and getting her undergraduate degree at the time at Texas Christian University, Mimi was a fun-loving nineteen-year-old who wasn't afraid to let her emotions show. Mimi met Ana one night at a restaurant when she overheard one of her new classmates speaking passable Spanish. When she learned that the chatty American girl had Puerto Rican parents, they immediately bonded. Mimi and Ana became roommates and shared the same expectations for their year ahead. "We did not want to eat at Burger King. We wanted to absorb the atmosphere around us," Mimi said.

Mimi kept a diary, which recorded their epic adventures. One night, they got drunk with a bunch of girlfriends at a packed Madrid bar and decided to bolt without paying. They ran away, tripping and laughing hysterically. At a friend's hotel room in Paris, they were unpacking when the bathroom door opened. A guy, a total stranger, emerged in only his underwear. "We laughed so hard, we were falling on the floor." On another boozy evening abroad, they stayed out dancing to Latin music all night. When Ana mocked Mimi for her uninhibited dance moves, Ana admitted, "I'm just jealous" and said she found it difficult to reveal herself and let go. Mimi was almost scornful, and wondered what kind of Puerto Rican girl was afraid to dance with abandon.

But the most impactful day was when the friends were on a train, headed back to Madrid from Barcelona, when Ana, then twenty, met a handsome traveler. Ricardo Fernandez Eiriz was from Buenos Aires and had sensitive eyes and curly dark hair. He was living in an apartment on the outskirts of Madrid with good friends from Argentina, Eduardo Fernández and his wife, Silvia, and their two young children. "Ricardo met Ana on a trip he went on with the Eurail pass," Eduardo recalled in an interview in 2022.

It was common for Argentinians of that era to retreat to Spain to escape the violent repression of the dictatorship back home.

On March 24, 1976, a military junta led by General Jorge Rafael Videla staged a coup and formally took power in Argentina, removing Isabel Perón as president of Argentina. Just a year later, when Ana met her boyfriend Ricardo, an estimated 760 Argentinians had "disappeared," kidnapped by right-wing squads and government thugs. "Most of the victims are described as political liberals or moderates," the *New York Times* reported.[43] In its "dirty war" against Communism, the Argentine government "hunted down, tortured, and killed suspected leftists—sometimes throwing their bodies out of helicopters into the sea," one reporter wrote.[44] Official records show that at least nine thousand people were killed and disappeared from 1976 to 1983, and likely many more.

Ana was intrigued by the dreamy-eyed Ricardo and respected his political pedigree. There had been street rallies almost every week in Madrid, and she and Mimi had become protest regulars. "There was a highly [charged] sentiment against the USA" for supporting Franco for so many years, Mimi said. "It was the first time that I was being exposed to so many anti-USA feelings. And after every protest, Ana used to explain to me the 'atrocities' that the USA government used to do to other countries." The friends watched a new documentary, *The Battle of Chile*, which movie reviews dismissed as an "admittedly biased, pro-revolutionary film." It chronicles the last months of the democratically elected Marxist regime of Chilean president Salvador Allende, who was ousted in a coup in 1973 by the right-wing General Augusto Pinochet. "The documentary explicitly implies the involvement of the American military in the coup," said Mimi, now a retired teacher living outside Washington, DC. After watching the film, "I was enraged, and Ana continued explaining how the USA interfered with other countries and would not let them live a free life."

Ana began dating Ricardo, about five years her senior and more politically aware than his new American girlfriend. She fell hard for Ricardo, and learned firsthand how the US man-handled its Latin American neighbors and frequently propped up brutal dictators who killed, tortured, and kidnapped leftists and other pro-democracy activists. "He was in love with her, and he brought her home several times," Ricardo's friend, Eduardo, confirmed in the 2022 interview.

Living with Ricardo and Eduardo provided better instruction in revolutionary theory and history than any classroom, Mimi added. Ana became "attracted to the social Communist parties in Europe during her junior academic year in Spain in 1978," the Pentagon Inspector General later wrote in a 180-page report on the Montes case.[45] "She described herself at the time as a leftist, but not a follower of classic Marxist orthodoxy." Mimi recalls hearing that Ricardo once burned his books, out of fear that his library of leftist tomes would expose him to authorities.

But Ricardo was more than a chronicler of American atrocities. Ana made time for romance, too. The young couple traveled to Granada to see the majestic Alhambra palace. Ana boasted in a postcard to Mimi, "It's so romantic and Ricardo and I are taking full advantage of it."

The discussions at the apartment in the Móstoles neighborhood of Madrid often got heated. And Ana took it all in. "They spent a lot of time talking about politics. And they hated America," Mimi said. "Ana was absorbing all of this. That was the atmosphere. You couldn't escape it. For an American girl, she was surrounded by people who hated America."

Ana felt torn. "She was so hungry to belong. She didn't know if she was Puerto Rican, if she was American or who she was," Mimi believes. Mimi began writing letters to Ana's mother, Emilia, back in Baltimore and was struck by the pride Emilia felt for Puerto Rico and the homeland she had deserted—for its poets, food, and history. So when Ana's new friends in Madrid attacked the US role in supporting authoritarian regimes around the world, Ana seemed caught in the middle. "When people would criticize the USA, I could tell she was embarrassed and she did not want to admit that she was partly American," Mimi said.

Ricardo lives in Buenos Aires today with his wife and did not respond to requests for comment. His friend Eduardo, now seventy-five, reluctantly sat down for an interview in a café in the Caballito neighborhood of Buenos Aires with an Argentinian investigative reporter I hired to find him. Eduardo brought his adult daughter, Laura, with him and seemed nervous discussing a friend involved in such a notorious case.

After living in Madrid in the late 1970s, Eduardo explained, he moved back to Argentina where he worked as a tinsmith and performed as an amateur actor. Eduardo is a large man, and his bushy hair and beard have long since gone gray. He spoke about Ana, haltingly, with a nostalgic smile. "I admired her commitment and her strong will," he said. He praised Ana for being "responsible and committed" in her politics and morality, but denied ever knowing about her secret work for Cuba until her arrest. He said the FBI never interviewed him.

Eduardo also rejected claims that he and Ricardo were leftist radicals. "I obviously was against dictatorship in Argentina, but I never was enrolled in any political party," he said. (However, an FBI special agent who oversaw the Montes case said that Ricardo and Eduardo "were definitely leftists and very political.") In the interview, Eduardo said he moved to Madrid legally in the late 1970s because he's of Spanish descent. Although reliable records from that era are hard to come by, the Argentinian investigative reporter could find no records showing that the police ever arrested Ricardo or Eduardo. She also could not find evidence that they ever joined any of the notorious leftist political parties of the 1970s and 1980s.

Eduardo made clear that he's still loyal to his old friend. He said that Ana is "unfairly imprisoned" in the United States and that she was locked up because "she wouldn't talk for money."

While being careful to come across as apolitical, he couldn't resist getting in a dig at Ana's homeland. "Americans believe that everything is fixed with money."

Eduardo said he's only traveled once to Cuba, just a year before Ana's arrest, and has no connection to the revolutionary island nation. He gets nostalgic talking about his friend who became Castro's most prominent spy. "We would love to see her before we die."

Back home in Baltimore in the late 1970s, Emilia missed her girls. Lucy was out of the house, pursuing her undergraduate degree as a Spanish major at the University of Massachusetts in Amherst. And Emilia worried about her confidante, Ana, so far away. In a letter to Ana's friend Mimi in 1978, Emilia wrote: "I'm so glad that Ana Belén was able to go. I'm scared of that world, foreign and wide as it is. Who would my daughter meet? Would she be safe at night?" Just a year removed from her divorce from Alberto, Emilia offered Mimi life advice and took a potshot at her ex. "Your future husband will not always give you happiness, no one can give you that… Ana Belén knows well that those who are miserable with themselves can't make anyone else happy." And she hoped that Lucy would soon have a foreign adventure of her own. "I'm encouraging Lucy to make the trip to Spain next year, so that she can also experience the things you have. Lucy is a smart, intelligent and good girl. She's a bit disoriented right now and she could use a trip like this," Emilia wrote.

Ana tried to make her relationship with Ricardo work, but it ultimately flamed out. She confessed to her mother that he was "a good man but not a strong man." She turned down Emilia's offer to bring Ricardo to the States. When the political situation began stabilizing in Argentina, Ricardo moved back home, but stayed in touch with Ana for years, mailing letters and books glorifying Argentinian revolutionaries.[46]

After her arrest, the FBI seized Ana's diary from her year in

Madrid. The CIA eyeballed it, too. They concluded that her junior year abroad helped to solidify her burgeoning worldview. "Montes's private journal, written while she was studying abroad in Spain in late 1977, reflects her identification with aspects of Communism," the CIA writes. "She viewed various European Communist parties as most capable of responding to the population's social needs…her early sympathies may have enhanced her later desire to assist a Communist government, such as Cuba."

Chapter 6.

"OUR NATIVE LAND CALLS TO US"

"Yankee imperialism is decadent throughout the world and it will soon have to be defeated in Puerto Rico. Communism will collaborate in the struggle for national Independence."

—SPEECH GIVEN IN 1947 BY JUAN CORRETJER MONTES, ANA'S RELATIVE AND A LEADING PUERTO RICAN NATIONALIST, AS REPORTED BY FBI INFORMANTS[47]

Ana graduated from UVa and, soon after, Puerto Rico beckoned. The island nation had always been Ana's home away from home. It wasn't just the tropical breezes and beach vibes that enticed her. There were cousins and aunts and uncles to visit, a sprawling network of Montes and Badillo relatives who were happy to feed her and take her in. Ana, Lucy, and all the Montes children were never allowed to forget the importance of Puerto Rico in their parents' lives. Emilia, especially, had romanticized the homeland she had left as a twenty-one-year-old bride. "The place where we are born and spend our childhood leaves physical traces of unique minerals in our bones," Emilia once wrote. "If we accept this modern scientific fact, we finally understand why our native land calls to us and why the memory of it clouds our eyes and leaves us speechless. I can say that my bones hurt as much as my heart."

For Ana, Puerto Rico's allure transcended nostalgia. Her

mother's native land needed saving. Ana craved political independence for Puerto Rico and an end to its second-class status with the United States. In this regard, she was following generations of relatives in both the Montes and Badillo family tree who had fought for decades to free the island from US shackles.

For centuries, Spain controlled Puerto Rico, colonizing it and importing slaves from Africa to harvest sugarcane and tobacco. But in 1898, the US Navy bombarded Spanish troops in San Juan and easily won over the island, while simultaneously taking military control over Cuba. In the wake of the Spanish-American War, Puerto Rico was ceded to the United States under terms of the Treaty of Paris. (The government of Cuba was temporarily handed to the Americans in 1899, with Cuba winning independence in 1902.) Congress in 1917 extended American citizenship to Puerto Ricans, but kept it as a US territory with limited rights. Puerto Ricans would have to register for the draft and fight on behalf of the US military but were denied statehood.

To this day, Puerto Rico's relationship with the United States is unequal. Puerto Ricans are US citizens but have no right to vote for president if they live on the island. The island's residents have been clamoring for greater freedoms for more than a century, spawning a fearsome nationalist movement fighting for Puerto Rican independence. In 1950, it all came to a head. That's the year that Pedro Albizu Campos, the then-leader of the violent Puerto Rican Nationalist Party, led his followers in seizing towns and attacking police stations on the island. Days later in Washington, DC, Campos's nationalists staged an unsuccessful assassination attempt on President Harry Truman at Blair House, where the president had been living during renovations on the White House. "Quick-shooting White House guards cut down two assassins this afternoon when they attempted to invade Blair House in a Puerto Rican Nationalist plot to assassinate President Truman," the *New York Times* blared on November 1, 1950. Truman was not injured and kept his afternoon appointments. "A president has to expect those things," he said of the failed attack.[48] The messianic Albizu Campos was arrested with dozen of his followers and sentenced to decades in prison.[49]

Four years later, four of Albizu Campos's devotees attacked Washington again. They entered the US Capitol and opened fire on congressmen, wounding five of them before being overwhelmed by police. "Albizu Campos, who had received a pardon a few months earlier, was immediately rearrested and spent another decade in prison before his death, in April, 1965," the *New Yorker* reported in 2017.

Like Puerto Rico itself, Ana Montes's extended family has its share of political radicals but has always been somewhat divided on the crucial question of Puerto Rican independence. Emilia favored greater autonomy. She recalls the nationalist attacks of 1950, when she was fifteen, and listening to live reports over the radio. "My mother was crying and my dad was silent. The nationalists had 'revolted' and it had all started with a mutiny at the state prison." Emilia was upset that "We could not even fly our own flag" to support Puerto Rican pride and nationalism, and she chafed at the country's dreaded gag law that "gave the government power to crush any opposition from the nationalists, communists" and other opponents.

Emilia's father had voted for the Independence Party, or Partido Independentista Puertorriqueño. Meanwhile, Emilia's mother's family had belonged to the Partido Popular Democrático, the mainstream party run by Luis Muñoz Marín that sharply opposed Puerto Rico's independence. But even Emilia's mother's family was split on the issue. "My mom worried about one of her sisters because her husband was known to belong or sympathize with the Nationalist Party, and a cousin was married to a Socialist leader," Emilia wrote.

As an adult in America, Emilia was sympathetic to independence, but not active or particularly outspoken. Her beloved brother, Coco, had lost his life in a car accident while campaigning for Vanguardia Popular, the radical youth party that was fighting for Puerto Rican independence, environmental justice, and an end to the US military draft. His untimely death seemed to temper Emilia's views. She would later write that her brother "lost his life for a cause." While proud of Coco's strong convictions, she would pine for her only sibling the rest of her life.

On the Montes side of Ana's family, there were rabid supporters of Puerto Rican independence, too. Ana's uncle, Carlos, a university professor, wanted Puerto Rico to be free of its colonial shackles. Carlos, the baby brother of Ana's father, Alberto, resisted joining the US military's Reserve Officers' Training Corps, or ROTC, when in college. Carlos and his wife, Gloria, defiantly flew the Puerto Rican flag on their balcony when that was not allowed. Their daughter Miriam Montes Mock, Ana's first cousin, says that the police opened secrets files on her parents, called "carpetas," and kept track of their activities.

Alberto was a believer in American exceptionalism and a huge supporter of Franklin Delano Roosevelt. "In my mind, he was always THE President," Alberto wrote. Lucy says that her father was always a moderate on the Puerto Rican issue. Although Emilia once told a reporter that, shortly before her ex-husband's death in 2000, he wrote a letter advocating independence for Puerto Rico,[50] Lucy says that's an exaggeration. She says the letter merely expressed the need for greater autonomy for Puerto Rico, but not a break from the mainland; Alberto's letter has been lost to history. Cousin Miriam Montes Mock lives in Puerto Rico and recalls talking to Alberto late in his life. "He stayed in my house for a couple of days, I believe, several months before he died. And he told me that he was interested in the decolonization process of Puerto Rico." Miriam believes that Alberto was interested in exploring statehood for his homeland, a more moderate position than independence.

If Alberto became a late in life supporter of greater political autonomy for his homeland, it would have delighted his radical cousin. Alberto's second cousin[51] Juan Antonio was a famous Puerto Rican political firebrand and Marxist who spent his life opposing US rule and is remembered by fellow revolutionaries as "the voice of the armed clandestine movement."[52]

Juan Antonio Corretjer Montes was one of the most consequential Puerto Rican revolutionaries of the twentieth century. He was also a prolific poet and is often called the National Poet of Puerto Rico. Today, a giant bronze bust of Corretjer Montes peers down from the highest point of his hometown of Ciales, Puerto Rico. In Chicago, a Puerto Rican cultural center also bears his name. Upon Corretjer Montes's death in 1985, a Marxist resistance group eulogized him with a gushing four-page magazine spread in *Breakthrough*, the political journal of the Prairie Fire Organizing Committee. "He endured many hardships, including exile and imprisonment. Yet he always retained his relentless optimism that Latin America would be free and that Puerto Rico would be independent and socialist. He never wavered in his conviction that uncompromising anti-imperialist politics and armed struggle were indispensable in achieving these goals," the obituary states.

"Don Juan" Corretjer Montes was born in 1908 in Ciales, the hometown of Alberto's father and the sprawling Montes clan. He became a nationalist at a young age. Don Juan joined the Anti-Imperialist League of the Americas in the late 1920s and "raised money and arms" to protest US involvement in Nicaragua. By 1930, he had joined the Puerto Rican Nationalist Party under the leadership of Pedro Albizu Campos. Corretjer Montes was named the group's secretary-general. "The Great Depression intensified widespread poverty across the island and contributed to growing numbers of Puerto Ricans embracing the Nationalist Party's demand for independence," explains historian Margaret Power in *Making the Revolution: Histories of the Latin American Left*. [53]

In 1931, in an unlikely foreshadowing of his relative Ana Montes's own activities, Corretjer Montes traveled to Cuba to protest President Gerardo Machado, the US-backed dictator. "On the radio, he urged Cubans to fight with arms in hand to repel a threatened US invasion. For this inciteful act he was jailed for several months," his obituary states.

In 1936, the US Justice Department charged Corretjer Montes, Campos, and six other Nationalist leaders with seditious conspiracy for attempting to overthrow the US government by force in Puerto Rico. They were found guilty and sentenced to ten years in federal prison in Atlanta.[54] It would be the first of at least three arrests for Don Juan.[55] Even after he was paroled, Corretjer Montes continued to attract the attention of US law enforcement. In once-secret FBI files on the Nationalist Party of Puerto Rico, the Bureau described Corretjer Montes as a "leader and Communist officer" of a Nationalist Party splinter group that demanded independence for Puerto Rico "by whatever means may be necessary." The 424-page document, released to the public through the Freedom of Information Act, lists dozens of bombings, assassinations of government officials, and terrorist acts that the FBI pinned on the Nationalist Party over the years. The report concluded that Nationalist Party members "vary in degree and type of cooperation, from financial cooperation to availability for assassination attempts and revolt."

Improbably, Ana's famous relative also championed Cuban leader Fidel Castro. After Fidel's armed revolutionaries ousted the US-backed Batista dictatorship in 1959, the Cuban government sent a plane to bring Corretjer Montes to Cuba to celebrate the victory. There he formed "a close friendship with Che Guevara," the fiery Argentinian who served as Castro's trusted lieutenant[56] and whose poster would later hang in Ana's basement.

Shortly after Castro took power, Corretjer Montes and his wife, Consuelo, formed the Puerto Rican Socialist League, or Liga Socialista Puertorriqueña. It brazenly advocated violence.

"The small size of the island made it imperative that the movement develop the capability to strike at the enemy and be protected from retaliation. [Don Juan] called for the formation of armed clandestine organizations to lead the struggle for independence."[57] The FBI had seen enough. In 1971, Corretjer Montes was jailed for conspiracy again.

Corretjer Montes died in 1985 and, to this day, is revered in Puerto Rico and in revolutionary circles. Thousands thronged his funeral in Ciales. "We will always remember him. Standing before us, tall, calm, dignified. A man who embodied revolutionary character, courage, and determination," his comrades wrote upon his death. Ana's aunt and uncle, Carlos and Gloria, knew Juan Antonio and respected him. "They liked Juan Antonio Corretjer. He was an important person for them," Miriam said of her parents.

Ana Montes arrived in Puerto Rico in the summer of 1979, toward the end of Don Juan's storied life. Ana surely knew of her famous relative Juan Antonio, but it's unlikely they ever met. The CIA would later write that Ana viewed Puerto Rico as "one culture in control of another." She argued that Puerto Rico "had no choice" but to be submissive to the United States. Ana's cousin Miriam is one of her closest friends and confidantes. "She was open about political views, about Puerto Rico's status. And she was openly pro-independence," Miriam said. But while Ana firmly believed that her family's birthplace would be better off without the United States, there's no evidence that Ana shared Juan Antonio's extreme views on how to achieve independence.

That summer in Puerto Rico, in 1979, Ana found a job as a receptionist at a law firm. Then she worked as a temp at the Universidad del Sagrado Corazón, or Sacred Heart University, in San Juan.[58] "She wanted to be Puerto Rican, she wanted to belong," her friend Mimi says. But the reality of Puerto Rico didn't match her idealism. "I met her there one time and I think she was already disillusioned," Mimi said. "When she actually lived on the island and saw the everyday life—the conservative people who are not striving for a cause in their lives—her bubble sort of burst." Ana was desperate for a cause; the people around her were just desperate to provide for their families.

After a few months in Puerto Rico, Ana leapt at a new opportunity. An acquaintance told her about an opening as a clerk-typist in Washington, at the US Justice Department's Office of Privacy and Information Appeals.[59] She wouldn't exactly be saving the world from behind her desk in the typing pool. But it was steady work in the nation's capital and just a short drive to Emilia back in Baltimore. Ana got packing.

Chapter 7.

"A SENSE OF MORAL OUTRAGE"

"Most of the other students and professors at Johns Hopkins shared her views about the unjustness of US policies... It was in this atmosphere that she developed a sense of moral outrage at the US participation in the hostilities in Nicaragua."

—DEPARTMENT OF DEFENSE INSPECTOR GENERAL REPORT ON THE ANA MONTES CASE, JUNE 2005

In December 1979, just as beleaguered President Jimmy Carter announced he would run for reelection, Ana Montes started her career with the Justice Department. She would remain a US government employee for nearly the next twenty-two years, following in her mother's footsteps.

Meanwhile, Lucy was spending her junior year abroad in Madrid, just like Ana. Lucy met a few times with Ricardo and Eduardo, whom Ana had described as avowed Communists. While Lucy recalls pleasant visits, she was struck by the glowing way Eduardo's wife, Silvia, spoke of Cuba. "She said, 'The people in Cuba have not rebelled, the people in Cuba have not revolted against their government. It couldn't be that bad,'" Lucy said.[60] For his part, Eduardo recalls meeting Ana's little sister in Spain, too. "Lucy was younger, she tried to copy Ana's ways," he said with a laugh.

In Washington, Ana began as a clerk with a lowly GS-4 pay grade. "I think initially she was like a receptionist," recalled

Margaret "Peggy" Irving, who was a line attorney in the same DOJ office as Ana and became a lifelong friend. As Montes found inexpensive housing in Northwest Washington, DC, the FBI conducted a routine background investigation of the Justice Department newcomer. In just four months, she sailed through. The FBI had failed to discover Ana's growing contempt of the US government and her love affair with Ricardo. It would be the first of many FBI failings in the case. Years later, when the Pentagon Inspector General studied the Montes security breach and looked back at the FBI's earliest scrutiny of her background, there was no hint of trouble. "This personnel security investigation was entirely favorable, with sources describing Montes as loyal, very moral, extremely independent, with a flawless reputation and compassionate personality," the Pentagon Inspector General reported.

In March 1980, based on the FBI's cheery assurances, the Justice Department granted Ana a top-secret security clearance. The clearance came with "Sensitive Compartmented Information (SCI) access," meaning Ana was now allowed to review some of the most sensitive national security files in the possession of both the FBI and DOJ. Ana quickly impressed her bosses. Supervisors praised her "excellent organization and attention to detail" and rated her as an "exceedingly rare" employee.[61] Peggy Irving recalls hearing that Ana "had very good analytical skills" and that she had been promoted to a legal technician.

Ana began analyzing DOJ records requested under the Freedom of Information Act and determining which documents could be released to the media and public. Originally passed by Congress and signed into law by President Lyndon Johnson in 1967, the Freedom of Information Act (FOIA) was intended to expand government transparency and to curb the misuse of overclassification of documents. Following Nixon's abuses of power exposed in the Watergate scandal, Congress beefed up the FOIA provisions in the 1970s, giving the public the right to request access to records from any federal agency. Ana became a FOIA expert with access to a broad range of secrets. She helped process FOIA appeals and advocated for or against the release of classified information in consultation with intelligence officials from the FBI, CIA, NSA, and National Security Council. During this time, Montes "first ventured into the world of sources and methods, counterintelligence investigations..." and had access to reams of classified information.[62]

Ana's relationship with her father had not improved. Shortly after the movie *Kramer vs. Kramer* came out, about a divorced father (Dustin Hoffman) who must learn how to take care of his young son after his wife (Meryl Streep) walks out, it spurred a Montes family debate on gender roles in modern society. Ana told her father that when she married, she expected her future husband to share in half of the household chores. Lucy recalls that Alberto pushed back. "That was the woman's job, the cooking and the cleaning and the laundry," he said. Alberto lost his temper and began screaming, Lucy said, and Ana walked out. "She didn't speak to him for ten months."

Nearly three years into her job, Ana was made a Justice Department paralegal at the GS-9 pay grade.[63] The promotion nearly doubled her salary.[64] With more financial flexibility, she began considering graduate school. Ana initially hoped to apply to the Defense Language Institute Foreign Language Center in Monterey, California, the famous school that trains US military personnel and select civilians to speak strategically important foreign languages. But Emilia interceded and asked Ana to stay closer to home and apply instead to the School of Advanced International Studies, or SAIS, run by the Johns Hopkins University in Washington. Mom's admittedly selfish plan worked. "She agreed, registered and was accepted," Emilia said.

Established during World War II to help students "cope with the international responsibilities that would be thrust upon the United States in the postwar world," the Johns Hopkins School of Advanced International Studies had become one of the elite training grounds for diplomats, scholars, and politicians seeking a deeper understanding of global affairs. Notable US officials and Cabinet members who have walked SAIS's halls include former secretary of state Madeleine Albright and former Treasury secretary Timothy Geithner. By 1982, when Ana began her two-year master's program with a concentration in Latin American studies, more than three thousand students had graduated from SAIS and were working in eighty countries.[65]

SAIS would prove to be the ideal incubator for Ana's stand-out career as a spy. The famed graduate school introduced her to other leftists who shared her increasingly radical worldview—social scientists call this a "reinforcing peer effect." Surrounded by like-minded students, many of whom were born and educated overseas, Ana's views on US policies toward Latin America "coalesced" at SAIS, the CIA found.

Life at SAIS in the early 1980s was colored by a galling series of events for many students, and much of the faculty, too. California's conservative governor, Ronald Reagan, had been elected president in a landslide in 1980 over Jimmy Carter and had started to flex his foreign-affairs muscles. Reagan began a massive buildup of the US military, declared the Soviets "the focus of evil in the modern world," and railed against Latin American governments and fighters "who've been armed to the teeth by the Soviet-Cuban-Nicaraguan axis."[66] At the start of Ana's second year at SAIS, Reagan even invaded the tropical island nation of Grenada. On the surface, the invasion was intended to protect American medical students enrolled at an island medical school before they could be taken hostage. But, more narrowly, Reagan was thwarting a Communist takeover of the government. Despite condemnation by the United Nations General Assembly, Reagan justified the US Special Forces assault on tiny Grenada. "It was a Soviet-Cuban colony, being readied as a major military bastion to export terror and undermine democracy," the president said.[67]

But it was Reagan's policies in Nicaragua that were the ultimate affront for most SAIS students in the 1980s. Ana and many of her classmates were enthralled by the Sandinistas, or Sandinista National Liberation Front, the Cuban-backed revolutionary Socialist political party that had overthrown Nicaraguan strongman Anastasio Somoza in 1979. Those same SAIS students were equally repulsed by the Reagan Administration's support for the Contras, the CIA-backed counterrevolutionary rebels trying to topple the Sandinistas. The violent excesses of Reagan's Contras in Nicaragua, in what became a proxy war between Cuba and the United States, solidified Ana's mindset. "Ana Montes gained her first real insight into what she described as the cruel and inhumane nature of US government policy supporting the Contra rebels in Nicaragua during her graduate studies at Johns Hopkins," the Pentagon Inspector General found. "She saw the United States as waging a war against that country, killing innocent people, and attempting to overthrow a legitimate government, all of which, in her opinion, was reprehensible." The US invasion of hapless Grenada only magnified those views.

Despite holding down a demanding day job in DOJ's FOIA office, Ana thrived at SAIS. Her graduate coursework at Johns Hopkins included extensive study of Latin American history and US policy. Classes included Introduction to Latin American Politics, Latin American History: A Survey, and Cuba Since 1959, a study of the Castro postrevolutionary period.

Montes aced classes led by the colorful Piero Gleijeses, SAIS's admittedly "most left-wing" professor.[68] The Italian-born scholar taught in SAIS's Latin American department, spoke five languages, and was the brother-in-law of the late John Lennon (Gleijeses's wife, artist Setsuko, is Yoko Ono's sister.) Although classroom memories from the 1980s are growing faint now, Ana clearly left an impression. "I remember that Ana Montes was a very good student," Gleijeses said in an interview in 2022. In the early 1980s, as an adjunct professor closely monitoring President Reagan's bellicose activities in Latin America, Gleijeses freely shared his misgivings with his SAIS students. "I was a person who was very critical of US policy." Even today, years after Montes's arrest and conviction as a Cuban agent, Gleijeses said he feels "respect" for Ana. "She did it for idealistic reasons. One can agree or disagree, that's a different story, but she did it for idealistic reasons," he said. "You had a very aggressive policy by the United States, by the Reagan Administration in Central America and against Cuba. And so whatever she did is also to be placed in the context of what the United States was doing."

All these years later, some of Gleijeses's former colleagues cringe at his coddling attitude toward Cuba. Riordan Roett was director of the Latin American Studies Program at SAIS for decades. Although he praises Gleijeses as a skilled and demanding teacher, he calls him "a bit of a bourgeois revolutionary" who stirred up SAIS's budding leftists. "Any left-of-center student would have gravitated toward Piero," Roett said. "There were always students who romanticized Fidel Castro."

Gleijeses was far from the only faculty member with a soft spot for Cuba. Another SAIS professor during Ana's time on campus was Walter Kendall Myers, who taught European Studies.[69] Dignified and patrician, Myers was sitting on a secret. He was enthralled with Castro and had begun spying for Cuba in 1979, three years before Ana enrolled at SAIS. Myers was not just a quirky academic with a bushy walrus mustache who had written in his private diary that Fidel was a "brilliant and charismatic leader" who had "helped the Cubans to save their own souls." He was also a European analyst at the State Department's Bureau of Intelligence and Research with a top-secret US security clearance. After a sting operation in 2009, the FBI arrested Myers and his wife, Gwendolyn, and charged them with spying for Cuba. The couple had been turning over US secrets to Cuba for three decades and had even had a private audience with Fidel Castro in January 1995. Gwendolyn Myers was sentenced to more than six years behind bars and died in 2015, shortly after her release.[70] Kendall Myers was sentenced to life in prison and remains incarcerated at the Supermax federal prison in Colorado.[71]

Professor Gleijeses wasn't a Cuba expert during Montes's SAIS years. But a decade later, the Castro brothers granted him rare and exclusive access to Cuba's historical archives, including thousands of pages of conversations between Fidel Castro, his closest aides, and foreign leaders. Gleijeses became the only foreign scholar allowed to read the previously closed archives of the Cuban Armed Forces, the Central Committee of the Cuban Communist Party, and the Cuban Foreign Ministry. Ana's SAIS mentor wrote several books and articles about Cuba after the Revolution, and earned generally positive reviews. When the *Washington Post* weighed in on a book Gleijeses wrote on Cuba's military adventures in Africa, it noted: "Gleijeses is clearly sympathetic to Castro's policies, devoting nearly as much space to Cuban doctors in Africa as to Cuban soldiers."[72] Montes was already working at the DIA in the 1990s when her former professor began combing through Cuba's archives. But she didn't miss a stitch. After Gleijeses wrote an article in 1996 on Cuba's decades-old military mission in Algeria, the phone rang. It was Ana requesting a meeting with her old professor. She stopped by SAIS and began pumping Gleijeses for his assessment of the Cuban Armed Forces. "I told her that I didn't know in reality, but, if I knew I wouldn't tell her because I didn't sympathize with her work" as a cog of the US Defense Department, Gleijeses said.

Years later, upon learning that Montes was a spy, he wondered if Havana had sent her to his office to gauge whether he was in bed with any US intelligence agencies. "I knew that there were people [in Cuba] who thought that I was a CIA agent," he said.

Gleijeses must have passed the loyalty test because in 2015, on a trip to Cuba, he got a special dinner invitation. Fidel Castro asked Gleijeses to join him at his home outside Havana, and they spent five hours dining and discussing Cuban history and politics. The name Ana Montes never came up once, Gleijeses said.

Ana was not on the same wavelength with all her SAIS professors. Riordan Roett taught at least six classes during Ana's SAIS years and had a reputation for being politically middle-of-the-road. Which meant that some students, including Ana, pegged him as a red-meat conservative. "She disliked me and my staff completely, and thought we were fascists," Roett told the author of *Spy Schools: How the CIA, FBI, and Foreign Intelligence Secretly Exploit America's Universities.*[73] "Every time I said something that was pro-America, pro-democracy, pro-NATO, she would protest."

Montes worked as both business manager and writer on the staff of *INFOBRAZIL,* a dry newsletter published by SAIS's Center of Brazilian Studies, which professor Roett also directed. Typical articles included "Poor Trade Performance Will Require More External Financing for 1983" and snooze-inducing reports on Brazilian frozen-concentrated orange juice prices.

But SAIS was anything but boring. Ana befriended both the American kids and the Latin American transplants. While she had a reputation as a diligent student who could be reserved and reticent, she was no wallflower. She went to parties and even snorted cocaine with friends at SAIS, common enough in the 1980s, but a potentially career-ending transgression for a Department of Justice employee with top security clearances.[74] And she fell hard for one of the most charming guys on campus, a handsome and gregarious older student named Roberto Álvarez Gil.

Roberto Álvarez cut a dashing figure at SAIS. The son of a successful diplomat from the Dominican Republic, he was a dozen years older than Ana and already had lived a big life. Prior to meeting Ana, he had trained as a lawyer, served in the foreign service of the Dominican Republic, and worked at the Organization of American States as a human rights specialist. SAIS was almost a finishing school for Roberto, and he added a master's degree at John Hopkins and completed all the course work toward a PhD in US foreign policy, too.[75]

Another young SAIS student at that time, Enrique Berruga of Mexico, recalls Roberto as the life of every party. "He was like the host. He was older than all the rest of us and far wealthier," Berruga said. Roberto had a record collection and good wines and was happy to share with his hard-pressed classmates. He kept in great shape and also was a devastating Merengue dancer, the national dance of his homeland. "He would say, 'Okay, next Saturday, we will have a Merengue night now.' And he would be the star of dancing, you know, and all the girls would go nuts about him with his movements," Berruga recalled. Professor Roett was more blunt. "Roberto Alvarez dated everyone," said Roett, the now-retired director of the SAIS's Latin American program. There was "always a string of young ladies" hanging on Roberto when he worked in the Latin American department, Roett added.

In an interview in 2016, Roberto Álvarez recalled first meeting Ana at a Portuguese language class at SAIS. "To class, she wore these cut-off jeans, very short jeans, which weren't the most appropriate at a Master's level at SAIS," he said. "She was a bit rural in her ways, let's say. She was lacking a little bit of finesse in her manners." But, for Roberto, there were other compensations. "The face wasn't all that attractive, but she had a very attractive body."[76]

Ana was even more smitten. "If you could try to make a move on her, she'll say, 'No, no, no. My heart belongs to another guy,'" Berruga said. Ana carried her affection for Roberto "like a shield" and was "utterly unapproachable," especially "if you tried to dance a little bit more horny," he added.

Ana confided to her mother about her strong feelings for Roberto. "I remember she fell in love with the son of an ambassador from the Dominican Republic," Emilia wrote. Meanwhile, Roberto took Ana's longing in stride. "We had a romance for a brief period," he said with characteristic understatement.

Ana could be unsure of herself, and Roberto recalls how uncomfortable she would get in front of his intellectual and politically astute friends at SAIS, including a boisterous ex-girlfriend. "I think she was a little taken aback with our group." The relationship soured, Roberto recalls, when he asked Ana if she would join him and other SAIS students on an exchange program to Cuba with the University of Havana.

Roberto acknowledges that he and his friends could be a bit much. We weren't "going around wearing Che badges," honoring Cuban folk hero Che Guevara, "but we were certainly sympathetic and understanding of the origins, the roots of the Revolution," he said. Given the chance to study Marxist theory in Cuba, a forbidden land with the hot Merengue guy at her side, Ana inexplicably said no. She "gave no impression of being interested whatsoever in any of this," Roberto said. Despite Ana's penchant for speaking her mind in class and lecturing her teachers on the evils of US policy, Roberto concluded that Ana "did not seem very politically inclined." For Roberto, that was the deal breaker.

Roberto thinks his trip to Havana took place in the early 1980s, during the Reagan Administration. When Ana turned her nose at the possibility, the magic was gone. "I do remember that she sort of had distance from us" after he returned from Havana. Ana was an outsider once again, a novice leftist struggling to fit in with the cool kids who more easily embraced the early '80s radical chic. "I think she saw us with a little bit of curiosity and a little bit of jealousy," Roberto said. He started to distance himself, crushing Ana. "I felt so sorry for her," her mother recalled. "It takes time to get over a rejected love."

Roberto Álvarez Gil has had a stellar post-SAIS career. He

opened a popular restaurant in Washington called Café Atlantico with an up-and-coming Spanish chef, José Andrés, the ac-
claimed restaurateur and founder of World Central Kitchen.
More recently, Álvarez was named Minister of Foreign Affairs
for the Dominican Republic.[77] After a distinguished career as
a diplomat, business consultant, and author, Álvarez became
his country's foreign affairs chief in August 2020, appointed by
President Luis Abinader. Álvarez openly discussed his romance
with Ana Montes years before becoming a top government official. When contacted in 2022 about his graduate-school romance with a woman who later became a notorious Cuban spy,
Álvarez left a friendly voice message confirming that he "said
everything I know about Ana" in the earlier interview.

SAIS classmate Enrique Berruga Filloy also found success
as a top diplomat for his country. Following graduation, Berruga worked his way up through the ranks to become ambassador of Mexico to the United Nations, ambassador of Mexico
to Costa Rica, and Mexico's undersecretary of Foreign Affairs
for South America.

Today, Ana's extensive book collection waits for her at
Lucy's home in South Florida. Among the hundreds of hardcov-
ers and paperbacks are presents that the future Mexican ambassador gifted to Ana. Some include intimate inscriptions. "With
much love for my 'Revolutionary Comrade,' from Enrique,"
Berruga wrote in August 1983, on a copy of *Pedro Y El Capitan*,
a famous play about a political prisoner and his torturer. "With
love for Miss Ana Montes," Berruga wrote on another paperback that he dated July 1983. Berruga says that the inscriptions
were meant to show his affection for Ana as a friend and nothing
more. The "Revolutionary Comrade" phrase was a cute nickname and "like a kids' type of thing," he said, and indeed was
written a year before Ana signed on as a Cuban spy.

In graduate school, Ana started hanging out at a group house
near Logan Circle in Washington with a couple of SAIS guys

from Texas and New York. She began dating Phil Pia, a friendly econ major and Italian American from Long Island. And then, seemingly out of the blue, a new best friend came knocking. The SAIS co-ed discovered Ana and hung on tight. It was a friendship from which Ana would never fully recover.

Chapter 8.

"A RICH ARRAY OF TARGETS"

"The Cuban intelligence services (CuIS) are known to actively target the US academic world for the purposes of recruiting agents, in order to both obtain useful information and conduct influence activities."

—FBI WHITE PAPER, "CUBAN INTELLIGENCE TARGETING OF ACADEMIA"[78]

To the casual observer, Marta Velázquez was just another SAIS student. Passionate about world affairs and indignant over the Reagan Administration's imperialistic meddling in Latin America, she blended in at the Nitze Building on Massachusetts Avenue in Northwest Washington. Former Capitol Hill staffer Horace Jennings dated Marta starting in 1984. "She's a very intelligent, very strong-willed person who also happened to be hot. Which is a great combination for me, you know, brains and beauty. That was the Marta I knew," Jennings recalled. Jennings had moved from Austin to DC in 1984 to take a job with Lloyd Bentsen, the Democratic US senator from Texas, and Horace crashed for a while at the Logan Circle group house with mutual friends. He met Marta and Ana through the group house and recalls Marta as being "a lefty in her politics" and "a fiery Latina from Puerto Rico," but not markedly more politically outspoken than her classmates.

★ ★ ★

SAIS Professor Gleijeses remembers Marta for her profession-
alism alone. He hired her as a research assistant for his book,
*Shattered Hope: The Guatemalan Revolution and the United States,
1944-1954*, and praised her "assistance and advice" in the book's
introduction. "I liked her. She was very good. She did excellent
work for me. On Guatemala, I think I thanked her in the [book]
acknowledgments and it was a very pleasant, professional relationship." Gleijeses said he never discussed politics with Marta.

If the teacher and his devoted pupil didn't talk politics, that
might have been one of the first times Marta held her tongue.
Born in Puerto Rico in 1957, Marta excelled in primary and
high school at Colegio Nuestra Señora de La Merced outside San
Juan. In her graduation yearbook, she is described as "the most
intellectual" and the "top prodigy in the class."[79] She was especially close to her father, a respected lawyer and judge named
Miguel Velázquez Rivera who "made no secret of his support
for the independence of Puerto Rico."[80]

Marta studied political science and Latin American Studies
at Princeton University, starting in 1975, and was a vocal student activist. She protested Princeton's investments in the apartheid regime in South Africa,[81] and was photographed at a 1977
rally, fist in the air, behind a sign reading "Apartheid Kills!"[82]
She signed a letter in the *Daily Princetonian* that condemned a
university provost for his "seeming disinterest" in minority students at Princeton,[83] and organized a Latino festival with Ac-
ción Puertorriqueña declaring "Independence and Socialism as
the Only Political Alternative for Puerto Rico."[84] While putting on the Third World Center's cultural festival at Princeton
one year, Marta told the school paper, "We are all part of op-
pressed nationalities throughout the world. Here at the university, which is very conservative and white-male-oriented, if we
can put together a performance as successful as this one was, it's
almost unbelievable."[85] For her senior thesis at Princeton titled,

Race Relations in Cuba: Past and New Developments, Marta, who has dark skin, described herself as "the descendant of an African woman" who lived at a sugar plantation in Puerto Rico.[86] Velázquez even traveled to Cuba with a Princeton group to conduct field research for her final paper.

Marta's Princeton thesis reveals the college senior's bias and naivete and could have been written by *Granma*, the official newspaper of the Cuban Communist Party. The 1959 revolution, she writes, "has guaranteed all workers—black and white—employment, education, health benefits and fair wages. Equality, therefore, now reigns in Cuba." Not only was racism magically wiped out as Fidel Castro took power, she argued, but the very concept of inequality was eradicated, too. "The socialist revolution, with the destruction of all forms of economic development that would thrive on the oppression of the workplace, erased all need for discrimination."[87] The thesis lambastes the United States for aligning itself with the ousted Cuban dictator, Fulgencio Batista, "the defender of a powerful racist class," while heaping praise on Castro. Castro's racial policies "proved to be the wisest course ever taken by a Cuban leader," Marta cooed, concluding that "the new state is indeed a blessing."

After Princeton, Marta headed straight to Georgetown Law School, where she earned a law degree. She moonlit as a managing editor and writer for the *Georgetown Law Weekly*, the student-run newspaper, and her story selection is telling. Marta investigated the law school's contract with a cafeteria operator that had business ties to the racist government of South Africa. She quoted from the Black Law Students Association, which labeled the food vendor "a racist business formation which supports...one of the most reprehensible, barbaric regimes known to humankind since the demise of Nazi Germany." Marta also covered more prosaic law-school happenings, exposing the chaos and "bunker mentality" of Georgetown's legal writing and research program, and the school's persistent funding woes. "The

Sex Discrimination Clinic at 604 G Street, NW, has been suffering for a lack of office furniture for more than a year," Marta railed in one article.

With degrees from Princeton and Georgetown under her belt, Marta went for the trifecta by enrolling at SAIS in the fall of 1982. While her teachers and boyfriend may not have zeroed in on her gushing enthusiasm for Fidel, the Cuban intelligence services most certainly did. After just a year at grad school, Marta flew from Washington to Mexico City "to clandestinely meet with Cuban Intelligence Service officers and/or agents," the US Justice Department would later divulge. She had become a Cuban agent.

It's not clear how the Cubans first learned about Marta Velázquez. They might have met her during her undergraduate trip to Cuba when she was researching her Princeton thesis. Or perhaps a sympathetic professor at SAIS or Georgetown heard about the "fiery Latina from Puerto Rico" and slipped a note to the Cubans. Either way, Marta was a grade A recruit. Infatuated with Castro and an Ivy Leaguer with multiple diplomas on her wall, Marta had everything a foreign intelligence officer could desire. And when the Cubans learned that their eager acolyte already was working as an intern for the US Department of State's Agency for International Development, they were sold.

José Cohen Valdés could have predicted that the Cubans would recruit Marta. The former officer in Cuba's Directorate of Intelligence, or DGI, once had a promising future in his homeland. "A University of Havana mathematics graduate with a specialty in cryptology, he had been recruited for the intelligence service as a young man and risen through the ranks," the *Miami Herald* reported.[88] But the more Cohen learned of Cuba's spy agencies, the greater his disenchantment. "There was a lot of corruption and incredible nepotism. The people who govern the islands are unscrupulous gangsters," he said. Cohen fled Cuba in 1994, leaving his wife and three children behind.

The star defector cooperated with the FBI and CIA and, for his efforts, a Cuban court sentenced him in absentia to death as a traitor. The Cuban government refused to let his family join him in Miami, and kept them separated for years.

Cohen understood the importance of American universities to Cuba's spy services and freely imparted his knowledge to US law enforcement. He wrote a white paper in Spanish titled "Castro's Intelligence Service and the US Academic Community" that details how the wolves encircle their prey.[89] Using Cohen's insider tips, the FBI issued a five-page unclassified report to make American colleges and employers aware of Cuba's underhanded tactics.[90] Academia "offers a rich array of targets" attractive to spy agencies around the globe. "The Cuban intelligence services (CuIS) are known to actively target the US academic world for the purposes of recruiting agents, in order to both obtain useful information and conduct influence activities," the FBI added. The Cubans often use flattery to appeal to students' political or ideological leanings. Once recruited, the idealistic students are put to work. Some are tasked with finding employment inside sensitive US government agencies to pass along classified information to Havana; they are called "agents in place." But others are simply asked "to pass on names of other potential recruits to their Cuban masters, regenerating the recruitment cycle."

As a wide-eyed recruit at SAIS, that was Marta's primary mission—to identify like-minded students and generate leads. Classmate Ana Montes must have seemed an easy mark. She was an outspoken critic of US foreign policy and a socialist ideologue with relatives who supported Puerto Rican independence. Ana had already "expressed her moral indignation about US actions in Nicaragua" to Marta and others in class.[91] As the Justice Department stated in a grand jury indictment that was unsealed in 2013, Marta assisted the Cubans "in spotting, assessing, and recruiting United States citizens who occupied sensitive national security positions or had the potential of occupying such posi-

tions in the future—including Ana Belén Montes—to serve as
agents of the Cuban intelligence service."

By 1984, Ana and Marta were inseparable at SAIS. While it's
unclear if their friendship was genuine or just a pretext for recruitment, they were a memorable duo. "Ana-and-Marta was
kind of a unique combination because Marta was as outgoing as
Ana was reserved," former boyfriend Horace Jennings recalled.
Ana invited her new friend Marta to the DC group house and,
one night over Peking duck in a Chinatown restaurant, she
played matchmaker with Horace. "Marta and I had a very, very
brief little affair," Jennings said.

There were other dinners. In spring of 1984, Marta began
grooming her eager recruit. At a restaurant in Washington, she
made a soft pitch. Ana, I have friends who can help you assist the desperate Nicaraguan people, Marta is thought to have
said.[92] They need someone to translate Spanish-language news
articles about Nicaragua into English, and would love to meet
you, Marta added.[93] Ana was no fool. She must have had an in-
kling that this was how it worked, how one becomes an agent
of a foreign power.

A few months later, Ana and Marta walked in the SAIS graduation ceremony. It was a pretty day, and friends took snapshots
and celebrated their final hours together. Ana, however, had
been handed an empty diploma. She still owed SAIS $2,300 in
tuition, which she had refused to pay. She claimed that the school
had treated her unfairly and had reneged on some financial aid,
and she had no intention of ever paying her debt.[94] In the days
ahead, she would lie to government job recruiters and claim
that she had fully graduated from SAIS, a portent of more consequential deceptions to come. It wasn't until four years later, at
the urging of her Cuban handlers, that she settled up with SAIS
and received her graduate degree and diploma. The Cubans re-
imbursed Ana for her final tuition payment, rare compensation
made to the ideological spy.

Just after graduation, Marta wrote Ana a formal letter consecrating their new arrangement. It said, in Spanish, "It has been a great satisfaction for me to have had you as a friend and comrade [compañera] during this time we've spent as students." She added, furtively, "I hope our relationship continues outside the academic sphere."[95]

As Ana contemplated seriously ratcheting up her political activism, she checked in with some old friends. She flew in August 1984 to Buenos Aires to see the Argentinian mentors who had made such an impression on her during their magical year together in Madrid. At the airport, Ana's old boyfriend Ricardo was there to greet her. He had married by then and was expecting his first child. Ana quickly grew annoyed when Ricardo still seemed attracted to her and couldn't forget the past. Ricardo "needed to realize that we've been over for a long time, that on my part there is nothing more than just affection,"[96] Ana wrote to Mimi in 1984.

There was plenty of sightseeing on the trip, but politics, too. Ana attended the weekly protest by the Mothers of the Plaza de Mayo, a group of grieving women who had lost children and grandchildren to Argentina's repressive regime, and she listened to a concert by a political singer. Ana and her friends also went to lectures about the plight of indigenous Argentinians. It's unclear if she hinted about her pending offer to assist the Sandinistas in their struggles against the US, but the visit reaffirmed her standing with the Argentinian leftists. Ana came away wondering if she should live outside of the United States for good.

Back in DC, Marta got a new job at the US Department of Transportation and quickly received her first "Secret" security clearance. Like Ana, she swore an oath to protect classified information. Although SAIS had ended, Ana saw Roberto again, meeting him for lunch. "I feel so confused in regard to him," she reported to her friend Mimi.[97]

Just as Ana was getting restless handling FOIA requests for

the Justice Department and considered applying for jobs at international aid organizations, Marta cooked up a fun girls' trip. President Reagan had won a runaway reelection against Walter Mondale, carrying forty-nine of fifty states and ensuring the continuation of aggressive US policy in Latin America. Let's hop on the train to New York to meet my friend right before Christmas, Marta is thought to have said, so you can help the Nicaraguans once and for all as they battle the Contras.

Marta's friend, of course, was a Cuban intelligence officer. For decades, the Cubans have used the cover of their offices at the United Nations Mission to conduct espionage and find idealistic Americans willing to help the cause. And that's how, at a popular Manhattan restaurant on Sunday, December 16, 1984, Ana Montes became Fidel Castro's greatest recruit. The twenty-seven-year-old "unhesitatingly agreed to work through the Cubans to 'help' Nicaragua," Defense Department investigators later reported. Marta congratulated her on her decision to spy, telling Ana that their New York dinner companion had predicted that she "would be one of the best" agents to ever assist the island nation.

In postarrest debriefs, Ana almost casually described her momentous decision to turn against her country. "Although she claims she would not have 'volunteered' to spy, she spent little time debating her decision," the CIA wrote. "She felt flattered and empowered by the Cubans' request to assist them with aiding the Sandinistas' cause." Ana strongly disputed that the Cubans had manipulated her. "I hadn't thought about actually doing anything until I was propositioned," she said. It was as if a "force of destiny" had approached her at the same moment she was feeling outrage over Reagan's foreign policy. As a "nobody" far from the action, she was thrilled to help the Sandinistas in their epic struggle against the Reagan-backed Contra forces in Nicaragua. "I was in a position to help, unlike millions of others. Once offered the opportunity to help illegally, it would be more than I could do legally."

The CIA interpreted the recruitment more darkly. Montes was made to believe that Cuba desperately needed her help, "empowering her and stroking her narcissism," the Agency wrote. "Her handlers, with her unwitting assistance, assessed her vulnerabilities and exploited her psychological needs, ideology, and personality pathology to recruit her and keep her motivated to work for Havana."

Another possible rationale for Ana's spying was revenge. The Cubans recruited Ana after SAIS's big man on campus, Roberto Álvarez Gil, jilted her and questioned her commitment to leftist causes. Álvarez, now the minister of Foreign Affairs for the Dominican Republic, says he has sometimes questioned whether Ana decided to secretly assist the Cubans just to prove him wrong. "This is sheer speculation, but I always wondered if she saw us precisely as this bunch of intellectual lefties and 'I'm gonna show them,'" Álvarez said in 2016. But the explanation seems too simplistic. If that were the case, why didn't Ana ever take her victory lap and show Roberto who was the true leftie now? A decade after they split up and Ana was deep into her spying career, she ran into Roberto at the well-regarded DC restaurant he owned, Café Atlantico. She kept her mouth closed. Roberto has no proof, but he wonders if Ana was savoring the moment. She was a master Cuban spy in the service of Fidel; Roberto, at the time, was a simple restaurateur. "We just exchanged pleasantries very briefly. And she was, what can I say? Fine, normal," Álvarez recalls. But something felt off. "I always wondered about that brief moment, whether she was smirking at me."

Whatever Ana's motivations, she and Marta got busy. Marta lent Ana a typewriter and suggested that she provide the Cubans with a simple autobiography. It may seem like a trivial request, but any spy agency would desire the life story of a fresh recruit. First, it creates incriminating evidence ripe for blackmail should the rookie get cold feet. Second, it provides a road map of vulnerabilities for future psychological manipulation. Marta cheered her friend on. Don't forget to include a description of your job at the Justice Department and your top-secret access, she reminded Ana, for good measure.

Chapter 9.

HEADED FOR A COLLISION

"NSA employees receive outstanding benefits that offer a better quality of life, both on the job and off."

—NSA'S JOB RECRUITMENT WEBSITE

In the early 1960s, six-year-old Elena Valdez fled Havana with her parents and young sister.[98] "My Dad left first because they were rounding up all the men," said Elena, who asked to be identified with a pseudonym to protect her identity. Like so many other Cuban families run out of Cuba after the Revolution, Elena's parents sought refuge in Miami. And it was there that they began to rebuild, leaving behind a big network of friends and relatives to make a better life for their daughters in America.

Money was always tight and, at first, her father and mother found work in local factories. Later, they saved enough to open a home-decor store in Miami. They rented apartments instead of buying because Mr. Valdez always fantasized about returning to Cuba once Castro was gone.

Elena was smart, a diligent student, and became the first in her family to attend college. She even won admission to a prestigious US graduate school. She had a facility for languages

and, in the early 1980s, heard about openings at the Drug Enforcement Administration and the National Security Agency.
DEA wanted to send Elena to Colombia to help investigate the
drug cartels. Hard pass. NSA needed Spanish-speaking linguists,
which sounded much more appealing. After a polygraph and a
seemingly endless background investigation, Elena finally was in.

NSA wasn't the most welcoming place for a Cuban immi-
grant, and Elena said she endured at least seven polygraphs over
the course of her three-decade career at the supersecretive organization once jokingly called "No Such Agency." The NSA
security team routinely kept her out of certain meetings that her
colleagues could attend, and she felt she was subject to greater
scrutiny than US-born employees. "They found ways of ex-
cluding me," she said in the first interview she'd ever given to
a reporter. "They were worried about the risk."

But Elena persisted, driven by loyalty to the nation that had
adopted her as a girl, and a desire to make Americans more aware
of the brutal and vindictive Communist regime that had taken
her homeland hostage. "A lot of people think that the Cuban
government is a sugar republic, oh, it's a fun place to go and
smoke cigars," Elena said. "But they have an intelligence service
that is comparable to the Israelis, except of course they are very
poor. But they are serious and get their stuff done."

In 1984, as Ana Montes signed on to give away US secrets to
her comrades in arms, Elena was making a name for herself as
one of the most hard-charging counterintelligence analysts at
NSA. While Ana was full of romantic notions about the Revolution, Elena harbored a burning contempt for the Communists
of the Castro regime. The two women, who joined the US Intelligence Community just a year apart, never met. And yet they
were on intersecting paths, headed for a collision.

Chapter 10.

DESTINATION HAVANA

"Cuba will not be allowed to earn hard currency from American tourists at a time when Cuba is actively sponsoring armed violence against our friends and allies."

—STATEMENT BY AN AIDE TO PRESIDENT REAGAN, IN APRIL 1982, UPON ANNOUNCING THE US GOVERNMENT'S NEW TRAVEL BAN TO CUBA[99]

As Ana wrapped up her dazzling academic career, Lucy did what a lot of twenty-somethings do and moved back home. After graduating college in Massachusetts and then getting a master's degree in bilingual education, she worked for a year as a second-grade teacher in Holyoke. But teaching wasn't for her, so Lucy regrouped. She found a job in Towson selling women's designer clothes at Hecht's, the once-dominant department store chain that originated in Baltimore. Since her mother was living in a one-bedroom condominium, Lucy moved in with her father and his second wife, Nancy, and her kids in their much more spacious home in Baltimore's Roland Park.

Alberto was happy to take Lucy in, and their relationship improved. Briefly. But once Nancy realized that her stepdaughter planned to live with them for more than a summer, she began to clash with Lucy. "She was jealous. She was insecure," Lucy said. "I didn't like living in the same house with her." Alberto hadn't changed his stripes, either. He yelled at Lucy once in front of a boyfriend, and in protest she moved out and slept on the couch at Emilia's.

After two weeks, Alberto coaxed Lucy to come back, but relations with Nancy only deteriorated. One morning, Nancy confronted Lucy in the kitchen and said "some really vicious things" to her. Unforgivable things that Lucy won't repeat. Lucy was ready. "I told her, 'I felt sorry for you when you married my dad, because I thought you have no idea what he's like. And I felt sorry for your kids too. But now I don't feel sorry for you at all. I only feel sorry for your kids.'"

Alberto heard about the blowup and was forced to pick sides. A few days later, he announced his decision. "If you can't get along with my wife, you'll have to leave." Lucy felt betrayed by Alberto's ultimatum, but steeled herself to carry on. She began reading newspaper classifieds and was drawn to the federal job listings. "There were translator positions opening at the FBI and the NSA. I thought, 'Oh, maybe I could be a translator. I think my Spanish is pretty good.' And so I applied to both of them."

To her delight, the FBI accepted. Unfortunately, their only openings at the time were far away in Miami. Lucy wanted to stay closer to her family and asked Alberto for his advice. He had always admired the FBI. Predictably, he counseled her to move. "Take it, take the job," he said.

Lucy had to act quickly to start work in Miami by January 1985. She was excited to share the surprise news with her big sister. Ana had the reputation in the Montes family as "the older, smarter, wiser, more experienced sister," and was frequently condescending to Lucy. But now, Lucy imagined, Ana would be overjoyed to hear that her sister also would be working for the Justice Department. The shared experience would bring them closer.

Lucy called Ana from her mother's condo and was floored by Ana's reaction. "She just had a fit," Lucy recalls. "I told her I had accepted a job with the FBI, and she got all upset. I couldn't understand why my sister would get upset because I took a job with the FBI." When Lucy questioned her, Ana snapped: "Well, I've met agents from the FBI and they're just jerks." The conversation stunned Lucy. "I was really surprised that she would be so against it. I didn't understand it at all."

Despite Ana's misgivings, Lucy began prepping for the move. It clearly had been a stressful time for everyone. On the very night she left for Miami, Alberto suffered a heart attack, the first of three he would have in his lifetime. He asked his other children not to tell Lucy, and they stayed silent. Alberto said he didn't want Lucy to feel guilty as she was starting a new job. Lucy remained in the dark for six weeks—another Montes family secret.

For Ana, Lucy's foray into law enforcement could not have come at a worse time. Within a week or two of accepting the Cubans' offer to spy, Lucy had upended everything. The sibling she had so frequently discounted went, overnight, from selling lady's blouses to becoming a Fed. Adding to the disaster, Ana and Marta were planning a covert trip to Cuba to meet their handlers. It was not especially comforting to know that, back home, Lucy was joining the FBI. She would be working for a major field office dedicated to rooting out Cuban spies. "It made her very nervous," Lucy realized, much later.

Ana and Marta, the budding criminals, soldiered on. Their *Thelma & Louise* adventure could not wait. Marta headed back to New York to meet with her shadowy Cuban friend and get final travel instructions. It was finally time for Ana to experience the revolutionary mecca firsthand, after having turned down Roberto's earlier offer.

On Friday, March 29, 1985, Ana and Marta took what appeared to be an innocuous spring break trip to Madrid. They flew to Spain using their own identification. But once on the ground, the ruses began. They met a Cuban cutout in Spain who provided them with phony passports. How far Ana had come since her junior year abroad in Madrid, seven years earlier.

The friends flew next to Prague, hopscotching throughout Europe to cover their tracks. In Communist-controlled Czechoslovakia, then a close partner to Cuba, two new operatives were waiting. At a safe house, the Cubans handed Ana and Marta travel clothes and a new set of false passports. One of the men, later nicknamed "F" by the FBI, accompanied the novices on the long flight to Havana.[100] The precautions were standard tradecraft to protect the identities of Cuba's promising new recruits. Cuba's intelligence service, or DGI, had a lot on the line, but so did the two young US government employees. Just three years earlier, President Reagan had banned most American tourists from visiting Cuba and designated the country a state sponsor of terrorism.[101]

Once safely delivered to Havana, Ana and Marta could relax. The DGI built an itinerary that mixed work with island fun, keeping in mind that their trainees were single women in their late twenties. Ana and Marta were enrolled in a master class in spycraft taught by some of the best in the business, who in turn had been trained by the Soviets. The young Americans learned how to communicate covertly with their handlers by receiving encrypted high-frequency shortwave radio messages sent by Havana. They practiced being followed, and how to artfully lose a tail. And they insisted on taking practice polygraphs, so they could outsmart security teams when applying for classified positions inside sensitive US government agencies.[102] The old hands at the DGI taught Ana and Marta how to fake their way through a lie detector test. The trick involved the strategic tensing of the sphincter muscles to affect blood pressure. It's unknown if the ploy worked or merely gave them the confidence to keep bluffing, but Ana and Marta passed every government-administered polygraph they took after their Havana training sessions.

For more than sixty years, Cuba has operated a sophisticated and resourceful espionage service that is surprising for a country of its size. Intelligence experts acknowledge that Cuba's DGI is extremely capable and determined to place spies deep within the US military, exile, and intelligence communities. "The Castro regime has long targeted the United States for intensive espionage activities," the State Department wrote in a fact sheet in 2003.[103] "Over a fifteen-year period from 1983 to 1998, fifteen members of the Cuban mission to the United Nations were expelled for espionage activities," the State Department added. Cuba's paranoia is well-founded. The CIA's numerous attempts to assassinate Fidel Castro or destabilize his regime date back to the Kennedy Administration and the thwarted 1961 invasion of Cuba at the Bay of Pigs. Many more attempts became public in 1975, when Senator Frank Church of Idaho conducted hearings on the CIA's plots involving foreign leaders. The Church Committee concluded there were "at least eight plots involving the CIA to assassinate Castro from 1960 to 1965."[104] Some were absurd, involving poisoned wet suits, toxic cigars, and aerosol attacks. Others were more sophisticated and called for the use of mafia figures to take out the Cuban leader. In 1960, one of the mobsters asked his CIA handlers if he could be furnished with "some type of potent pill that could be placed in Castro's food or drink," according to CIA records that were declassified in 2007. The 702-page data dump, the CIA's so-called "Family Jewels" report, details twenty-five years of misdeeds by the spy agency and helps to explain Castro's fear of US meddling, and worse, in Cuba.[105]

As Ana toured Cuba under the command of the DGI, she had a brief affair on the island with a guy she described as "gorgeous." He proudly showed off his country and even took her to military bases, which likely means he was an intelligence agent himself or a hunk-for-hire. Ana was impressed with her beefy tour guide, but couldn't help but notice Cuba's pervasive poverty.

After nearly two weeks of instruction, Ana and Marta headed

home, retracing their steps from Havana to Prague to Madrid, and using both sets of phony passports again. They stopped in Madrid long enough to pose for photos of themselves in front of famous tourist destinations. In case any pesky customs agent came asking, they were just two American girls on a sun-soaked Spanish holiday.

Despite her Tradecraft 101 courses, Ana was not yet a master of deception. Or discretion. Upon arriving home in DC, she couldn't help dishing to her old girlfriend, Mimi Colon. Ana was "beaming" and disclosed to Mimi that she had vacationed in Cuba, attended lectures by fascinating Cuban professors, and met all kinds of wonderful people. But mostly, she shared details on the hot guy who had chaperoned her. "We were talking about men, not about politics," Mimi said. "She knew I was a very naive listener... I was very safe."

In the middle of a travel ban to Cuba, it would have been verboten for a Justice Department employee with a top-secret security clearance to visit the Communist stronghold. But Ana took it one step further. She volunteered to Mimi that she had visited Cuban military bases, destinations that clearly would have been off-limits for any regular American tourist. Ana must have quickly realized her novice mistake. Shortly after their gab session, she abruptly cut Mimi off. She stopped phoning Mimi or taking her calls and permanently closed the door on their friendship. Mimi was devastated and wondered—for the next sixteen years—if she had done something to cause the split. "Prior to this we used to write to each other all the time," Mimi said. But after Ana's confession, "she never wrote again, ever. I wrote to her for 2½ years after that and eventually stopped. I could not understand the sudden change."

There was another reason why Ana needed to clean house. She was about to start interviewing for jobs at US government agencies that required high-level security clearances. She couldn't afford to let investigators stumble upon a chatty old friend who could blow her cover. Better to just cut Mimi out of her life completely and hope that no one ever asked her about Ana's two-week mystery trip, not to mention the lefties she and Mimi had befriended in Spain years ago.

Ana started to hunt for jobs that would grant her access to classified information, particularly on the civil war in Nicaragua. The high-level security clearance from DOJ she had already acquired—Washington's coin of the realm—made her a desirable candidate. She applied to the Office of Naval Intelligence and the Arms Control and Disarmament Agency, now-defunct.[106] She claims that she never really wanted to work in the Intelligence Community to "help our government carry out policies in Latin America that I vehemently disagreed with. I wanted something more palatable and less extreme."[107] But when she didn't immediately get an interview at a human rights group, she never reapplied. And so it was that, in June 1985, Ana filled out an application to work for the Defense Intelligence Agency, or DIA. She listed Marta, her fellow traveler, as a character reference.

After Ana's arrest, she "continuously and vehemently" denied to her debriefers that the Cubans played any role in directing her to find work at DIA. However, as part of the plea bargain negotiations, Ana's lawyers openly contradicted their client. Ana's legal team provided an attorney proffer "that she was specifically targeted by the Cubans to apply for a position at the DIA." Not only had the Cubans suggested that Ana apply to the US military's largest intelligence agency, but they even "assisted her in preparing her application."[108]

Ana's Justice Department supervisors had been dazzled by her talents, with one boss describing her as "an outstanding worker and delightful person." When he learned that Ana was seeking employment elsewhere in the government, he paid her the highest compliment. He said "recruiting her was one of the smartest things I ever did. If you can get her, take her."[109]

After two interviews, that's precisely what DIA recruiters did.[110] On September 30, 1985, Ana began work as an entry-level analyst for DIA, the nation's primary producer of foreign military intelligence.

Today with more than sixteen thousand employees worldwide, DIA is the main intelligence arm for the Secretary of Defense, the Joint Chiefs of Staff, and the combatant commands. It's the CIA for the Department of Defense, if you will, disseminating highly classified information to American warfighters. The DIA closely tracks foreign militaries to protect the United States and its allies. There's a need for an honest broker. In the 1950s, the Army, Navy, and Air Force were known to inflate assessments of Soviet capabilities and to inefficiently produce duplicative assessments of foreign forces. President John F. Kennedy's Secretary of Defense, Robert McNamara, established the DIA in 1961 to provide impartial and integrated intelligence for the entire Department of Defense. The new agency proved its worth just a year later, during the Cuban Missile Crisis, when DIA's Chief of the Latin American Division helped to discover Soviet nuclear missiles in Cuba—seventy-foot SS-4 medium-range ballistic missiles hidden in the woods on the western end of the island.[111] It was an early indication of the importance of the DIA to winning, or preventing, wars around the globe. Ana was now a fully recruited Cuban spy, an agent in place, deep behind enemy lines.

The media would dub 1985 as "The Year of the Spy." That's the year the FBI arrested retired US Navy Warrant Officer John Walker Jr., and his family members for spying for the Soviets. It's also when the Bureau nabbed US Naval Intelligence officer Jonathan Pollard for passing classified materials to the Israelis, and NSA specialist Ronald Pelton for spying for the KGB. "The Cold War was on its last gasps, but you would have never guessed it by all the moles in the U.S. government who were passing secrets," the FBI said of the Year of the Spy.[112] The FBI wouldn't learn it for fifteen more years, but Ana Montes (and the FBI's own Robert Hanssen) also had joined 1985's rogues' gallery of US officials who had turned their backs on the home team.

Once at DIA, it took Ana time to adjust. "I did not know the difference between a corporal and a colonel, and I'm not kidding," she said. "I didn't even know which Service was wearing the green uniform and which Service was wearing the blue..."[113]

Prior to her employment at DIA, one female colleague from the Justice Department had ratted her out to the FBI's background-check investigators. The unidentified coworker "suggested that Montes was disloyal to the United States" because of her vocal opposition to US policy in Nicaragua.[114] That might have been helpful information for the DIA to consider before they hired Ana—and before they made her the DIA's principal Nicaragua analyst.

Marty Scheina spent nearly thirty years at DIA and retired in 2006 as the staff director for DIA's Counter Narcotics Office. When Scheina, then a supervisor of DIA analysts overseeing Latin America, hired Ana in 1985, he said he never heard anything negative about her. He accepted Ana based on her SAIS degree, DOJ track record, and strong job interviews. It didn't hurt that Ana was Puerto Rican. "I felt, what better person to be able to judge the minds of a Latino than another Latino?" he said. DIA didn't conduct polygraphs then.

Scheina hired Ana as a longform analyst. Like a reporter embedded inside DIA, she would be researching and writing reports and articles about the militaries of Central American countries and their political intelligence capabilities. It was a boom time for hiring at DIA, with the Reagan Administration's hyper focus on Central America, and Scheina had to fill slots quickly. If everyone got polygraphed back then, he said, "we were never getting anybody in the door."

Ana spent eight months on the job before the Defense Investigative Service got around to asking her about her political critiques of US actions in Nicaragua, as reported much earlier by a former DOJ colleague. Ana brushed off the accusations, affirming that she had a First Amendment right to disagree with her government. She professed loyalty as a US citizen and added, helpfully, that she had never advocated the overthrow of the government. The Defense Investigative Service was satisfied and checked the box. Meanwhile, Ana had learned an important lesson. She could no longer speak her mind as she had in graduate school. To get by with the DIA officials working at Bolling Air Force Base, with their crew cuts and medals and well-pressed uniforms, she needed to sublimate her personal beliefs. And blend in.

Chapter 11.

MIAMI VICE

"Force, violence, including murder, bribery of police officers and attempts to induce false testimony before a federal grand jury were all utilized by the Enterprise to protect and conceal its affairs from interference from law enforcement authorities…"

—FROM THE FEDERAL INDICTMENT OF FLORIDA DRUG KINGPIN MARIO S. TABRAUE, JULY 1988

Down in Miami, Lucy had started her own adventure. Just as NBC's *Miami Vice* was breaking ratings records with its MTV soundtrack and Armani-clad cops chasing down local drug thugs, Lucy began assisting a real-life federal task force trying to save southern Florida from a cocaine-fueled explosion of violence. On the day Lucy started at the FBI's Miami Field Office in January 1985, the FBI and local police arrested four men for drug trafficking and seized $20 million of cocaine at a home in South Dade. It was the second major Dade County cocaine bust in two days.[115]

Almost immediately in Miami, Lucy got a top-secret security clearance and began translating Title III wiretaps of drug dealers and gunrunners under federal investigation. She was a GS-9 Language Specialist, earning $21,804 a year, with health care and a retirement fund. She missed her family but couldn't have been happier in Florida. Lucy was deputized in 1986 to translate for a federal Organized Crime Drug Enforcement Task Force, and traveled to Atlanta for a month to help the FBI and federal prosecutors crack down on rampant drug dealing in Georgia.

After just three years on the job, Lucy was earning accolades. William Sessions, then the director of the FBI, gave her a cash award and his personal thanks in 1988 for her "outstanding contributions" on the DOJ drug task force that had brought down Mario Tabraue, the Cuban American kingpin of a Miami cocaine empire.[116] Tabraue was a machine-gun-toting archvillain straight out of *Scarface*—if Tony Montana also owned a pet giraffe and cheetah. Federal prosecutors alleged that Tabraue had been the "chairman of the board" of a cocaine and marijuana trafficking network worth $75 million and arrested him in December 1987 as part of Operation Cobra. "At one point, investigators charged, he had stored ten thousand pounds of marijuana at the Parrot Jungle, a Miami-Dade tourist attraction," the media reported.[117] Tabraue was sentenced to one hundred years in prison[118] but was released on appeal in 2000 after just a dozen years behind bars.[119] More recently, Tabraue gained fame in Netflix's *Tiger King* TV series as one of the owners of an exotic animal business.[120]

Lucy had been surprised when Ana took the job at DIA, and always expected her to work for an international charity group. But she was excited to share her triumphs and thought that Ana would want to hear a sanitized version of her Miami escapades. After all, Ana also worked in the Intelligence Community and had a security clearance, so Lucy assumed their new positions might bring them closer. Again, disappointment. Ana showed zero interest in hearing war stories about the FBI and was even more guarded about her own DIA experiences. Ana's reluctance to open up, or even tell an innocuous workplace story or two, triggered memories of the sisters' inability to connect starting at adolescence. "She shared very little about herself with me. I guess

I'm the kind of a person, I've always been an open book. She was the opposite," Lucy said. "I guess she was always secretive."

Like Lucy, Ana was making a name for herself at her new job. The Cubans had done their homework well. Ana became DIA's principal analyst for El Salvador and later for Nicaragua, just as the Cuban-backed civil war in Nicaragua was heating up.

DIA's security failings were remarkable. The Personnel Security Division accepted Ana's flawed FBI background investigation from 1980, the one that apparently had missed or discounted her relationship with Ricardo and Ana's strong feelings about Puerto Rican independence. The DIA security pros granted Ana an interim top-secret clearance on October 2, 1985, just two days after her start date. She wasn't polygraphed or given psychological testing, since DIA didn't yet have a polygraph capacity; by contrast, CIA and NSA already did.[121] She wouldn't undergo a DIA counterintelligence polygraph, now standard at US intelligence agencies, for nine more years.

In the meantime, Ana's supervisors were in a pinch. More analysts were needed to support the US military's growing role in El Salvador under Reagan. Ana's new bosses formally requested that she be given SCI clearance, even higher than "top secret," granting Ana access to some of the most closely held secrets within the possession of the Department of Defense. Remarkably, just four months after stepping foot inside DIA, Ana was granted a waiver and allowed to read SCI documents about El Salvador, Nicaragua, and US military operations in-country. Ana's illegal trip to Cuba was still a fresh memory.

Even more disturbing, DIA's investigators missed two blatant lies that Ana told during her application process. First, she claimed that she had received a master's degree from SAIS in 1984. In reality, she was still beefing with school administrators over tuition and never formally graduated. DIA never bothered to confirm with SAIS. Second, Ana lied about drugs. While she admitted to some marijuana and cocaine use in college, she claimed that she had last used drugs in 1979 at UVa. In reality, Ana had snorted cocaine with SAIS friends in 1982, after gaining a top-secret security clearance with the Justice Department.[122] "I intentionally lied about the cocaine as my use was so recent," Ana later confided to CIA profilers. "I did not want to get rejected."

DIA's personnel security team conducted a background investigation of Ana nine months after her start date and remained unaware of both lies. Ana herself revealed them to DIA years later, in a preemptive move in 1991, volunteering that she had fudged on her job application regarding drug use and her phony diploma. But by then she had earned so much respect within the agency that her lies were quickly forgotten.

As Ana settled in as a DIA analyst, Lucy shared some exciting news. Less than two years after arriving in Miami, she had fallen in love. Her fiancé was Chris Mangiaracina, a painter with a small art studio on South Beach.[123] Chris also managed the auto fleet at the FBI's Miami Field Office and was preparing to work for the Bureau as a white-collar financial crime investigator. They had met on the job and the romance was quick. Soon Ana would have two family members who worked for the nation's top law-enforcement agency.

The wedding news only heightened growing differences between the sisters. Lucy noticed that Ana had become somber and lost her sense of humor. She declared that she wasn't interested in marriage and refused to date anyone from work. What's more, Ana volunteered, she generally ate lunch at her desk and didn't enjoy socializing with coworkers. "That was the beginning of where I found myself disagreeing with my sister over and over again about things," Lucy said. "And I couldn't understand why she would say a lot of the things that she said."

Lucy began planning her wedding in the evenings and off-hours, while eavesdropping on drug dealers on court-authorized wiretaps during the day. In December 1986, she gathered her friends and family for a joyous bridal shower in Baltimore. Ana invited a sidekick for the festivities. It was Marta Velázquez, her Cuban coconspirator. In a photo of that day, Lucy and Marta sit shoulder to shoulder on a couch, flashing pearly white teeth and big smiles all around. At the far end of the couch, dressed in black with matching black pearls, Ana looks distressed with a distant gaze in her eyes. On her sister's big day, she struggles to muster a grin.

Chapter 12.

A WARRIOR MONK DEEP WITHIN
THE BUREAUCRACY

"When you finish studying this book you, too, will have a better understanding of what your memory is and what it can do; you will be aware of basic principles to guide you in improving your memory…"

—FROM THE BOOK, YOUR MEMORY: HOW IT WORKS & HOW TO IMPROVE IT, FOUND ON THE BOOKSHELF IN ANA'S WASHINGTON, DC, APARTMENT[124]

Ana's new dual assignments were equally demanding. By day, she pored over classified intelligence reports on El Salvador, looking for long-term patterns. At night and over the weekends, she was on the clock for Fidel.

For the first three months at DIA, Ana met her handlers in New York City, usually at restaurants recommended by the Cubans. Marta tagged along at least twice. But meeting in New York with intelligence officers assigned to the Cuban Mission to the United Nations was risky. The FBI frequently identifies Cubans working in the UN Mission, and special agents follow them on a regular basis. Ana wisely insisted that, moving forward, she would only meet her handlers in Washington. And she requested that her Cuban contacts no longer be so obvious. No one could be tied to the UN Mission in New York or the Interests Section in DC. (The building was called an "Interests Section" because Cuba and the US did not have formal relations in the 1990s and 2000s, and thus the stately Cuban-owned mansion could not fly a country flag or properly be identified as an embassy.)

The Cubans were happy to accommodate Ana with an illegal officer or NOC, meaning an operative under Non Official Cover, without known ties to the Cuban government or DGI. Ana's new handlers would meet her at Chinese restaurants in Washington near Metrorail stations. They began dining together once every two to three weeks, generally on the weekends. Ana had a fear of street crime, particularly during the crack epidemic in Washington, and insisted on meeting in blue-chip DC neighborhoods.

To avoid detection, Ana decided early on to limit the number of documents she removed from DIA. She presented her handlers once with a DIA phone book, plus the occasional classified photograph or memo.[125] But handing off hard documents was rare. She knew that DIA security guards conducted random bag searches, and didn't want to be caught taking a classified document off premises. "She believed that she would not leave a paper trail if she communicated intelligence information to the Cubans by memorizing her recollections," the Defense Department learned.[126] This strategy was safer, but necessitated mentally storing reams of data; Ana is believed to have read tens of thousands of highly classified documents in her career, at least.

Ana bought a book on memory techniques that stressed using mnemonics, visualization, and repetition of key phrases.[127] "*Your Memory* is the essential guide for everyone on the quest to improve their memory," the book promises. Although CIA psychologists would later assess her as having "superior" intellectual functioning as measured by the Wechsler Adult Intelligence Scale, and "superior, novel nonverbal reasoning ability," they noted her relative weaknesses in retention. "Montes displayed an average ability to hold and process information in memory," the CIA found. "When pressed for time, Montes has difficulty processing visual information quickly." Retaining loads of information would turn out to be an exhausting side hustle for someone with an average memory. By sheer will and discipline, Ana improved her ability to collect and disseminate information. She would churn out priceless secrets to her handlers, week after week. There was a secondary advantage to locking all that data in her brain—ego. Ana was not merely stealing papers like Robert Hanssen, the disgraced FBI turncoat, who stuffed trash bags full of classified documents and left them for the Russians at dead drop locations in Virginia in exchange for cash and diamonds. She was gathering raw intelligence and then appraising its value, acting as a seasoned analyst for both the American and Cuban sides. "Significantly, this scheme played to Montes' grandiose perception of herself as a comrade-in-arms with the Cubans," the Defense Department said. "By passing classified information verbally and constructing notes from memory, Montes saw herself as an equal with her Cuban comrades, not as a menial espionage tool extracting classified documents from 'enemy' installations."

Ana typically took lunch at her desk, absorbed in quiet memorization of the latest briefings. She informed the Cubans that she would not attempt to gain access to classified information that was outside her assigned duties at DIA. But that left plenty of runway, especially with the heightening civil wars in Nicaragua and El Salvador. She would focus on learning and sharing secrets of strategic value to the Cubans, while her handlers could worry about meeting-site security and countersurveillance to ensure they weren't being followed by the FBI.

Her intense attention to detail began to pay off. DIA supervisors continually praised Ana in her first few years of employment, commenting on her "high intelligence and positive attitude."[128] Ana was a longform, foundational analyst responsible for identifying trends in Salvadoran military capabilities. She would write top-secret reports, often the "Defense Intelligence Summary," for review throughout the Intelligence Community. During these early years, the directors of the Defense Security Assistance Agency congratulated Ana for her outstanding translating skills at a conference with the US-backed Salvadoran Armed Forces.[129]

Marty Scheina, DIA's former Chief of the Latin America Division, remained Ana's supervisor for most of the rest of her DIA career, just shy of sixteen years. He remembers being immediately impressed with Ana's nonstop drive. "She was an outstanding analyst. She was a phenomenal writer, extremely prolific, typically producing about two to three times as much as the average analyst."[130] Ana expanded her analytical knowledge by taking several DIA technical courses as well as a three-day orientation course in Signals Intelligence, or SIGINT, taught by the NSA. By the late 1980s, she was earning widespread notice. Her reports were "praised by policy makers, the Military Departments and the Intelligence Community for their timeliness and clarity."[131]

As Ana burrowed deeper into DIA, Marta was making her mark in government, too. "Marta Velázquez has been traveling all over the world, negotiating international maritime and aviation agreements as a lawyer for the US Department of Transportation," the *Princeton Alumni Weekly* trumpeted in an alumni roundup.[132] Little did they know that their former classmate, now code-named "Barbara," was double-timing as a Cuban agent, according to Justice Department prosecutors. Marta was indeed traveling all over the world—passing classified government secrets to her handlers "with the intent and reason to believe they would be used to the injury of the United States."

Marta and Ana stayed close until 1988, when Marta "provoked a dispute" with Ana and publicly broke off their friendship, prosecutors alleged in an indictment of Marta made public in 2013. She concocted an argument with Ana just before taking a high-level job as a lawyer with the US Agency for International Development and shipping off to the US Embassy in Managua, Nicaragua. The faux breakup was meant to "effect compartmentation" between the two friends, the DOJ claimed, or to clean the records of both conspirators as they advanced in their government careers.

Ana's mother, Emilia, recalled how Ana used to bring Marta to holidays and family parties in Baltimore until one day she abruptly disappeared. "I realized they were not on speaking terms anymore but Ana refused to say why," Emilia said. Piero Gleijeses, the SAIS professor, recalls that Marta volunteered to him that her friendship with Ana was over. Ana had joined the dreaded DIA and "had become very conservative and basically the friendship has gone astray," Marta told Gleijeses. It wasn't until after Marta's indictment became public that the professor discerned the truth. "Probably Marta was selling me a lot of lies."

The dustup was just another bit of OPSEC theater. After Marta gave birth to a boy, Ingmar, a Cuban intelligence officer was instructed to share the good tidings. In 1998, he quietly passed the happy news to Ana back in Washington, a decade after their friendship supposedly had imploded.

The contrived fight with Marta wasn't the only cleanup project. In the late 1980s, Ana's friend and former SAIS classmate Enrique Berruga was working in Washington as a press attaché at the Mexican Embassy. Ana invited him out for lunch. Over sandwiches, in a somewhat funereal tone, she made it clear that this was to be their last interaction. "She told me, 'Because of the sensitivity of my job, I cannot have a social life as a normal human being,'" Berruga recalled. "She said, 'Well, because of what you're doing for life professionally, and what I do, we cannot see one another.'" Berruga, then just a junior aide, thought Ana was joking. He asked, "Are we going to exchange Mexican secrets with the American secrets, or what is going to happen?" But Ana was serious and held firm. That was the last time they ever talked.

Upon reflection, Berruga wonders if Ana was trying to protect him. Perhaps, he said, Ana thought "he's not aware of how dangerous I can be." And since she cared about him, she determined to stay far away for the rest of her career—even though the future ambassador to Mexico would have been a juicy intelligence target for Cuba. "That's a possibility," he said, because Ana always struck him as "an innocent, sort of a noble person." Berruga, who once gave Ana a book with the inscription, "With much love for my 'Revolutionary Comrade,'" now thinks Ana was doing him a favor. "Perhaps she thought to herself... I'm going to jeopardize his position or his life just by having sandwiches."

Chapter 13.

DEATH OF A GREEN BERET

"Gregory A. Fronius, SFC US Army, NOV 3, 1959—MAR 31, 1987"

—CEMETERY MARKER FOR STAFF SGT. GREGORY FRONIUS, US ARMY SPECIAL FORCES

Apparently, not everyone merited the same protection. In early 1987, Ana took her first DIA-authorized trip outside the country. She traveled to Guatemala for one week and to El Salvador for five. It was her lengthy stay in El Salvador, at the height of the conflict for control of the nation, that could have relegated her to a life sentence.

The civil war in El Salvador is a distant memory for many Americans, a footnote conflict long since forgotten by Hollywood. But there was a time when Americans cared deeply and picked sides in the struggle for El Salvador. Progressives were sickened by the killing and torture carried out by Salvadoran government forces, often in concert with death squads and army units trained by the United States. Conservatives were alarmed by the territorial ambition of the rebels, Marxist guerrillas propped up by the Soviet Union and Cuba to export Communism throughout the Americas. President Reagan once spoke live from the Oval Office, in prime time, about the threat he believed El Salvador's Marxists posed at America's doorstep. "San Salvador is closer to Houston, Texas, than Houston is to Washington, DC," Reagan warned. "What we see in El Salvador is an attempt to destabilize the entire region and eventually move chaos and anarchy toward the American border... El Salvador's yearning for democracy has been thwarted by Cuban-trained and-armed guerrillas, leading a campaign of violence..."[133]

Montes, the DIA's premier Salvadoran analyst, found herself in the middle of the action. Inwardly, she loathed how, in her view, the US always seemed to back murderous authoritarians in foreign lands. But around her chest-thumping DIA colleagues, she had learned to bury her personal feelings, all in the name of the greater good. The Pentagon had sent US military trainers to El Salvador to prop up the regime's feckless army. Ana was perfectly positioned to share every last detail with her Cuban superiors.

In January and February 1987, as part of analyst orientation,[134] Ana traveled to El Salvador to get a lay of the land. She briefed US service members in the field, interviewed top US Embassy officials in the capital, San Salvador, and helped assess the capabilities of the Salvadoran Armed Forces, or ESAF, at bases throughout the country. As first reported by DIA investigator Scott Carmichael in his book *True Believer: Inside the Investigation and Capture of Ana Montes, Cuba's Master Spy,* Ana also paid a visit to the El Paraiso military base, a showcase compound manned by the Salvadoran army's 4th Infantry Brigade. Located thirty-six miles north of San Salvador, it was on the edge of a major battle zone. Ana received briefings on base security and operations to thwart guerrilla attacks.

American Special Forces advisers had designed El Paraiso in 1982 to be impregnable, but it wasn't. The Marxist-led Farabundo Marti National Liberation Front guerrillas, or FMLN, had already attacked it once, nearly destroying it. In the early-morning hours of March 31, 1987, they came back. At around 2:00 a.m., rebel sapper units penetrated the fence line and rained mortars on the center of the base. They raced in with satchel charges, the *New York Times* reported, "blowing up barracks and raking dumbfounded soldiers with automatic weapons, according to survivors."[135] At least forty-three Salvadoran soldiers were killed in the ambush and more than thirty-five wounded. Among the dead was Staff Sergeant Greg Fronius, a US Special Forces soldier and the first American military adviser to die in combat in El Salvador.

Fronius was a Green Beret, just twenty-seven years old, and had only been in El Salvador for three months. The married father of two young children grew up in Ohio and Pennsylvania and had always wanted to serve his country. "He wanted that Green Beret," his brother, Stephen, told the *Philadelphia Inquirer* in 1987. "He asked them for the toughest outfit. He just loved the service, and he didn't want to be in the rear echelon."[136]

Given the precision of the El Paraiso ambush, military experts have long speculated that the rebels had help from an inside source. The Chief of Staff of the Salvadoran army told reporters he suspected that some of the guerrillas had "infiltrated the army to gather intelligence for the attack."[137] An FMLN commander who helped attack El Paraiso later admitted that the Cubans had helped train him how to fire a mortar.[138]

We now know that a trained Cuban spy—Ana Montes—visited El Paraiso just weeks before the attack and had received briefings on the camp's security measures. Is it possible that Ana shared those classified details with her Cuban comrades after her trip, imperiling the lives of Greg Fronius and his Salvadoran trainees?

After Ana's 2001 arrest, military and civilian debriefers spent days interrogating her about her trip to El Paraiso. They were desperate to know if she provided details to her Cuban handlers about the security profile at El Paraiso and whether she met Fronius and pumped him for information. If so, Ana could face murder charges.

The FBI and DIA walked away frustrated. Ana said she could no longer remember meeting Fronius or what she might have told the Cubans about El Paraiso. "She never acknowledged or admitted that there was any possibility that her information caused the death of anyone, let alone US service people," one FBI debriefer and case agent said. DIA counterintelligence officer Mark Ritter agrees. The trained interrogator spent weeks in an FBI conference room interviewing Montes postarrest, and says that he and his team "keyed in" on Ana's visit to El Paraiso. "We asked her about it a lot," Ritter said. "I came away with nothing." Ritter says that, even when he printed out DIA reports that Ana had written and highlighted key sections to ask if she had shared those classified details with Cuba, Ana would punt. "In most cases she would say, 'Well, I don't remember because you're talking 10 years ago or 15 years ago.'" Carmichael believes Ana knew more than she led on. "I would say that she may have been fluffing it a little bit because she doesn't want to take responsibility for somebody's death." Her legendary memory got shaky when talking about the death of an American, he said.

While the interrogators got Ana to concede that El Paraiso's weapons, troop figures, and defense capabilities were the kinds of meaty details she absolutely would have shared with Cuba, the admission was too circumstantial. Although one DIA debriefing team member felt that Ana had admitted to "being an accomplice to murder" and clearly showed contempt for the lives of the soldiers and the risks they were taking, he was an outlier. There wasn't enough to bring back to prosecutors to add to the twenty-five-year prison sentence she had agreed to in a plea deal.

When judging Ana, the abstract technicalities of the law should just be one consideration. Most observers would agree that Greg Fronius, the Green Beret, father, husband, brother, and son deserved better. As he put his life on the line at El Paraiso for his nation, Ana was inside the same compound's walls in service of an enemy. Scott Carmichael, who would later play an instrumental role in bringing Ana to justice, will never forgive her. "It's the betrayal, it's stabbing him in the back. I'm certain that she turned over information about that particular camp to the Cubans. I mean, there's no doubt about that. That's what she was down there for is to get all that information." Carmichael adds that Fronius happened to be the only Green Beret at El Paraiso when the firing started, but others could just as easily have been there with him. "By turning over that information, she knew she was putting those guys in danger. And she may not have given a shit about the El Salvadoran soldiers, but she should have given a crap about the Green Berets." The death of Greg Fronius, he adds, exposes the inherent immorality and dark side of spying. "That's what espionage really is all about, you know, death of warfighters. It's not just giving an advantage to an adversary. It's an advantage in what? In warfare, and that's what this is. And then in warfare, young people die."

After her trip to El Salvador, Ana's colleagues remained in the dark. She won another award, this time for her help debriefing a Salvadoran intelligence asset. The US Army Operational Group presented Ana with a plaque celebrating her "exceptional area knowledge" and praising her "interpersonal skills."[139]

Chapter 14.

SURROUNDED

"In order to defeat your enemy, you must first understand them."[140]

—DEANNA TROI, THE HALF-HUMAN AND HALF-ALIEN ON STAR TREK: THE NEXT GENERATION, WAS ONE OF ANA'S FAVORITE TV CHARACTERS

In the mid-1980s, the FBI was still trying to overcome its reputation as a stodgy bastion of White men in crisp white shirts. There were only 373 Hispanic special agents in the Bureau at the time, or just 4 percent of the total. Women, first allowed to become agents in 1972, fared slightly better. There were 733 female FBI agents in 1987, less than 8 percent of the boys' club total.[141] When 311 Hispanic special agents won a class-action lawsuit against the FBI alleging rampant discrimination in hiring and promotion, the Bureau knew that structural changes were coming. "The FBI, and I as director, are committed to increasing the number of minority and female agents within the FBI ranks," Director William Sessions announced on the day of the court ruling. "It is absolutely essential that our nation's racial and ethnic composition be reflected in the FBI's ranks."[142]

As the Bureau embraced a more diverse workforce, Lucy had an inspired idea. Joan, her brother Tito's wife, would be the ideal FBI candidate. The couple had secretly married in 1981 while attending St. Mary's College in Maryland. Tito was a college senior and Joan just a sophomore. "We actually eloped and nobody knew. Nobody knew for over a year," Joan said. Lucy realized that Tito's young bride was clever and as clean-cut as they come. It wouldn't hurt her chances, either, that she had been born in South Korea. Joan had been adopted by her stepfather, William DeArcangelis, a US Army staff sergeant stationed in Seoul. He and Joan's mother raised Joan in Maryland and Virginia, where she grew to love America and admire the FBI. Growing up, "there was an FBI person that lived across the street from me and I was always fascinated by it," Joan said.

When Lucy called her sister-in-law to broach the idea of becoming a special agent, Joan was working for the Magnavox human relations department in Pennsylvania and looking for a more stimulating career. "I immediately liked the idea and wanted to do it because I've always wanted to put bad people away."

Joan ran to Tito with the good news and was amazed by his reaction. Even though Tito had recently graduated from Westminster Theological Seminary outside Philadelphia and was about to become a Presbyterian minister, he said he wanted to become a lawman, too. The seminary internship he had arranged was a dud, and the couple was struggling financially. "He was at a loss at that point of what to do," Joan said. Working for the FBI would be just another form of service. *If not a pastor, why not be a guy that puts bad people away?* Tito asked himself.

Lucy was ecstatic. Her younger brother would be the perfect G-man. He was a born-again Christian who had spent his teen-age summers at bible camp. Together with Joan, they were dream recruits for the new-and-improved FBI—a church boy with Puerto Rican roots and his patriotic Korean-American wife.

The FBI brass agreed. In late 1987, the Bureau offered Tito and Joan jobs as clerks at the Miami Field Office, where the

Montes family was building a dynasty. The young couple moved to Miami Beach and started in the FBI mailroom, learning the system as they applied to become full-fledged agents. Tito graduated first from the FBI's Training Academy in Quantico, Virginia. Joan, Ana, Alberto, and Lucy were on hand for the ceremony in 1989. Ana even posed for photos inside the FBI Academy with her family, her hair cut drastically short like the good soldier she had become. The Farrah Fawcett locks from college were long gone. Joan graduated from Quantico a year later. She and Tito were assigned as young agents to the FBI's Atlanta Field Office, where they would spend their entire careers.

For Ana, all the FBI recruitments must have seemed a cruel joke. In just a few short years after deciding to spy for Cuba, Ana now had four close relatives in the storied FBI. Her brother Tito and sister-in-law Joan were special agents with handguns and handcuffs and powers to arrest, while her sister Lucy and new brother-in-law Chris did the less glamorous but equally important work supporting hundreds of Miami-based crime fighters. Ana was surrounded.

Joan recalls one Thanksgiving when Ana, Emilia, Lucy, and her husband, Chris, all joined Joan and Tito at their new home in Atlanta. The young couple had invited as many of their Atlanta-based FBI friends as they could fit at the table. In almost any direction Ana looked, there was a badge. Castro's secret agent put on a good show, smiling and laughing while passing the mashed potatoes and cranberry sauce. "She was comfortable, not awkward at all," Joan recalls. Years of working shoulder to shoulder with military commanders and Pentagon apparatchiks had prepared her well.

Tito and Joan had first started dating in 1979, the year Ana graduated from UVa, and the Montes family took a while to warm up to Tito's secret bride. When Alberto learned that Tito had eloped, he refused to keep paying for his tuition at the seminary postcollege. "As soon as he found out we were married, he says, 'Well, if you're old enough, if you're man enough to be married, then you can pay your own way,'" Joan recalled. Emilia was chilly at first, too. Joan was from blue-collar roots, the first in her family to go to college, and was sure that her new mother-in-law believed that Tito could do better. Ana was also standoffish. "She was also not easy to get to know, and seemed formal in the beginning, very serious-minded," Joan said.

The sisters-in-law began to bond over working out and then learned of their shared love of cheesy sci-fi. Tito and Joan had begun obsessively watching *Star Trek: The Next Generation*, and it turns out Ana was a Trekkie, too. "She watched every show. We started talking about the shows all the time," Joan said. Ana had a sweet spot for English actor Patrick Stewart, who played Captain Jean-Luc Picard. But her favorite character was Deanna Troi, a half-human, half-Betazoid with a preternatural ability to sense emotions. An empath with supernatural abilities to read the human heart. Troi also happened to be a mental health counselor, with an advanced degree in psychology. She was the Alberto Montes of the USS *Enterprise*. Ana liked Troi, the empath, and officer Will Riker. "They had a relationship. She liked their relationship together," Joan said.

One year, Joan and Tito invited Ana on a vacation to St. Thomas in the US Virgin Islands. They liked the vibe so much that they bought two condos at the Bluebeard's Castle resort, with a time-share deal that allowed Ana to stay affordably at resorts throughout the Caribbean. Later, she would meet her Cuban handlers at Caribbean locales, mixing work with a bit of pleasure.

Joan ultimately won over Emilia, too. Her mother-in-law began to appreciate Joan's quiet calm and they remain friendly to this day, even though Tito and Joan divorced in 2003. But Joan realized early on that there were conversations best left un-spoken. She and Tito had admired President Reagan, a sentiment that could easily start an argument with Ana and Emilia. "So we never talked politics."

Throughout their marriage, Joan says there clearly was tension in the Montes family, especially with Alberto. But Ana and her siblings weren't big sharers, and that included Joan's husband. "As a family, the kids really didn't talk much about growing up as kids around the parents." Tito revealed that "he was afraid of his dad" when he was younger, but Joan could never get much more out of him. "He did say that his dad was very much a disciplinarian. But he didn't go into details."

Joan and Tito settled in at the FBI's Atlanta Field Office. Tito handled drug cases, helped solve high-profile art heists, and served for years with the Special Operations Group or SOG, the undercover surveillance unit made of special agents that the FBI uses to track suspects in sensitive terrorism, intelligence, and criminal investigations. Joan had an even more high-profile Bureau career. The five-foot-three-inch dynamo became a hostage negotiator, an undercover informant in drug cases, a counterterrorism supervisor, and an investigator on the deadly truck bombing of the Alfred P. Murrah Federal Building in Oklahoma City in 1995 and the Olympic Park bombing in Atlanta a year later. Given her Korean background, the FBI also tapped her to work undercover on sensitive foreign counterintelligence cases. Joan recruited Vietnamese, Chinese, and Korean sources to work as assets, or spies, against rival Asian nations.

Joan would have been a tempting intelligence target for Ana and her Cuban masters, who have a long history of selling classified US secrets to American adversaries. But Ana never pumped her sister-in-law for any FBI scuttlebutt, and Joan never volunteered. "I got used to never talking about work with my family. So nobody knew what I did. They knew I worked for the FBI, but I never talked to them about cases," Joan said.

There's discretion and then there's deception. After Ana's arrest, Joan had time to reflect on their twenty-year friendship, the countless dinners and family holidays together, and the phone-call marathons spent indulging their *Star Trek* obsession. It only left her with questions. "Did I really know Ana at all?" Joan wondered. "Was any of the Ana that I saw or interacted with, was it really her or just a facade?"

Chapter 15.

A METEORIC RISE

"Ms. Montes has accomplished all duties in an exemplary manner, established an outstanding record of personal achievement, and inspired others to improve the quantity and quality of their work performance."

—DIA AWARD FOR MERITORIOUS CIVILIAN SERVICE, PUBLIC CEREMONY, 1990

With her military-grade haircut and no-nonsense pantsuits, Ana began to fit right in with the war planners around her. She was meticulous, demanding, and could at times be brusque, arrogant, and downright rude. But even coworkers who didn't particularly like her learned to respect her. Former DIA analyst Steve Smith shared a cubicle with Ana for years and considered her a friend. "In the time that I knew her, I didn't see anything that brought to my mind a suspicious thought about Ana Montes. I really thought she was loyal, highly professional, and I don't think there was any single incident, not even a single incident that I could point to that would've driven me to think that maybe there's something wrong here," he said. Marty Scheina, Ana's longtime supervisor, felt the same. "She got kudos from all over. She got kudos throughout the Intelligence Community. One US ambassador in Latin America commented on her saying that she was an outstanding analyst."[143]

Ana was impressing her bosses in both Washington and Havana. Over her meteoric DIA career, she received cash bonuses and piles of special recognitions. Her unsuspecting superiors nominated her for the DIA Meritorious Civilian Service Award,[144] which they presented to Ana in a formal ceremony in 1990. They of course had no idea that, just the year before, she had traveled to Cuba on her second clandestine trip to the island. In a private ceremony, her Cuban spymasters also had presented their star student with a medal—and then took it away for safekeeping. It was both an ego stroke for their narcissistic agent and a private token of appreciation, an award that Montes could never take home or display.

In 1990, the DIA reassigned Ana to work full-time as a long-form Nicaragua analyst. She had developed a near-encyclopedic knowledge of the Nicaraguan military forces run by the Sandinistas, the Socialist political party that overthrew dictator Anastasio Somoza in 1979 and had established a revolutionary government. It was a useful assignment. The Cuban government and its DGI spy service were thoroughly in bed with the Sandinistas, having helped to train their guerrilla leaders prior to the Revolution and maintaining close ties once the Sandinistas ran Nicaragua throughout the bloody 1980s. Ana had an equally impressive understanding of the military capabilities of the Contras, the rebel forces supported by Reagan and the CIA that were battling the Sandinistas for control of Nicaragua.

Just as Ana was given her new assignment, the civil war ended. Beaten down by a decade of bloodshed and poverty, the Nicaraguan people in February 1990 voted Sandinista leader Daniel Ortega out of office. His replacement was Violeta Chamorro, the first elected woman president in the Americas, who quickly ended the military draft and disbanded the Contras. After her arrest, Ana told her debriefers how ironic it was that she had gotten the full-time Nicaragua assignment the same year that the Nicaraguan people had democratically elected a new president. Overnight, "the basis for her initial moral outrage at US policy toward that country was no longer relevant."[145]

Now that the Sandinistas were out of office, President George H. W. Bush ended the US embargo with Nicaragua and offered other assistance. The DIA sent Ana to meet new Nicaraguan President Chamorro and to brief her, twice, on her own country's military capabilities. Scheina picked Ana to play "the female card," he said. "You know, trying to say, 'Hey, you know, she's one of our best. Oh, and by the way, she's a female.'" Chamorro had been kept in the dark about her country's operations because, even after the historic elections, the brother of ousted President Daniel Ortega remained in charge of the Nicaraguan military. So it fell to Ana to brief President Chamorro about her own troops and weaponry and to fill in the many blanks that Minister of Defense Humberto Ortega had left out. Naturally, Ana passed every detail of her private conversations with Chamorro straight back to Havana.

When handing out the US government's Meritorious Civilian Service Award, unsuspecting DIA supervisors thanked Ana for her outstanding assistance to President Chamorro. "Ms. Montes distinguished herself by meritorious service as the Nicaraguan Military Capabilities Team Leader," the award states. "An example of her outstanding performance was her very well received May 1990 briefing to the Nicaraguan head of state."

In 1991, as part of a standard Periodic Reinvestigation, Defense Investigative Service agents grilled Ana for hours about her foreign travel, foreign contacts, drug use, and finances. Ana handily lied about her job moonlighting for the Cubans. But, in an attempt to sanitize her record, she revealed that she had previously provided false information about her drug use and SAIS master's degree. The gambit worked. After a review, a DIA adjudicator noted that while Ana had a tendency to "twist the truth" to save her skin, taking action against her was not warranted because the deception had happened six years earlier.

Ana, the DIA concluded, had broken the rules, but learned her lesson. Years later, the CIA was not impressed. "These lies became personnel matters, and Montes was not sanctioned."

With the end of the civil wars in both Nicaragua and El Salvador, Ana's early justifications for helping Cuba had fizzled. And yet she gamely kept spying. In February 1993, Ana was selected to run DIA's Cuba account.[146] She was now in the middle of the action as a longform Cuba analyst for the DIA, with unparalleled access to classified secrets on America's undersized rival. The Berlin Wall had come down in 1989 and Cuba's benefactor, the Soviet Union, had collapsed two years later. Ana had a new rationalization for betraying family and country. Cuba was "in big trouble" and desperately needed her again. "Montes explained that her moral realignment from helping Nicaragua via the Cubans to directly helping Cuba stemmed from a realization that the United States might find a pretext to invade that island," the Defense Department concluded.[147] "The US invasions of Grenada and Panama, along with the reduction of Soviet/Russian military and economic support to the Castro regime after 1991, made it clear to Montes that Cuba" needed her behind the scenes to even the score, the military's Inspector General found.

Chapter 16.

SPYING GETS LONELY

"You should go to the WIPE program and destroy that file according to the steps which we discussed during the contact. This is a basic step to take every time you receive a radio message or some disk."

—INSTRUCTIONS ON HOW TO DELETE ENCRYPTED MESSAGES, RECOVERED FROM ANA'S HARD DRIVE

Fueled by her need for "validation, recognition, and control,"[148] Ana threw herself at her new dream assignment. She invited herself to any briefings that might conceivably concern Cuba, studied with a renewed intensity, and dominated meetings inside DIA and out. Ana "tried to influence high-level audiences with briefings and analytic papers and by serving on highly compartmented, interagency committees and task forces," the CIA wrote.

In short order, Ana became the Intelligence Community's leading expert on Cuba's military leaders, weapons systems, and overall capabilities. She picked up the nickname the "Queen of Cuba," a sobriquet that hinted both at her unassailable expertise but also the imperial manner with which she imparted her wisdom.

The added responsibilities during the day kept her even busier at night. Ana would clock out at DIA, exercise at the gym, grab a bite, and then start her real job. Her tradecraft was a mash-up of KGB *Spy vs. Spy* classics reconfigured for a new digital age. On computers, including a refurbished Toshiba Satellite Pro 405CS laptop she purchased at CompUSA, Ana would type in Spanish the key passages she had memorized from the dozens or even hundreds of classified intelligence reports she reviewed daily. "Continue writing along the same lines you have so far, but cipher the information every time you do, so that you do not leave prepared information that is not ciphered in the house," the Cubans had instructed her. "This is the most sensitive and compromising information that you hold."[149]

Using a bespoke software program provided by her handlers, Ana would then encrypt these nightly dispatches onto floppy disks purchased from a local Radio Shack. Later, over egg rolls with her handlers in Washington restaurants, Ana would casually slide the diskettes to "Ernesto" or another handler without missing a beat. "Give 'E' only the ciphered disks," the Cubans reminded Ana. "Do not give, for the time being, printed or photographed material."

When the Cubans wanted to pass along sensitive information to Ana or suggest a new tasking order, sometimes Ernesto or another handler would return the favor and furtively pass Ana a floppy disk. More commonly, Ana got her orders the same way spies have since the Cold War: through numeric messages transmitted anonymously over high-frequency shortwave radio.

Ana had lived alone in Washington, DC, apartments for years, first at 2331 Cathedral Avenue, NW, just outside the National Zoo. In fall 1993, she purchased a second-floor co-op at 3039 Macomb Street in the Cleveland Park neighborhood of Northwest DC. She clearly had to scrimp and save. Her father gifted her $13,000 for the down payment, and Ana signed a promissory note to the condo's owners, television producer John Bredar and his wife, agreeing to pay them $911, in twelve monthly installments of $75.92, to help complete the sale.

From the privacy of her new co-op, and with an earpiece at the ready, Ana would turn on her Sony ICF-2010 shortwave radio and tune it to a preestablished frequency at precisely 9:00 p.m. or 10:00 p.m. on Tuesdays, Thursdays, and Saturdays. On Saturdays at 9:00 p.m., for example, she would program in AM frequency 7887 kHz. A female voice would cut through the otherworldly static declaring, "Atención! Atención!" She would then spew out 150 seemingly random numbers into the night. "Tres-cero-uno-cero-siete, dos-cuatro-seis-dos-cuatro," the voice would drone. Montes would key the digits into her computer, and a Cuban-installed decryption program would transform them into Spanish-language text.

Known as "numbers station" broadcasts, these shortwave transmissions were the backbone of spy communications for decades. They enabled spy services to communicate with operatives deep in the field, without fear of detection. "Numbers messages were used extensively during the Second World War. The British Special Operations Executive (SOE), the American Office of Strategic Services (OSS), and many other wartime intelligence agencies used them to communicate with their espionage and sabotage teams, operating behind enemy lines," cryptology expert Dirk Rijmenants writes.[150] The messages reached Ana in Washington all the way from Havana, where the Cubans operated a powerful shortwave, high-frequency transmitter.

The numeric messages were practically impossible to break without a unique cryptographic key. And since they were sent out broadly, for anyone with a cheap shortwave radio to hear, the numbers station broadcasts made it harder for enemy spy services to pinpoint the intended target. Radio amateurs for years have hunted for the eeriest broadcasts, nicknaming them according to their quirks. The Cuban station Ana listened to is called "Atención," since every transmission starts with the word "Atención," or "Attention," in Spanish. There's "Swedish

Rhapsody Child," named for the mechanical voice of a child used by a numbers station operated by the Polish secret services. And there's "Yankee Bravo," in which a German woman, probably with the KGB, introduces her numbers with the call sign "Yankee Bravo."[151] Not only do hobbyists scan the airwaves for numbers station messages, but so do the US spy services. The NSA has been blindly recording other nations' numbers stations broadcasts for years, hoping to find the keys to decode indecipherable messages collecting dust on a shelf.

Coincidentally, Marty Scheina was one of those amateur shortwave radio geeks, also called a "DXer." One day at work, at the tail end of a meeting, Scheina regaled his DIA section chiefs and analysts with war stories about his beloved hobby. "I mentioned that I'd listened to a lot of shortwave radio, and I'd logged over 40 countries and found it a good way to practice my Spanish," Scheina said. Ana, who was listening attentively in the crowd, decided to play dumb. "Ana looked at me and she says, 'Oh, it's way too technical. I couldn't figure it out. I wouldn't be able to figure it out.' Come to find out, she knew a hell of a lot more about it than I did."

To get her thrice-weekly instructions, Ana would tune into the numbers station broadcasts. When she needed to convey an urgent message, she reached for an old-school pager or pay phone. Back when there were public pay phones everywhere, she would seek one out at the National Zoo, in Metrorail subway stations, or by the old Hecht's department store in the Chevy Chase neighborhood of DC. Even though she often had a cell phone in her purse, Ana would use pay phones to call pager numbers controlled by the Cubans. One beeper code would mean "I'm in extreme danger"; another, "We have to meet." Schooled in spycraft by the Soviets, the Cubans relied on the storied tools of the trade. Montes's pager codes and shortwave-radio notes were written on specially treated paper. "The frequencies and the cheat sheet for the numbers, that was all on water-soluble paper," an FBI case agent would later explain.[152]

Ana was mastering her craft. In 1993, she took her third of four trips to Cuba. Two times already, she had used phony passports and sometimes disguised herself in a wig on circuitous flights to Havana. In 1993 and again in 1998, she got Pentagon approval to visit Cuba on official DIA fact-finding missions. She would meet at the US Interests Section in Havana during the day and take meetings with colleagues. But during downtime, she would slip away to brief her Cuban superiors in perilous in-person sessions at DGI safe houses.

Despite all the derring-do, Ana passed a DIA-administered counterintelligence polygraph examination in March 1994, answering questions designed to ferret out espionage, sabotage, or unauthorized disclosure of classified information.[153] It was the one and only polygraph test the DIA gave her in her sixteen-plus-year Department of Defense career. Some investigators believe that Ana defeated the lie box by using the sphincter-muscle trick the Cubans taught her. Others point out that Ana's ease in beating the system exposed the inherent weakness of polygraphs, investigative tools that are not admissible in US courts of law. After Ana's arrest, DIA interrogator Lisa Connors spent days asking Ana how she beat the "lie box." The Cubans had told Ana that American-administered polygraphs were easy to fool, and Ana kept repeating in her head that the test was flawed. "What I really wanted to know was, did she really believe what they told her about how ineffectual a polygraph was, or was she a sociopath?" Connors said. She never answered her own question.

Regardless of how Ana pulled it off, she was now truly in the clear. When colleagues later raised doubts about her, the successful lie-detector results kept them off the scent. "The polygraph test in 1994 made her even more dangerous by deflecting suspicion away from her. She was freer to pursue her espionage," the DIA would later admit in an internal training film, *The Two Faces of Ana Montes.*

Ana did indeed become more dangerous. Just two months after acing her polygraph,[154]she disclosed to the Cubans the true name of a covert US intelligence officer who was headed to Cuba in an undercover capacity. It was a fellow spy likely working for the CIA. The Cubans overseeing Ana thanked her for this "tremendously useful" information and let Ana know, hauntingly, "We were waiting here for him with open arms." Investigators do not believe the US officer was harmed or imprisoned, but Ana's identification of him clearly botched whatever grand plans he had in store for the Castro regime.

Despite her unparalleled successes, spying got lonely. Ana's social circle contracted. She refused to befriend anyone she worked with, for fear they would expose the charade. Her family was equally dangerous, loaded as it was with FBI loyalists. Lucy had two young children by now, Emily and Matthew, and the babies were always a safe topic. But Ana still felt she could never let down her guard. "She was becoming, I would say, increasingly tense," Lucy said. "There were no lighthearted topics, no jokes, no goofing around."

The pressure of maintaining dual identities was adding up. "Montes immersed herself in her work at the DIA and her espionage, most likely as a way to block out her loneliness," the CIA psychologists wrote. Marta was gone and there was no one to come clean to, no one who truly understood the intense stress her Oscar-level acting job had created. By default, Ana's handlers became her comrades, her social life. And her de facto therapists. Every week or so, Ana couldn't wait to unload her pent-up frustrations and fears to them over dim sum or whatever cuisine was next on the rotation. "They were emotionally supportive. They understood my loneliness and wanted to do something to help," Ana said.[155] But even her handlers would not be around forever.

Chapter 17.

ROYAL FLUSH

"The object of the conspiracy was for coconspirators to function as covert spies serving the interests of the government of the Republic of Cuba within the United States by gathering and transmitting information to the Cuban government…"

—FROM THE FEDERAL INDICTMENT OF TEN CUBAN "WASP" SPIES ARRESTED BY THE FBI'S MIAMI FIELD OFFICE

In Miami, Lucy had spent years almost exclusively eavesdropping on drug dealers and street hustlers, translating live and taped recordings of South Florida's robust cocaine underworld. Occasionally, she'd work a kidnapping or major financial fraud. "My workday typically consists of listening to recordings of conversations from phone taps and body recorders. When I started, some of these were still done on reel-to-reel tapes," she explained once in an "Up Close and Personal" profile of a typical language specialist, for the FBI's website.[156] "Many times an Agent will depend on you to determine the truthfulness of the person they are interviewing. This can be critical in their assessment of the reliability of the source. You become, in essence, their eyes and ears."

One day, Lucy's supervisors came to her with a very different eyes-and-ears assignment. She was placed on the Royal Flush Task Force, a then top-secret operation run by the FBI, NSA, and the Navy to investigate Cuban spies operating in the shadows in Miami. It was an espionage case, her first, and it became the most significant investigation of her career. Lucy won't discuss what she heard on those court-authorized wiretaps, called Title IIIs, but filings in the case establish that her colleagues in the Miami FBI's Cuban Squad began busting up a major Cuban spy ring as early as May 1995.

Operating from Miami Beach to Big Pine Key, the spy ring had been code-named "Red Avispa," or the Wasp Network. It was an ambitious but low-budget operation, run by the DGI in Havana. The goal was to infiltrate US military bases in South Florida including US Southern Command—which oversees US military activities in Latin America and the Caribbean—and MacDill Air Force Base. "This spy ring was sent by the Cuban government to strike at the very heart of our national security system and our very democratic process," prosecutors would later say.[157] At least a dozen Cuban operatives used code names, phony accents, fake identity papers, shortwave radio broadcasts, two-way radios, laptops, and encrypted diskettes to infiltrate Cuban exile groups and try to gain classified information about top American military installations. Lucy and her fellow language specialists had their hands full, translating hundreds of supposedly secure communications between the sprawling Wasp Network and their masters back in Havana.

Lucy knew the rules and never thought about telling Ana that she was working on an exciting new Cuban case. If she had shared any investigative details, the Cubans likely would have rolled up the Wasp Network immediately. They would have temporarily shut down Ana, too, ensuring the future safety of their prize recruit.

For now, though, Ana was in the dark. And seriously on edge.

On Saturday, February 24, 1996, Lucy was at home when local TV stations began reporting major breaking news. The Cuban air force had just shot down two unarmed airplanes belonging to a Miami-based Cuban exile group called "Brothers to the Rescue." Cuban MiG-29 fighter jets had fired air-to-air missiles at the two civilian planes, instantly killing three US citizens and one permanent resident alien. Lucy immediately thought of her sister. "I called Ana at her apartment and was surprised to find her at home. I asked her why she wasn't at work, and when she asked me why, I said 'Because a Brothers to the Rescue plane was just shot down by Cuba.' There was complete silence at the other end."

Ana had every reason for concern. Castro's air force had just murdered Americans helping a beloved Cuban émigré group. "Cuba Downs Two Rescue Planes," the *Miami Herald* reported on its front page the next day. "The Brothers have sponsored thousands of missions across the Florida Straits, generally steering clear of Cuban airspace as they searched for wayward rafters."

Started in 1991 as an air search and rescue force to provide humanitarian assistance to refugees fleeing Cuba in small boats and unstable rafts, Brothers to the Rescue had recently shifted its focus. Once the number of Cuban migrants slowed in 1994, the Brothers to the Rescue president began flying his Cessna 337 over or near Havana, dropping propaganda leaflets below. The Cuban government was not amused by the provocations. Fidel Castro had warned that planes flying over Cuban airspace risked being shot down.

On February 24, three Brothers to the Rescue planes departed Opa Locka Airport in Miami. At about 3:00 p.m., just before the aircraft crossed the 24th parallel marking the boundary between US and Cuban Air Defense Identification Zones, two Cuban air force fighters launched from San Antonio de los Baños Airfield southwest of Havana. Radio communications between the MiG-29 and the military control tower in Havana capture what happened next:[158]

Cuban MiG-29: OK, the objective is in sight; the objective is in sight. It is a small airplane. Copied; small airplane in sight...

Cuban Military Control Tower: Go ahead...

MiG-29: It is a small airplane, a small airplane...

Control Tower: What type and color?

MiG-29: It is white and blue. White and blue, at low altitude, a small airplane. Give me instructions...

MiG-29: We're locked on. Give us the authorization. It's a Cessna 337. That one, that one. Hell, give us the authorization.

Control Tower: Fire.

MiG-29: Hell, give us the authorization! We got it!

Control Tower: Authorized to destroy.

MiG-29: We copy. We copy.

Control Tower: Authorized to destroy...

MiG-29: First shot... We blew his balls off! We blew his balls off!

Seven minutes later, the MiG-29 fired again, destroying a second civilian plane. The Cubans took no action against the third Brothers' plane, which landed safely back in Miami at 5:08 p.m.

Almost as soon as Lucy hung up, Ana's phone rang again. Her bosses needed her to come into the Defense Intelligence Analysis Center, or DIAC, early the next morning, to help weigh options. A US military strike against Cuba seemed likely. President Bill Clinton was already publicly fuming. "I condemn this action in the strongest possible terms," he said that Saturday evening, decrying "the shooting down today in broad daylight of two American civilian airplanes by Cuban military aircraft."[159]

Montes arrived at the DIAC at about 6:00 a.m. Sunday morning to read incoming message traffic about the incident. The Joint Chiefs of Staff quickly formed a task force and Ana was needed. This was her moment. She arrived at the Pentagon at about 11:00 a.m.

Ana would spend the rest of the day at the Pentagon, briefing the Joint Chiefs on Cuba's military preparedness and learning more about the shootdowns. What happened next would put her in the crosshairs, too, for the first time making her colleagues seriously question the loyalty of the Queen of Cuba.

Working on a Joint Chiefs Task Force inside the Pentagon is both an honor and a duty. Tradition states that you are at the beck and call of the generals and do not leave your post until dismissed. And so it came as a surprise when Ana, claiming exhaustion, left the Pentagon sometime around 8:00 p.m. on the evening after the shootdown. "According to the secondhand recollections of a coworker, Montes should have worked until 10:00 p.m., but received a phone call, became visibly agitated, and left early at 8:00 p.m.," Pentagon investigators later reported.[160]

If Ana took a personal call at the Pentagon that Sunday evening, there's no evidence that the Cubans were on the other end of the line. Dialing into the Pentagon directly, where all calls leave a computerized record and many are monitored, would have been absurdly risky. Even calling her on a cell phone would have violated every principle of sound tradecraft. Mark Ritter, the DIA counterintelligence officer who helped interrogate Ana after her arrest, is skeptical that Ana even took a personal call during the crisis. In debriefs, Ana flatly denied it. "The Cubans would really never have risked even using a cutout to call the Pentagon, for crying out loud," Ritter said. "You're risking hostile discovery, and the Cubans aren't that stupid."

Ana did admit to Ritter that she met several times a week with her Cuban handler during the Brothers to the Rescue crisis, so why would she lie about an initial phone call? Ritter reports that on Monday morning February 26, less than forty-eight hours after the deadly shootdown, a Cuban handler broke protocol by waiting for Ana on the street. He flagged her down in Cleveland Park as she was about to drive to work, to get an impromptu briefing. "She said her Cuban handler contacted her by standing on a street corner on her way to work," Ritter said. "She pulled over and they went for a walk." Ana made plans to meet her handler again for dinner the next evening, but this time, she could not leave the Pentagon early. "She said she was supposed to meet [him] Tuesday night but couldn't, so he again flagged her down Wednesday morning for a very brief meeting," Ritter said. Ana said she didn't have any emergency beeper codes that were specific enough to keep her handler up to speed on fast-moving events, so she waited for him to find her again. He was desperate to know if the US was about to launch cruise missiles at Cuba or retaliate in some other deadly way, and whether American investigators had determined that at least one of the civilian planes was outside of Cuban airspace when the MiGs shot it down. Her handler "was very concerned about what the United States was going to do, what sort of strikes they were going to make on Cuba," Ritter added.

Leaving the Pentagon early just a day after an international crisis is bound to raise eyebrows. Taking a personal call and then scurrying home, well, that's a whole other level. Reg Brown, a DIA Latin American counterintelligence analyst, had been scratching his head for years over Ana's behavior, but had always kept his doubts to himself. But after he heard that Ana had taken a phone call and rushed out of the Pentagon during the biggest emergency of her career, that was an anomaly he couldn't ignore. The DIA counterintelligence analyst simply had to tell someone.

Chapter 18.

THE KMART SECURITY GUARD

"He is a father, a grandfather, an author, a Vietnam-era veteran…
He's done a lot of crazy things in his life; traveled all over the world;
worked as a cop, as an NCIS Special Agent, and as a spy-catcher for
Uncle Sam."

—FROM SCOTT CARMICHAEL'S FACEBOOK BIO

With his round face, easy smile, and plus-size Macy's suits, Scott Carmichael defies the stereotype of the sophisticated, Georgetown-trained mole hunter. The former cop from Wisconsin's dairy belt laughingly describes himself as "a Kmart security guard," but in reality he hunted spies for more than a quarter century for the DIA. And was pretty good at it. While Carmichael can turn on the bumbling Columbo shtick when needed, he's a relentless investigator who won't be charmed or bullied into looking the other way.

And that's why, in April 1996, the phone rang in Carmichael's office. It was Reg Brown, the counterintelligence analyst, with little more than a hunch. He told Carmichael that he had some concerns about Ana, a few too many incidents and coincidences he couldn't easily explain away. Carmichael had never heard of Ana but welcomed the call.

First, Brown said, Ana had been "unusually aggressive" in

accessing classified information and sometimes weaseled her way into meetings that she had no business attending. Sometimes these meetings involved Cuban counterintelligence matters, which was Brown's turf. "I knew Ana. And when I saw her involved in a lot of things that the Cubans were interested in, it began to make me quite nervous. And so I had a good feeling that something wasn't quite right, but I never suspected her of being spy," Brown said in the DIA internal training video.

Appearing in silhouette and identified under the pseudonym "David," Reg Brown, now retired, said that it was his job to look for Cuban influence campaigns. "We had a lot of information from Cuban defectors that Cuba had spies working within the United States government. What caused me concern is that if they had agents within the Department of Defense, what kind of information we were losing, what kind of information they were interested in, and who were those spies?"

In the call to Carmichael, Brown built his case. He had heard that Ana had voiced her opposition to US policy in Cuba,[161] and he couldn't explain why some once-golden Cuban intelligence sources had magically dried up. But mostly Brown focused on the Brothers to the Rescue incident. He explained, based on a tip provided to him secondhand by a colleague, how peculiar it was for Ana to slip out of the Pentagon during a five-alarm fire and take what appeared to be a personal phone call. And then he outlined Ana's quiet role in protecting Cuba even before the MiGs fired their deadly rounds.

Brown explained how, in early February 1996, a Washington think tank called the Center for Defense Information, or CDI, sent a delegation of retired American flag officers to Cuba. The Center believed in fostering international cooperation and tasked the retired officers with finding ways that Washington and Havana could work together to solve their long-standing regional differences.[162] Retired US Navy admiral Eugene Carroll, deputy director of CDI and a vocal proponent of nuclear disarmament, was on that trip to Cuba. The Cuban armed forces told him that they were upset with all the Brothers to the Rescue flights over their sovereign territory, and asked Carroll what the repercussions would be if they shot down a plane. They were rattling the sword.

Reg Brown, who didn't respond to interview requests, learned that Ana had arranged for Admiral Carroll to brief US officials about Cuba's threats—in meetings just one day before the planes were shot down. The timing all seemed fortuitously staged, as laid out by Brown and relayed by other sources:

- On February 23, Admiral Carroll warns the Americans that a disaster is bound to happen if the US doesn't stop the Brothers to the Rescue overflights.

- The next day, the 24th, the Cubans carry out their threat and shoot two civilian planes out of the sky.

- And then a day after that, on the 25th, Carroll states in a TV interview that he had warned US officials to take the Cuban threats seriously.

The sequence seemed calculated to protect the Cubans from retaliation and position them as victims, even though they had just blasted two civilian planes out of the sky. "All of a sudden, the public's view of the shootdown was that it was America's fault. It was our fault," Carmichael said. "We failed to stop the aircraft from taking off from Florida on route to Cuba. And we'd been told what was going to happen and we allowed it to happen. So therefore the United States government was at fault for this."

The many coincidences, and signs of Ana's hidden hand, convinced Brown that he had unraveled a classic influence campaign. "[Brown] believed that the Cuban Intelligence Service orchestrated the events to influence US public opinion, and he believed that Montes was involved," the Pentagon IG said. Brown found it curious that Ana seemed to be avoiding him. "She knew I was a counterintelligence analyst. She couldn't always look me in the eye. She stayed away from me," he said. "Why is she staying away from me? And all of these things are coming together. One plus two plus three plus four. All of that comes together, okay, in a sequence of events that causes concern."

Carmichael listened intently and, he said, then brought Brown's concerns to the FBI's storied Washington Field Office, or WFO. They weren't particularly excited. It was a highly circumstantial case. Six months later, when Brown pinged Carmichael again and shared some new warning signs, the FBI relented, Carmichael said. For the first time in her career, Ana was about to be grilled by a seasoned mole hunter.

Chapter 19.

THE INTERVIEW

"Scotland Yard Detective: Is there any other point to which you would wish to draw my attention?

Sherlock Holmes: To the curious incident of the dog in the night-time.

Detective: The dog did nothing in the night-time.

Sherlock Holmes: That was the curious incident."

—*FROM "THE ADVENTURE OF SILVER BLAZE," BY SIR ARTHUR CONAN DOYLE*

When Ana agreed to an interview on November 7, 1996, she assumed that Scott Carmichael was updating her top-secret clearances. Routine. Carmichael knew how nonthreatening he appeared. Here's the schlubby guy from security with yet more questions, she probably thought.

Ana was five minutes late and immediately tried to rush him, stressing how important she was as the new acting division chief in her section. She couldn't possibly have time for this distraction. In multiple interviews and in his 2007 memoir, *True Believer*, Carmichael explains why some people mistakenly discount him. "Some of my friends tell me that I bear a striking resemblance to the late comic Chris Farley," he wrote. "I do not look like…James Bond, or any other ruggedly handsome G-man type… I'm not threatening in my appearance. I'm not intimidating. I seem to be easy."

But underestimating Carmichael is not without risk. When

Ana made it clear she wanted to get back to work as quickly as possible, she was challenging Carmichael for control of the room. For dominance over the interview. So, to get her attention—and with zero evidence to back it up—he told one of DIA's finest analysts he thought she could be a spy.

"And that's when I hit her between the eyes. It's like, I've got to get her attention to focus that this is serious," Carmichael said. "And so what I said to her is, 'Look, this is not a routine interview. I'm not conducting a background investigation. I don't do that sort of thing. I'm a counterintelligence specialist. And I've been watching you for a while. And I have reason to believe that you participated in a Cuban intelligence influence operation. And we need to talk about that.'"

The strong-arm tactic worked. Ana instantly turned compliant, and now had time for Carmichael's endless questions. "She's getting more and more relaxed. And she's no longer feeling as threatened by me as she was in the very beginning when I hit her right between the eyes," he said in an interview.

Carmichael said he would seek to corroborate any information she provided, and began to quiz Ana on the Brothers to the Rescue incident. Together, they started making lists of names of people she had met that first night of the crisis, and key times. "I said: 'Well, you left the Pentagon. That's a little unusual under the circumstances.' She said, 'Well, you know, I got hungry, it's a long day… I was hungry. So I just told everybody I was leaving.'" Ana denied ever receiving an outside phone call at the Pentagon, as Reg Brown had heard, and Carmichael didn't have the goods to challenge her on it. She even had perfectly reasonable answers for Carmichael's insinuations about Admiral Carroll. Ana hadn't devised the plan to ask Admiral Carroll to brief US officials about Cuba's threats before the shootdowns; another DIA employee had come up with the idea. Two dead ends.

Now Ana was working hard to demonstrate her innocence.

First, she told Carmichael that she had been working closely with one of the FBI's top counterintelligence officials, William Doherty, on a "Hard Target" interagency intelligence group. The Hard Target group discussed covert US operations in the most unwelcoming places, including Iran, China, North Korea, and Cuba. Doherty oversaw all Cuban counterintelligence efforts run out of FBI headquarters and had an unimpeachable reputation. "She goes, 'I even work with William Doherty. You can trust me because William Doherty trusts me,'" Carmichael said. Second, Ana volunteered to Carmichael the name of a female professor at Georgetown University whom she thought might be spying for Havana. Ana "was trying to deflect suspicion away from her," Carmichael said. "She said, 'Hey, if you want to talk about a Cuban agent, let me tell you about this woman over at Georgetown.'"

After an hour, Ana and her Chris Farley stand-in were getting along, even smiling. But when Carmichael began to press Montes on her whereabouts after that first evening in the Pentagon, everything changed. "We were joking and getting along great one minute, and the next thing you know, all of a sudden she's like a mouse and a hawk is circling her," Carmichael said. He sensed deception and went into cop mode, asking rapid-fire questions. "I said, 'There's a market on the corner. Where did you park the car? Did you use a spot? Bump into anybody that you know?'" Carmichael pressed further. "'You've lived in the same building for [several] years. There's only so many apartments there. You know everybody there, right. Did you bump into anybody?'"

Carmichael said he could tell she "was hiding something," but didn't have enough evidence to do much about it. "That entire time, she was just scared to death and just staring at me. And I mean, I felt like she was staring at my lips to catch every word." He wrapped up the interview and let Ana leave. The Pentagon Inspector General would later assess that Carmichael had tried, but failed, to corroborate any of Reg Brown's suspicions. "The Special Agent could not substantiate the allegations lodged by Montes' coworker," they wrote.

It wasn't until six years later, after the arrest and during the debriefings, that Ana's change in behavior that day made sense. Carmichael had stumbled upon a fear, a serious insecurity. As DIA counterintelligence officer Mark Ritter learned during his interrogation of Ana, her Cuban handler broke protocol by showing up on the street in Cleveland Park, just outside Ana's DC apartment, on that Monday morning in 1996. Her handler was indiscreetly waiting for Ana, less than twelve hours after she departed the Pentagon early the previous evening. It's likely that Ana was frightened someone had spotted her with her Cuban contact. Or maybe she just felt nervous and guilty as Carmichael drilled deeper. "She was hiding something, it was operational. We had accidentally tripped across it. And we just didn't know it at that time," Carmichael said.

There was something else Carmichael missed. When he accused Ana of possibly being a spy, or an unwitting dupe in a Cuban influence operation, she never protested. Ana was DIA's exceptional analyst, the Queen of Cuba. She had just passed a polygraph two years earlier. Why didn't she stand up, grab Carmichael by his collar, and declare her innocence? Or at least express indignant disbelief? Carmichael didn't realize until much later that he had missed a tell. The cardinal rule of counterintelligence investigators, he said, is to believe that the spy exists. "So the dog didn't bark," Carmichael said. "She didn't do anything. She didn't say a word. She just stared at me." Sherlock Holmes, he said, he is not.

Recently, Carmichael acknowledged that Reg Brown had probably been wrong in believing that Ana had received a mystery call in the Pentagon, or even that she had orchestrated the Admiral Carroll episode. Brown couldn't remember who tipped him off about the phone call, so Carmichael never could find anyone who could corroborate the allegation. And there is no evidence that Ana manipulated Admiral Carroll to give the Cubans cover for the Brothers to the Rescue shootdown. Regardless, Carmichael insists that Reg Brown was key to solving the UNSUB case. "Reg was right. He just wasn't right about the right stuff," Carmichael said. If Brown had never called with his doubts about Montes, Carmichael never would have interviewed her. And if Scott had not interviewed her, he never would have caught her lying about something that happened on the street outside her apartment building. "The entire investigation wouldn't have gone any place at all. The reason that it went any place at all is because Reg said something to me about her that caused me to have personal contact with her."

After the 1996 interview with Ana, Carmichael briefed his supervisors. They weren't impressed. As a courtesy, he said he verbally shared what he had learned with the FBI's WFO Cuba Squad, too, and they were equally unenthusiastic. (The FBI's lead case agent later said he does not recall any mention of Ana in FBI files from 1996.) Carmichael knew the WFO Cuba Squad because, a few years earlier, they had asked him for help in locating tech manuals for the "SAFE" System, an electronic information-sharing database used by both DIA and CIA. The Cubans had stolen an unclassified copy of the manual, the FBI disclosed, and needed Carmichael's help in finding a version and interviewing the vendors who created the classified messaging system.

By Thanksgiving of 1996, Carmichael was out of options. He officially closed the case. Ana Montes would continue spying for nearly five more years.

Chapter 20.

"ONE OF THE MOST DAMAGING SPIES"

"Cuban intelligence operations in the United States have been enduring, aggressive and painfully successful."

—MICHELLE VAN CLEAVE, CHIEF, MONTES DAMAGE ASSESSMENT TEAM

Cleared of suspicion, Ana recommitted to her work. As she turned forty, she marked the occasion with a master class in deceit. She personified the insider threat, coolly bluffing her way into an ever greater cache of national security gems.

The DIA made it easy. The agency went out of its way to help Ana learn about, or be "indoctrinated" into, a highly secretive program run by the National Reconnaissance Office (NRO), the US organization that designs, launches, and operates reconnaissance satellites and provides signals intelligence to the NSA and other spy agencies. By May 1997, DIA granted the impostor the access she craved.[163]

The NRO's satellite project was so highly classified, called a Special Access Program (SAP), that only the most trusted insiders at DIA were read in. We know this, in part, because Ana once boasted to her Cuban bosses about the exclusive club she had just joined. "In addition, just today the agency [DIA] made me enter into a program, 'special access top secret.' [First name, last name omitted] and I are the only ones in my office who know about the program," Ana wrote to a Cuban intelligence officer in a message that the FBI later recovered from the hard drive of Ana's Toshiba laptop.[164] After her arrest, the DIA confirmed to investigators that Ana and the colleague she outed had been briefed into the Special Access Program, together, on May 15, 1997.

No government agency, charging document, publicly available report, or news article on the Montes case has ever identified the classified programs that Ana freely turned over to the Cubans. There have been tantalizing clues over the years that have described the overall damage she caused, but without providing much texture. Until now.

In 2012, the government official who ran the multiyear Ana Montes damage assessment task force testified before Congress. Michelle Van Cleave, who previously had served as head of counterintelligence under President George W. Bush, labeled Ana "one of the most damaging spies in US history."

"Few people realize the extent of the damage her 16 years of meticulous espionage caused this country—including putting lives at risk," Van Cleave said. She testified that Ana "compromised all Cuban-focused collection programs, calling into question the reliability of all US intelligence collected against Cuba." But then Van Cleave left a hint. "She also compromised programs of broader scope—highly sensitive intelligence of limited value to Cuba, but potentially very high value to other adversaries," she told the House Committee on Foreign Affairs.

Van Cleave is retired from the government now, after having served as Director of Security for the United States Senate during the calamitous January 6, 2021, riot on the US Capitol. In a recent interview, she made clear that her views on Montes have not softened. "Ana, based on what she compromised, causing in all likelihood the loss of American and other lives in Central America, that's a check mark in her column that I would never overlook." But as the keeper of government secrets for decades, Van Cleave refused to name the programs that Ana turned over to Havana; the Montes damage assessment that Van Cleave helped to author in 2005 remains highly classified.

Others, however, have helped to fill in the blanks.

Multiple sources with knowledge of the Montes case reveal here for the first time that Ana compromised one of the most expensive and significant classified programs in recent US history. Montes divulged to the Cubans intricate details about US stealth satellites that can orbit the earth undetected. Conventional satellites can be tracked and their orbits identified, allowing countries to hide troops and ground-based weapons when the satellites fly overhead. But US stealth satellites in the 1990s and 2000s, as part of an NRO black program code-named "MISTY," used cloaking technology that made them nearly impossible to detect—with much more advanced technology than the sleight of hand that allowed the old F-117A Stealth fighters to remain hidden on enemy radar.

The secret MISTY satellite program that Ana compromised had a price tag in the billions, and was designed to be untraceable by the Russians, Chinese, Iranians, Cubans, and other American adversaries. When members of the Senate Select Committee on Intelligence met in closed session in 2004 to debate whether they should continue funding the program, the *Washington Post* reported that the latest generation of the MISTY satellite had almost doubled in projected cost to nearly $9.5 billion.[165] "With the amount of money we're talking about here, you could build a whole new CIA," one unnamed official fumed. Four Democratic senators objected to the unidentified "major acquisition program" in the 2005 intelligence authorization bill, code for the MISTY stealth satellite program.

Senator John D. Rockefeller IV of West Virginia, then vice chairman of the intelligence committee, took the unusual step of discussing his opposition to the program on the Senate floor—without name-checking the program he was bashing. "My decision to take this somewhat unprecedented action is based solely on my strenuous objection—shared by many in our committee—to a particular major funding acquisition program that I believe is totally unjustified and very wasteful and dangerous to national security," Rockefeller said in December 2004. "Because of the highly classified nature of the programs contained in the national intelligence budget, I cannot talk about them on the floor."[166] Senator Ron Wyden of Oregon was more pointed. "I, like the vice chairman, do not support the continued funding of a major acquisition program which is unnecessary, ineffective, over budget, and too expensive." Wyden added that "the original justification for developing this technology has eroded in importance due to the changed practices and capabilities of our adversaries."

It's likely that Montes was responsible for some of our adversaries' changed practices. By late 2004 when the Senate debate went public, Ana had pleaded guilty and told government investigators all about the Special Access Programs she had divulged to the Cubans years earlier. Senator Rockefeller and fellow members of the Senate Select Committee on Intelligence presumably would have known that someone had jeopardized the MISTY program and shared details with US enemies, news of which likely added to the senators' reluctance to approve the program's ballooning price tag. "I can't go into this, but when we look at satellites, one or the other of us has questions," Senator Dianne Feinstein of California told her Senate colleagues at the time. "I'm concerned these are tens-of-billions-of-dollar items and we sure as heck better know what we're doing."

America's spy agencies have longed for stealth capabilities in the sky almost since the beginning of the US satellite program. In April 1963, just six months after the end of the Cuban Missile Crisis, the deputy director of the CIA's Office of Special

Activities first began discussing the need for a "covert reconnaissance satellite," or stealth system. In a memo reflecting Cold
War fears, the CIA determined that the Russians had already
made it next to impossible to conceal American satellites.[167] If
we rely solely on conventional satellites, the CIA warned, "an
intense Soviet effort will seriously reduce our coverage, and
may deprive us of coverage completely." To keep spying over
Soviet territory, the agency argued, a secondary eye-in-the-sky
was urgently needed. "This, then, is the justification for a development of a backup covert system which would rely, above
all, on concealment."

The NRO itself relies on concealment. Its name was classified "Secret"[168] for years, and the government didn't even acknowledge its existence until 1992.[169] Consequently, reliable
news about development of stealth satellites has been rare. Every
so often, however, there have been glimpses.

In the early morning hours of February 28, 1990, NASA
launched the space shuttle *Atlantis* from Kennedy Space Center.
The astronauts were on a secret flight called "Mission 36." But
blasting a 122-foot space shuttle with dual solid rocket boosters
over the Florida coastline was bound to attract attention. "Atlantis Lofts AFP-731 Reconnaissance Satellite," *Aviation Week*
scooped a few days later. The 37,000-pound satellite, a pet project of the CIA and NSA, was equipped with receivers to scoop
up Soviet signals "ranging from secure video to microwave to
telephone conversations" in most populated areas of the Soviet
Union, the magazine reported.[170]

Despite the revelations, reporters were kept at a distance and
had no idea that Mission 36's payload was code-named MISTY,
had a unique stealth mode, and an absurd price tag. NASA's
cost just to launch the shuttle was $115 million, not to mention
the satellite's astronomical R&D and operations budget.[171] Even
after three employees of the Strategic Defense Initiative Organization filed an open-source US patent application in March

1990 for a "Satellite Signature Suppression Shield," operational details on the new reconnaissance satellite remained a mystery. The patent, for an inflatable shield for "suppressing the characteristic radiation signature of a satellite,"[172] angered the NRO.

Amateur satellite spotters around the world are obsessed with finding spy satellites and posting their altitudes and azimuths on public websites including Heavens-Above.com.[173] Aided by math smarts and tricked-out telescopes, the hobbyists drive the NRO to exhaustion. "If we had our druthers, we would prefer that these things not end up on the internet," Rick Oborn, an NRO spokesperson, once told *WIRED* Magazine.[174] "It's no secret that other countries stop doing what they're doing when the satellites are overhead."

In February 1990, satellite spotters in Scotland and Alaska noticed an unusually bright object in the sky just after the launch of the space shuttle *Atlantis*. But soon, many of the same trackers described an apparent explosion associated with the mystery AFP-731 satellite. "Within weeks, both US and Soviet sources reported it had malfunctioned and would make a 'fiery reentry... in the next thirty days,'" author Jeffrey Richelson revealed in *The Wizards of Langley: Inside the CIA's Directorate of Science and Technology*. The Soviet news agency Novosti wrote that the new spy satellite had broken up, with Soviet space experts tracking what were thought to be four large pieces from the spacecraft falling to earth.[175] Meanwhile, newspapers quoted an anonymous US intelligence official who described the malfunction as a "serious setback."

They were all wrong. The new MISTY satellite was operational but cleverly hidden. Richelson, a senior fellow at the National Security Archive until his death in 2017, thought that the "explosion" may have been a trick to confuse the Russians and give the satellite time to vanish.

That stealth satellite remained a phantom until May of 1997. That's when Ana got a briefing on MISTY and promptly leaked details to the Cubans. She learned that part of MISTY's charm was that it appeared mostly to be a SIGINT collector, scooping up signals intelligence, or electronic communications, as it circled the globe. In reality, it was an IMINT collector, slyly taking detailed images or photos of the landscape below. "This thing was disguised as something other than what it was," one knowledgeable source explained. So even if enemy commanders figured out that a US stealth satellite was overhead, they would be tricked. "They would shut down their communications when really they should be putting the tanks in the garage."

Revealing details of the ingenious MISTY program to the Cubans is concerning enough. But the Castro brothers have a long history of brokering US secrets. Sources familiar with the Montes case presume that the Cubans quickly sold or traded Ana's information to the Russians, their old patrons, or to other interested parties. "There is a continuing market for such stolen U.S. secrets, which can be sold or bartered to third party states or terrorist organizations that have their own uses for the information," Michelle Van Cleave explained during her 2012 testimony. She added that the damage to the US from the loss of sensitive national security information to Cuban espionage "is not bounded by the national security threat presented by Cuba alone, but also by its value to potentially more dangerous adversaries."

In the MISTY example, it's highly possible that the Russians knew all about the stealth satellite without help from the Cubans. The Russians had their own spies inside America's intelligence agencies, of course, and their own pipeline to US government secrets. A former top US intelligence official reveals for the first time that FBI traitor Robert Hanssen is believed to have shared details on the MISTY program with the Russians during his epic two-decade career as a spy.

Terry Holstad was an FBI supervisor and special agent for twenty-eight years. He officially retired on September 1, 2001, just days before the 9/11 terror attacks. Holstad reveals on the record that he was one of a very few FBI investigators who knew about the mysterious MISTY Special Access Program— and Ana's successful efforts to help the Cubans defeat it. "I got briefed into the program because during one of the FISA court-approved searches, the [Montes] agents discovered" messages on Ana's laptop regarding the MISTY program, Holstad said, referring to the Foreign Intelligence Surveillance Act court that approved a physical search of Ana's apartment in the summer of 2001. "Then we went out to the NRO, and they explained to us what the program was."

Later, when the CIA needed help conducting its damage assessment of Hanssen following his 2001 arrest, Holstad seemed a good fit. In the first interview he's ever granted, Holstad recounted how he personally questioned Hanssen about the super-classified NRO MISTY program. "I went to work for the Agency for about 15 months as a contractor on the Hanssen damage assessment team. And I ended up interviewing him extensively really while he was still here in Virginia and taking a couple trips out to Supermax to talk to him out there," Holstad said, referencing the maximum security Supermax facility in Colorado where Hanssen is serving a life sentence. Holstad said that one of the first times he was at Supermax, a CIA officer joined him for the debrief. Hanssen hinted he knew about the MISTY satellite program and was willing to discuss it. But since the CIA agent also in the room had not been cleared to learn about MISTY, Holstad couldn't discuss it in front of him. "He hadn't been briefed. So I said, 'I need to go back and talk to him [Hanssen] in depth alone.' And I did and I got a lot of information," Holstad said. "I was briefed into it as the Unit Chief in the FBI. So I had to interview him by myself about that program."

Holstad concluded in his final CIA report that Hanssen compromised the MISTY satellite program. "Hanssen passed that information, but passed it to the Russians," he said. "As best I can recall, he didn't deny it. He didn't confirm it. And I told my bosses that and I said, 'I would err on the side of caution and say he passed it.'" Holstad said he made his determination about Hanssen "in light of his history" in passing along so many secret documents, failing polygraphs post-arrest, and his overall deceptive nature.

Before Ana was briefed on MISTY, she had to sign a "Sensitive Compartmented Information Nondisclosure Agreement" acknowledging that unauthorized disclosure of the program would violate federal criminal law and "could cause irreparable injury to the United States or be used to the advantage of a foreign nation."[176] That's precisely what happened, Holstad and other sources said.

The MISTY satellite "was unpredictable and for that reason, it was like we could sneak up and take a look and [the Cubans] wouldn't be ready," a well-briefed source said. "But by her passing this information to them, they could become even more cautious than they were." The source added: "Certainly this is extremely serious. The money that's invested in the program to me is secondary compared to the intelligence that could have been lost because of her compromising information."

John Pike is an expert on the space industry and sophisticated military systems, and runs the GlobalSecurity.org website. He explained that the MISTY satellite was hardened to survive enemy attacks during a nuclear war—and built to blend in. "The theory was that they were going to give it various stealth, low-signature attributes that would make one look like a piece of space debris." The NRO's pricey show horse had one major advantage over conventional military satellites. "If you don't know when this satellite is going to be overhead, it gives you a better chance of catching people with their pants down," Pike said. While Congress would have wanted to know if a spy or spies had blown MISTY's cover, the senators would be even more interested to learn whether China and Russia were sophisticated enough to find MISTY on their own. "The controversy, the question was, how robust Russian and Chinese space surveillance capabilities were and whether they would be able to pick the satellite out of a lineup."

When asked recently if Ana divulged secrets on the MISTY program, Van Cleave would not comment. But then she volunteered this: "Do we have very sensitive satellite programs? Yes. Would Ana have had access to that information? To be sure."

Holstad, the FBI's former Cuba Unit Chief, confirmed that it caused "tremendous" damage to national security when one, and likely two spies, compromised the program. "It just goes to the capabilities that this government had at the time, as to what they could do with this device, this piece of equipment. And it would go into the realm of potentially hindering terrorist investigations, intelligence, and all kinds of things. So it was just a tremendous amount of damage," he said.

MISTY was not the only important intel program Ana revealed. She is estimated to have read tens of thousands, or perhaps even hundreds of thousands, of classified intelligence memos in her nearly seventeen-year career. She had carte blanche access to the SAFE System, an electronic information–sharing database that stood for "Secure Analyst File Environment." DIA analysts and collectors in the field uploaded articles and raw intelligence reports daily to the SAFE system, as did their counterparts in the CIA, NSA, NRO, Defense Department, and many other major spy agencies. Using keyword searches, Ana had access to an almost unlimited smorgasbord of secrets prepared by the US Intelligence Community. She would pick and choose what was of interest, memorize it, and pass it along to her friends on encrypted diskettes.

In 1999 and 2000, Ana was granted access to additional Special Access Programs.[177] Sources familiar with the Montes case reveal that Ana learned about, and likely exposed, one other inventive collection system that had been bearing fruit for years.

The FBI is the primary US agency that tracks the activities of foreign intelligence officers operating in the United States, often with technical support from the CIA and NSA. It's the job of the FBI to keep an eye on spooks and everyday diplomats for Cuba, Russia, China, Iran, and dozens of other countries—foes and allies alike—who work out of their embassies, consulates, and offices in Washington, New York, and other US cities. It's a constant battle for insider knowledge and electronic supremacy. Our enemies know that we spy on them in the US, and they return the favor at our embassies overseas.

Consider the sprawling Russian Embassy at 2650 Wisconsin Avenue, NW, in the Glover Park neighborhood of Washington. For years, the FBI occupied a single-family home on Wisconsin Avenue directly across from the front gate of the Russian compound. Locals called it "The Spy House." No one ever seemed to live in the brick and stucco home, which public records easily showed was occupied by an FBI surveillance specialist who used his true name.[178] For years, it had three video cameras peeking out of three attic skylights, capturing all the action below. These days, technology has replaced the need for the Spy House. At least forty-one domed surveillance cameras are mounted today to light poles ringing the Russian Embassy. The unmanned cameras monitor multiple entrances and exits to the embassy grounds, plus nearby intersections, feeding live video footage nonstop to the FBI.

That's the surveillance that's easily observable on the outside. In March 2001, the *New York Times* revealed that the US government had constructed a secret tunnel underneath the Russian Embassy.[179] "The secret tunnel operation, which officials indicated was run jointly by the FBI and the National Security Agency, was part of a broad United States effort to eavesdrop on and track Soviet—later Russian—facilities and personnel operating in the United States," the *Times* reported. The tunnel cost several hundred million dollars but was betrayed by Hanssen, the rogue FBI agent. Hanssen, a twenty-five-year FBI veteran and Russian counterintelligence expert, mailed an unsigned letter to a DC-based KGB agent on October 1, 1985—coincidentally just a day after Ana began working for DIA.[180] In the letter, Hanssen asked for a $100,000 fee, provided the names of three KGB line officers that the FBI had recruited as agents in place, and revealed the existence of a "highly sensitive and classified information collection technique" that is presumed to be the then-secret tunnel under the Russian Embassy. After receiving Hanssen's letter, Moscow executed two of the KGB double agents he identified and imprisoned the third.[181] If the sophisticated listening devices in the tunnel worked before Hanssen exposed them, they ceased functioning after the KGB received his missive.

Ana also compromised a highly sensitive and classified FBI collection system. Sources familiar with her case say that she became aware of a tricked-out Chrysler Corporation van that the FBI was using to bug the conversations of intelligence officers operating out of the Cuban Interests Section in the Adams Morgan neighborhood of Washington. Ana learned that the van looked normal, except for a minor alteration. "The roof was raised, but it was raised in such a way that you couldn't tell that the roof was higher than the standard van unless you had another van right next to it that was the same model and year," a source said. US intelligence agencies had crammed special antennas into the van's roof to make it easier for the FBI to conduct surveillance. "So they could actually drive by different places and pick up phone conversations" or listen in to Cuban officers dining in nearby restaurants.

When Ana informed the Cubans about the slightly taller Chrysler van, their intelligence agents immediately knew what to look for in DC or New York and would clam up when it was around. It's likely the Cubans shared their good bounty with friends, too. After all, a van that the FBI used against the Cubans would work just as well against other foes. "Of course, it was probably more targeted against Russia at the time," the source added. "It could be targeted against anybody, really."

Emilia and Dr. Alberto Montes were living on a US Army base in West Germany when Ana Belén Montes was born on February 28, 1957.
Photo Credit: Montes Family

The Montes family moved to Topeka, Kansas, in 1958. Ana is on the right.
Photo Credit: Montes Family

Celebrating Christmas with baby Carlos, 1963.
Photo Credit: Montes Family

Behind closed doors at the family home in Topeka, Dr. Montes was "the king of the castle," Ana said, "and demanded complete and total obedience."
Photo Credit: Montes Family

Dr. Alberto Montes received his diploma from famed psychiatrist Dr. Karl Menninger in 1963 and trained to become a psychoanalyst.
Photo Credit: Montes Family

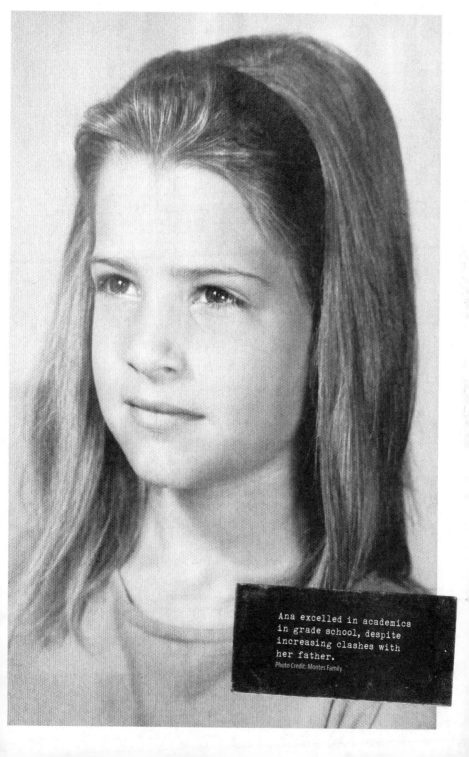

Ana excelled in academics in grade school, despite increasing clashes with her father.

Photo Credit: Montes Family

Ana graduated from Loch Raven High School in Towson, Maryland, with a 3.9 GPA and headed to UVa for college.
Photo Credit: Montes Family

Lucy, L, Ana, and Tito in
the suburbs outside Baltimore.
Photo Credit: Montes Family

Ana's boyfriend her junior year abroad in Spain,
Ricardo Fernandez Eiriz, helped shape her politics.
Photo Credit: Ana Colon

Ana's look in college would change
dramatically once she began working
for the DIA, the so-called "war machine."
Photo Credit: Montes Family

Ana celebrated her twenty-first birthday in Spain, 1978.
Photo Credit: Ana Colon

Lucy Montes began work for the FBI as a translator in Miami in 1985, just weeks after Ana accepted the Cubans' offer to spy.
Photo Credit: Montes Family

Ana, far right, forced a smile at sister Lucy's wedding shower in 1986. She brought her friend and accused Cuban agent Marta Velázquez, far left. Seated between Lucy and Ana was sister-in-law Joan, who would later become an FBI agent. Photo Credit: Montes Family

The sisters at Lucy's wedding, 1987. Photo Credit: Montes Family

By 1989, Ana was winning awards at the DIA and had dramatically altered her look.
Photo Credit: Montes Family

Tito became an FBI special agent in 1989. Ana attended the ceremony inside the Bureau.
Photo Credit: Montes Family

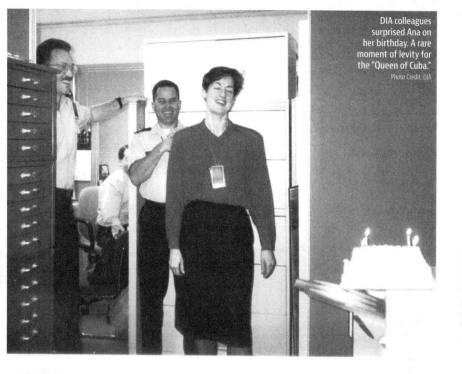

DIA colleagues surprised Ana on her birthday. A rare moment of levity for the "Queen of Cuba."
Photo Credit: DIA

Ana's boss and champion, Marty Scheina, said he "knew less about Ana" than almost any employee who had worked for him at the DIA for such a long time.
Photo Credit: DIA

In 1997, CIA Director George Tenet awarded Ana a Certificate of Distinction for her "strong sense of Intelligence Community responsibility."
Photo Credit: DIA

FBI Director J. Edgar Hoover, center, posed in 1970 with the McCoy family. Steve, far left, would go on to become the FBI's Blue Wren case agent, following his father into the family business.
Photo Credit: Steve McCoy

FBI special agents Steve McCoy, L, and Pete Lapp.
Photo Credit: Charlie Archambault

Even the FBI concedes that DIA investigator Scott Carmichael was first to identify Ana Montes as a likely spy.
Photo Credit: Mike Morgan

The FBI covertly tailed Montes and watched her make suspicious calls on public pay phones, even though she carried a cell phone in her purse.
Photo Credit: FBI

The FBI arrested Ana ten days after the 9/11 terror attacks. They were worried she might faint, but Ana walked out "calm" and composed.
Photo Credit: FBI

ANA BELEN MONTES
DOB 02-28-57
65J WF 220371
FBI WFO 09 21 2001

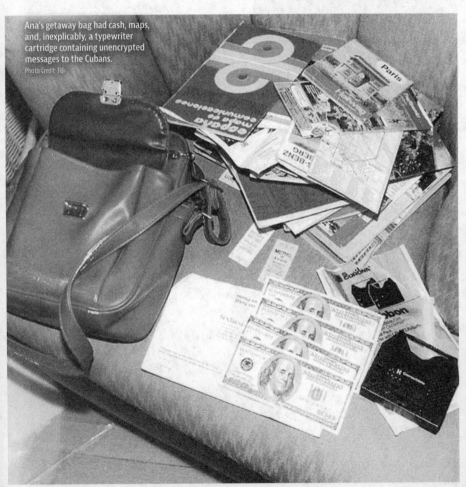

Ana's getaway bag had cash, maps, and, inexplicably, a typewriter cartridge containing unencrypted messages to the Cubans.
Photo Credit: FBI

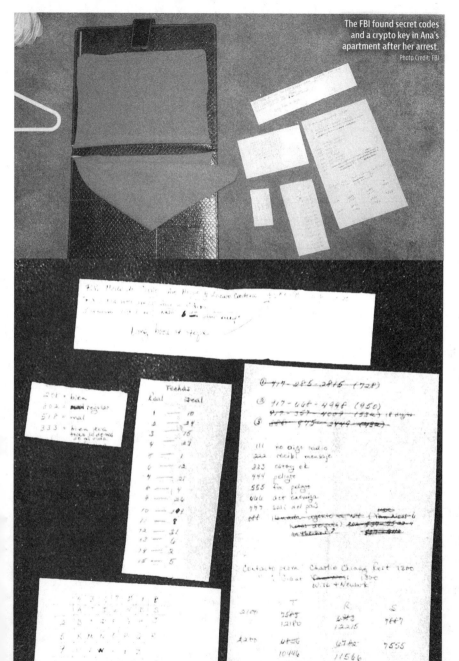

The FBI found secret codes and a crypto key in Ana's apartment after her arrest.
Photo Credit: FBI

The DOJ accuses
Marta Velázquez,
right, of working for
the Cubans and helping
to recruit Ana as a spy.
Marta lives freely
today in Sweden.
Photo Credit: Lina Nydahl

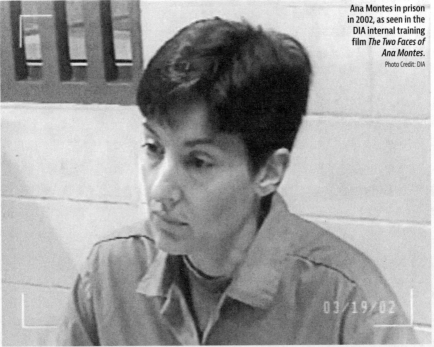

Ana Montes in prison
in 2002, as seen in the
DIA internal training
film *The Two Faces of
Ana Montes*.
Photo Credit: DIA

03/19/02

Chapter 21.

BOTTOMING OUT

"Who are you? Where is the meaning(s) in your life? Struggling with decisions? We all are."

**—ANA'S PSYCHIATRIST,
WRITING IN *PSYCHOLOGY TODAY***

As Ana fed ever-more valuable intelligence to Cuba, America's spymasters could not have been more oblivious. Or appreciative of her cover work. The congratulations reached an absurd peak in 1997, when the Director of Central Intelligence awarded Ana with the National Intelligence Certificate of Distinction. Within the spy community, there are few higher honors than the Certificate of Distinction. Ana must have been pinching herself as she paraded into the CIA to be lauded by George Tenet, who ran the CIA from 1997 to 2004. The photo of Tenet smiling next to Castro's greatest spy is one for the history books. The CIA's now-comical citation states, "Ms. Montes' strong sense of Intelligence Community responsibility fostered the strengthening of a collegial strategy among analysts working (Cuba), reflecting great credit upon herself and the Defense Intelligence Agency."[182] Tenet declined an interview request about Montes.

Down in Miami, Lucy's hard work in the Wasp Network case

was paying off. Over the previous few years, Lucy and members of the Royal Flush Task Force had gathered massive amounts of evidence against ten members of the Cuban spy network and were ready to round them up. "Spies Among Us," the *Miami Herald* splashed across its front page in September 1998. "US Cracks Alleged Cuban Ring, Arrests 10."[183] The Miami Field Office of the FBI announced that it had broken up the biggest spy ring in years from the Communist island, stopping the Wasp Network from infiltrating US military bases in South Florida.

Lucy's bosses and the Cuban community in Miami took notice, and Lucy earned praise from the FBI brass and an award from the local Latin Chamber of Commerce. But the most effusive congratulations came from George Tenet himself. Not long after lauding one Montes sister, the CIA director awarded Lucy and members of the Royal Flush Task Force with a Meritorious Unit Citation for exceptional service. Director Tenet praised Lucy and the team for "devotion to duty, perseverance, and cooperative excellence in investigation." Lucy's hard work "corroborated the membership, tradecraft, and objectives of a Cuban Intelligence Services network..." Tenet said.[184] He added that one of the spies, later convicted, had infiltrated the Brothers to the Rescue organization and delivered a secret message that helped the Cuban MiGs locate and shoot down two civilian airplanes in international airspace, killing four.

But there was another coincidence to the FBI's breakup of the Wasp Network in Miami that was not immediately apparent but would prove critical to Ana's well-being. Prior to arresting the Cubans, the FBI obtained search warrants to remove the spies' computers and electronic files. They found files, lots of files. "The amount of information they had left on floppy disks or given away in intercepted radio messages fills fourteen hundred pages—three fat folders of prosecution evidence—and that is just the highlights," one reporter noted.[185] The FBI also recovered the "crypto keys," or cryptographic keys, that could unlock the numbers broadcasts that the Cubans used to communicate with their spy network via shortwave radio. The NSA would later use these keys to code-break years of high-frequency messages from Havana to agents operating in the US—including the UNSUB who later was revealed to be Montes.

As soon as Ana's Cuban superiors learned that the FBI had walked away with all those juicy files in Miami, they did what all scared spy agencies do. They went to ground.

In September 1998, Ana's handlers brusquely cut her off. To stanch the bleeding, all Cubans illegally operating in the United States went silent or flew home. For Ana, there would be no more casual dinners in DC, no more egg-roll-fueled briefings. In fact, there would be no more meetings in the United States again. All Ana's future meets would take place overseas on island getaways.

The fallout from the Wasp arrests altered Ana's communications protocols, too. She stopped using her Toshiba to decrypt messages and type out encrypted memos on floppy disks. Instead, she mostly relied on memory to verbally pass along classified information during in-person meetings with her handlers in the Caribbean. To unravel the shortwave radio broadcasts, Ana went old school. She used a handwritten cipher, like a checkerboard, to decrypt the numbers station broadcasts.[186] After the arrests in Miami, an FBI investigator explained, the Cubans still gave orders to their far-flung agents using high frequency, or HF, radio broadcasts. "But they got away from the computers and the new floppy disks and all that stuff," he said, "and went with this more archaic kind of communication methodology."

Ana educated herself on FBI investigative tactics by talking her way into a law-enforcement-only meeting. FBI agents who had worked the Wasp case gave a classified briefing at the Bureau's training center at Quantico, sharing details on how they had rolled up the Cuban spies. "Ana was in the audience... And she's listening, taking mental notes," said DIA counterintelli-

gence officer Mark Ritter. "The next time she meets her handler, she says, 'Hey, this is how the FBI caught your Cubans.'"
Ritter said that Ana admitted her attendance at the closed FBI
briefing to him when he was interviewing her, postarrest, for
DIA. He said the anecdote is a good reminder about loose lips.
"One of the things that we as counterintelligence officers don't
discuss is how you actually catch the spy…what precise bit of
information led to it. And the reason why was born out in the
Montes case."

Ana was more alone than ever. Lucy had no idea at the time,
but the first espionage case she had ever worked on, the lucky
case that had earned her praise from the CIA director, was making her sister's life a joyless hell. "When contact with her handlers drastically decreased in 1998 due to several Cuban agents'
arrest, Montes was shaken," the CIA wrote. Ana felt trapped.
"Something that gave me fulfillment disappeared," she admitted. "I had a feeling I was very alone and was working in place,
doing things I did not want to do." Lucy's triumph had become
Ana's despair.

The fallout from the Wasp arrests only exacerbated the intense
psychological stress Ana had been feeling. Childless and single,
she had started to grow despondent around her fortieth birthday. "I was finally ready to share my life with someone but was
leading a double life, so I did not feel I could live happily."[187]

Ana's younger sister witnessed the breakdown firsthand. In
late June 1998, Lucy threw herself a fortieth birthday party at
her home near Miami. Her marriage with Chris had just ended
in divorce, and Lucy was ready to enjoy time with friends. She
invited Ana and was delighted that she came. And then instantly
regretted it.

At the party, Ana sat stone-faced. She was practically cata-
tonic, and no one could snap her out of it. "She never spoke the
whole weekend. There was something obviously wrong with
her," Lucy said. "I was embarrassed. I had to apologize to some

of my friends. She was in the house, but she wasn't talking to anybody." In retrospect, Lucy realized Ana was cut off from her handlers—her only true friends. "She must have been terrified."

The CIA psychologists later figured out what was happening. "After 13 years of spying, Montes's double life was causing her psychological distress," they found. Ana began struggling with anxiety and depression. For the next eighteen months, she was in treatment "for depressed mood, sleep difficulties, and crying spells," the CIA wrote.

Ana voluntarily sought psychiatric treatment with Dr. Joseph Tarantolo of Washington, DC, a self-described "psychoanalyst with Buddhist and existential proclivities." Dr. Tarantolo is an unconventional practitioner who has written passionately about the dangers of drugs commonly prescribed to manage psychiatric disorders. "I eschew drugs and will help you get off of antidepressants and other psychotropic drugs. I tend to be philosophical," Dr. Tarantolo wrote in a bio posted in *Psychology Today*.[188] In an email to the author, the first time he's revealed that Ana was his patient, Dr. Tarantolo added: "We are a drug driven culture. That can be problematic and sometimes dangerous."[189]

In online reviews, one former patient objected to his strategy—and personality. "He is openly anti-medication, which would be fine as a viewpoint, but he was loud, bullying, implied that I had been drugged my entire life..." the reviewer said. "I began halfway through the session to feel myself in the presence of a crazy person, at least someone seriously unhinged. His vehemence against antidepressants really took me aback, for someone reportedly trained in the field."[190] In an email, Dr. Tarantolo defended his approach. "I have seen patients who have been on psychoactive drugs most of their lives. If they are motivated, I try (sometimes succeed, sometimes fail) to wean them off," he said.

In a phone interview in 2021, Dr. Tarantolo took the unusual step of volunteering opinions on Ana, his former patient.

"This was a conflicted woman," he said. "She was dedicated to her country and to Cuba. And she felt that conflict powerfully." He added that he looked forward to speaking with Ana after her jail sentence and "my hope is she will be truly free." He said that Ana never admitted during any of their sessions that she was a spy and also "never discussed her work." Finally, Ana's psychiatrist defended his imprisoned patient. "Remember, Ana was not only a spy. She wanted her country to do right. I wish she had found a better way to soothe her patriotic conscience."

Despite Dr. Tarantolo's misgivings about the clinical overuse of drugs, Ana needed some extra help. According to the CIA, "She took an antidepressant for nine months and later took anti-anxiety medication for more than a year when she had panic attacks."[191] Dr. Tarantolo made clear that the drugs didn't come from him. "I believe she got the Benzo Rx from another physician. I did not give her an antidepressant," he told the author. "Now, of course, we/I can understand why she was so anxious, living a double life. As I have opined many times, drugs merely hide the problem(s), they don't address the underlying struggle."

Chapter 22.

"A LIMITED CAPACITY"

"Cuba has a limited capability to engage in some military and intelligence activities which would be detrimental to U.S. interests..."

—THE CUBAN THREAT TO U.S. NATIONAL SECURITY,
A REPORT TO CONGRESS, MAY 1998

DIA policy requires employees with security clearances to self-report mental health treatment and, for once, Ana came clean. Sort of. After she started seeing Dr. Tarantolo as a patient, Ana informed her supervisor, Marty Scheina, that she was getting mental help for work-related stress. "She came to me and she said that she was getting counseling. Seeing a shrink," Scheina said. He felt duty bound to report it up the line and briefed his boss, Dave Curtin. "I said, 'Dave, I just want to tell you that Ana is feeling like she's been under a lot of stress lately. And she has been seeing somebody professionally.'"

Ana of course didn't admit what was causing such intense pressure, and Scheina didn't press. His prized recruit kept taking on more and began work in the late 1990s on one of the most important reports of her career. She wrote the first draft of *The Cuban Threat to U.S. National Security*, an influential interagency analysis of Cuban military and intelligence capabilities that William Cohen, the defense secretary under President Clinton, presented to Congress in May 1998.

Ana is regarded by national security professionals as "one of the most damaging spies in US history" because of the longevity of her career, her nearly unlimited access to classified information, and the power she wielded as a Cuba expert inside the insular US Intelligence Community. Aldrich Ames at the CIA and Robert Hanssen at the FBI divulged intelligence to the Russians that crippled massive spy programs and led directly to the execution of well-placed operatives in the secret employ of the United States. Their double-dealing still has the power to shock. But as dangerous as Ames and Hanssen were, their crimes consisted primarily of selling the family jewels. Ana distinguished herself by not just giving away valuables to Havana, but simultaneously downplaying the Cuban threat. She's forever enshrined in the rogues' gallery of most harmful American spies by assuring generals in the morning that Cuba had become a paper tiger, while in the afternoon, robbing their SCIFs blind. Ana not only revealed the names of Cubans working undercover for the United States, a truly dangerous betrayal. She also "served as an agent of influence," Van Cleave said, allowing her briefings and analytic reports to be "colored by her loyalties to Cuba." The DIA's Lisa Connors spent four months interviewing Ana after her arrest. Connors said Ana should have gotten a life sentence for her crimes. "She wasn't just stealing information and revealing people and revealing our sources. But she also was influencing our policy," Connors said in her first interview about the case. "She was incredibly dangerous because she affected our policy. We were not looking where we should have been looking because she was directing our attention elsewhere."

Given its highly compromised author, *The Cuban Threat to U.S. National Security* offers a charitable interpretation of life in the Communist stronghold—and still sparks debate among knowledgeable observers. The unclassified executive summary states that Cuba "does not pose a significant military threat" and adds that the breakup of the Soviet Union in 1989 "triggered a profound deterioration of the Cuban Revolutionary Armed Forces (FAR)."[192] In a line that has stirred controversy ever since, the report concludes that Cuba "has a limited capability to engage in some military and intelligence activities which would be detrimental to U.S. interests and which could pose a danger to U.S. citizens under some circumstances."

Since Castro's own spy wrote the first draft of the 1998 report, it's been hard for many national security experts to see the "limited capacity" phrase as anything other than disinformation. "There is no doubt that Cuba poses a significant, dangerous, and hostile intelligence threat to the United States—and Ana Montes herself embodied it," one Army lieutenant colonel and former DIA military analyst said.[193] Even Defense Secretary Cohen seemed to undercut his own report to Congress when he sent a letter to Senator Strom Thurmond, Chairman of the Armed Services Committee, stating: "While the assessment notes that the direct conventional threat by the Cuban military has decreased, I remain concerned about the use of Cuba as a base for intelligence activities directed against the United States…" Cohen added that Cuba could be cooking up plans to make biological weapons.[194] "I remain concerned about Cuba's potential to develop and produce biological agents, given its biotechnology infrastructure."

Ana spent months writing *The Cuban Threat to U.S. National Security*, with contributions by analysts at the CIA, NSA, the State Department's Bureau of Intelligence and Research, and the Southern Command's Joint Intelligence Center. In that sense, it truly was written by committee. But Ana took the first pass and is recognized as its author. If the report goes easy on Cuba, as some believe, it was Ana who pulled the first punch.

Fulton Armstrong is a former CIA analyst and high-ranking Latin America expert who was first hired by the Agency in 1984.

He knew and respected Ana as "a good analyst, a rigorous analyst" and strongly rejects the notion that Ana soft-pedaled the 1998 report as a Cuban agent of influence. "The famous Montes Report, the very first draft was indeed written by her, but it was so bad that we completely rewrote it and coordinated it throughout the Intelligence Community with unanimous and enthusiastic support," he said. "It was not her paper, but it was used by the morons back when all this happened [to say], 'Oh, look at the evidence of her efforts to influence the Intel Community, to influence policy.' It's just bullshit." As the Deputy National Intelligence Officer (NIO) for Latin America at the time, Armstrong said that he was "in charge of coordinating" the report for the Intelligence Community, "all 15 agencies of which enthusiastically embraced it."

One of the so-called "morons" who still gets under Armstrong's skin twenty years later is John Bolton, the conservative icon who was President George W. Bush's US Permanent Representative to the United Nations and briefly served as National Security Advisor under President Donald Trump before turning on him. In 2002, in the run-up to the Iraq War, Bolton gave a famous speech to the conservative Heritage Foundation entitled, "Beyond the Axis of Evil: Additional Threats from Weapons of Mass Destruction." In it, Bolton suggested, provocatively, that "the United States believes that Cuba has at least a limited offensive biological warfare research and development effort." He then blasted Castro for denouncing the U.S. war on terrorism following the 9/11 attacks. "He continues to view terror as a legitimate tactic to further revolutionary objectives," Bolton said. "Last year, Castro visited Iran, Syria, and Libya—all designees on the same list of terrorist-sponsoring states. At Tehran University, these were his words: 'Iran and Cuba, in cooperation with each other, can bring America to its knees.'"

Bolton then hammered home his point. Why was the US government's report on Cuba, written by Secretary Cohen during the Clinton Administration, "so unbalanced"? Why did it seriously "underplay" the threat Cuba posed to the US? "A major reason is Cuba's aggressive intelligence operations against the United States, which included recruiting the Defense Intelligence Agency's senior Cuba analyst, Ana Belén Montes, to spy for Cuba. Montes not only had a hand in drafting the 1998 Cuba report, but also passed some of our most sensitive information about Cuba back to Havana," Bolton said.

Bolton has called Fulton Armstrong an "apologist for Cuba" known to Senate Republicans for "imposing his own pro-Castro biases on Cuban-related intelligence."[195] In a 2022 interview with the author, Bolton blasted Armstrong for not taking a harder line on Cuba in the 1998 report and during Armstrong's decades at the CIA. He claims that Armstrong was friends with Ana, but played down their friendship after her humiliating arrest. "As long as you've got what Lenin used to call 'useful idiots' helping, you don't even need to recruit spies," Bolton said. "You know, you have to ask yourself, if somebody is such a brilliant guy that he's a high-ranking intelligence analyst, how is it he's missing what Montes is up to?"

Armstrong is retired from government now and is an adjunct professor at the American University in Washington and at Syracuse University's Washington program. He says that Bolton's "disastrous record speaks for itself" and denies ever being a friend of Ana. "Never was, never will be." He brushed off Bolton's insults. "You take a liar at face value, and want me to rebut him?" Armstrong asked. "I was not, and never have been, anyone's 'useful idiot.' Not fact-based at all."

Looking back, Armstrong said it's clear that the 1998 Cuba analysis he supervised was on the mark. "The judgment was right. Cuba poses no threat to the United States, period." And he adds that it's unfair to tether Ana to the final version. "It's called the Montes Paper because she was the original task author, but this happens many, many, many times. Papers get rewritten almost completely and, in her case, I think it probably would be fair to say completely."

But a former DIA analyst who worked closely with Ana said that's missing the point. She said that the original author of any intelligence product typically exerts undue influence over the final version. "In my view, saying that the drafter of a consensus document is irrelevant is kind of like saying it didn't matter that Thomas Jefferson was the principal author of the Declaration of Independence," said Suzanne Shafford, a former Air Force captain who served as a Joint Staff officer and civilian DIA analyst from 1997 to 2010. "Yes, he received guidance/input from John Adams and Ben Franklin, and the other members of the Continental Congress made significant changes and deletions, but does anyone doubt that the Declaration would read differently if it had been drafted by Sam Adams? In addition to word choices…the author's voice and framing of a document matter."

When Ana wasn't holed up in her sixth-floor cubicle writing *The Cuban Threat to U.S. National Security*, she was out in the wild personifying it. In May 1997, she revealed the identity of a third and fourth covert US intelligence officer operating in Cuba, endangering the lives of two CIA assets operating under deep cover. And in January 1998, she visited Cuba for her fourth time, working out of the US Interests Section in Havana and slipping off to see her DGI superiors.

Ana's trip overlapped with Pope John Paul II's historic first visit to the island and was not without intrigue. In a suspicious email she sent to DIA investigator Scott Carmichael after the trip, she claimed that a mysterious Cuban had followed her in Havana. "I went across the street from my hotel into a botanical garden and kind of got lost in the maze," she wrote. "And I turned around and there was a man standing there, a Cuban in a three-piece suit. And I think he was following me." Carmichael said that Ana's unprompted email felt like a desperate student kissing up to a teacher and "triggered the alarms in me." It wasn't until years later, after her arrest, that Carmichael put it all together. He thinks Ana sent him the email in case any Americans had spotted her cavorting with a handler in Havana. Like the veteran spy she had become, she was building yet another cover story. It was an extra bit of insurance to preemptively protect herself from any do-good American snitches.

Chapter 23.

THE SEVENTH FLOOR

"The Exceptional Impact Promotion Program permits DIA to promote a small number of individuals who bring such extraordinary
knowledge, skill, and ability to their jobs that they function at a higher
level than normally expected...."

—LETTER FROM THE DIA DIRECTOR

In May 1999, a secretary was on the line. "Ana, could you
come immediately to the seventh floor?" she asked. "Mr. Curtin would like to see you." It was the phone call that Ana had
long been dreading.

She froze. Dave Curtin was Chief of DIA's Regional Military Assessments Group. He was a high-ranking official in the
Directorate of Intelligence Operations. A heavy hitter. Curtin
also happened to be Marty Scheina's boss, and was the supervisor to whom Scheina ran when Ana confessed that she was
seeing a psychiatrist. *My God, Ana must have imagined. This
is it. Handcuffs and orange jumpsuits.*

Ana's cubicle was only a floor away, and she was standing
in Curtin's outer office in no time, overlooking the Anacostia
Naval Air Station. "So we take her up to the seventh floor. We
don't tell her what it's about," Ana's direct supervisor, Scheina,
remembers. Ana had never been so visibly nervous. Curtin was

running late, so Scheina and Ana waited together for fifteen excruciating minutes.

By the time Curtin arrived, he sensed a problem. Ana was badly out of sorts. "She clearly looked concerned." So with one quick phrase, Curtin put her out of her misery. "Ana, congratulations, you've been promoted to 14."

Ana wasn't being arrested or interrogated. This wasn't that kind of a setup. Instead, she had been secretly promoted to GG-14, rare air for a DIA analyst. Ana's bosses had wanted to surprise her and announce the coveted promotion to the GG-14 level (called GS-14 elsewhere in the federal system), which included a significant raise and was the culmination of a fierce competition among thousands of other DIA employees hoping for a bump in pay and prestige. Without her knowledge, Ana's supporters had nominated her for the Exceptional Impact Promotion Program (EIP) and, after three tries, an independent board at DIA had selected her. "Please accept my sincere congratulations on the exceptional work you have accomplished in support of DIA and the nation. I am proud to have you on my team," the DIA director wrote.[196]

Scheina and Curtin had expected Ana to jump up and down and hug them after learning the fabulous news. For most analysts, becoming a 14 in the federal pay system was a lifetime achievement. Instead, Ana nearly fainted. "She went right down in one of those stuffed chairs," Curtin recalled. "She collapsed," Scheina added. "She just went down real hard." It wasn't until much later, Scheina said, that he realized what he had witnessed. Ana had been told to report to her boss's boss "and she's there waiting intensely for fifteen minutes or so until he comes back, the whole time thinking, 'Oh my God, I'm going to be in the slammer.'"

After a beat, Ana let out a big sigh and accepted the congratulations. But she was far from safe.

Across town, about a year earlier, the NSA had briefed about twenty FBI special agents and supervisors on promising leads in espionage cases they had developed from SIGINT interceptions and other sources. The NSA analysts were parceling out tips, many of which they had picked up from high-frequency shortwave radio broadcasts between Havana and Cuba's illegal officers operating in the US. The NSA had decrypted all kinds of secret messages using the disks that the Wasp Network had so carelessly left around in Miami—disks that the FBI had scooped up and provided to the NSA's code-breaking geniuses. Now the NSA was returning the favor, encouraging the FBI investigators with their arrest powers and ability to pursue criminal charges against US citizens to dig deep and start making cases.

Elena Valdez, who had escaped Cuba with her family when she was just a child and grew up in Miami, was one of the NSA's briefers at the big meeting. Now a trained counterintelligence analyst for the NSA and expert on Cuba and Latin America, she and her boss handed the FBI several detailed clues about an unidentified subject, or UNSUB, who appeared to be a senior US official on Havana's payroll. She couldn't provide a name or even a government agency, but she offered up several highly specific factoids to chase. "I briefed them [FBI]. I briefed a whole room of people. And I thought, 'Wow, this is going to get this going,'" Elena said in 2022, in the first interview that the now-retired NSA official has ever given. "There were certain points that my team and I had arrived at that gave us clues which we felt…were very detailed and we felt very strongly that this person could be identified."

Elena said it was clear "there were several penetrations" by Cuban intelligence. "We came to them [FBI] and said there's a problem. There was a big problem."

As she left the meeting, Elena felt a sense of relief. The FBI, the nation's premier law-enforcement agency, was now in possession of some truly meaty leads about a Cuban spy, or spies, who had infiltrated the upper echelons of the US government. We've done our part, Elena told herself, and the FBI will take it from there. "We assumed they were checking."

Chapter 24.

LA OTRA

"Those close to her view her as egocentric, manipulative, aggressive, dominant, arrogant, lacking in empathy, hardheaded, skeptical, competitive, cynical, and dishonest."

—CIA PROFILE OF ANA MONTES

From Ana's earliest days at DIA, her bosses had lauded her. "She was my most prolific analyst," Marty Scheina says. "The closer people were to working with her, organizationally, the higher regard they had for her." But that high regard didn't always trickle down. While Ana's coworkers respected her diligence and subject-matter authority, many bristled at her aloof and arrogant ways.

Inside the DIAC and at intelligence shops throughout Washington, Ana earned a telling nickname. Behind her back. Unbeknownst to her, she was given the nickname, "La Otra," the Defense Department's Inspector General reported. In Spanish, La Otra means "The Other." Within the insular world of US intelligence, after two decades of government service, the newly minted GG-14 was still an outsider.

Ana had always been a bit aloof. "She was an introvert without a doubt," Lucy said. But Ana's personality hardened over the years, and she began exhibiting classic loner traits at DIA. She would eat lunch at her desk, alone, practically every day and often beat a quick retreat when work meetings morphed into anything fun. Marty Scheina recalls hosting monthly luncheons for his Latin American analysts, where he would update them on DIA happenings and everyone would bring a dish to share. "Once I got through the main things and other people talked about those issues and it started to turn to social, she was out of there. She was out of the conference room, she was going back to her cubicle."

Colleagues who considered Ana a friend knew almost nothing about her. For years, Latin America analyst Steve Smith shared an open cubicle with Ana on the DIAC's sixth floor. "I would describe Ana Montes as socially reserved, and very careful about the information that she would share with people," he said.[197] Lourdes Talbot also worked a few feet away from Ana, starting in 1994, coming to DIA straight out of Princeton. Ana was older and became both a supervisor and mentor. "I had her on a pedestal," Talbot admits.[198] Both women shared Puerto Rican backgrounds, and Ana occasionally would tell Talbot about her mom or share warm stories about Lucy's young children. But in seven years of working so closely together, Talbot only saw Ana socially once, at a baby shower. "She was very protective of her personal life, and very adamant that nobody should ask about her personal life. I was definitely curious about what she did after work and you know, how she managed to balance work and her whole life, but we never interacted outside of the office," Talbot said.[199]

Ana could be "intimidating," Talbot volunteered, and "some of it was just anti-social." Ana would walk by colleagues in the hall without nodding or saying hello. "She was in her own damn world." Montes was competent and prepared, and never afraid to dress down anyone at a meeting who challenged her or didn't earn her respect. "She was pretty much a bitch," Talbot added in an interview.

Even Marty Scheina, who brought Ana to DIA and supported her over the years, found her to be impenetrable. "I would say of the employees who worked for me over the years and the ones who worked for me for a long period of time, I probably knew less about Ana than I did about others."[200] Scheina and other boosters were able to look past Ana's many idiosyncrasies. "It was not that she was trying to be rude," he said. "It's that she concentrated on her business."

In an appendix of the CIA's still-classified behavioral analysis of Montes titled, "Impaired Personality Functioning," the government psychologists who interviewed Ana postarrest offer harsh assessments. Considering their interview subject was the daughter of a Freudian psychoanalyst, the descriptions carry an added sting:

- "She demonstrates compulsive, avoidant, narcissistic, antisocial, and immature personality traits."

- "She harbors feelings of inadequacy and self-dissatisfaction, and she is uncomfortable in social interactions."

- "Montes is fearful of rejection and is thus heavily 'defended.' She is very cautious about expressing affection and uncomfortable when others attempt to become emotionally involved with her."

The CIA analysts conclude that Ana "had narcissistic and antisocial personality traits that are commonly found in spies." Unlike Aldrich Ames at the CIA and Robert Hanssen at the FBI, Ana "was not motivated by greed, frustration over poor work, low self-esteem, reckless behavior, lack of judgment, infidelity, fascination with the art of espionage, or other frailties," Defense

Department investigators found. After all, Ames was a CIA intelligence officer who pocketed up to $2.5 million from his Russian handlers over a nine-year period, while Hanssen took home more than $600,000 from his Russian friends. By contrast, Ana only accepted a few thousand dollars from the Cubans to pay off her SAIS graduate-school debt, help buy a modest car, and purchase a used Toshiba laptop. But the Defense Department Inspector General found that she did share some characteristics with her fellow traitors, including "poor interpersonal skills, a sense of intellectual superiority, and a dour demeanor."

Washington is teeming with Ana's former colleagues and other civil servants who can attest to all three character defects. Yvette Wooley started at DIA in 1983, two years before Ana, and became a "current" crisis analyst, helping to staff a command center in the Pentagon and reporting on the most recent happenings in Latin America. She recalls Ana as "very professional, highly regarded," but also territorial, imperious, and suspicious. Once when she asked a colleague how Ana was doing, he replied, "You know how Ana is, if you ask her, 'How was your weekend?' she'll say, 'Why do you want to know?'"

Ana also could be vindictive. During yet another Cuba crisis, Ana objected to an analyst's reporting and took her head off, Wooley said. "It took on enormous proportions because she began to criticize this analyst personally. Now analysts are all stuck in their environment, but we don't get personal. So Ana was unusual in that she didn't want anybody to question anything, anything, that she wrote on Cuba. And I mean, she took this analyst apart and it was totally uncalled-for."

That analyst was Kathy Weyenberg. From 1995 to 2000, she worked in the Pentagon as a current crisis analyst overseeing Latin American and Western Hemisphere events. She found Ana to be standoffish, at best. "If you had lunch with her at work, that was as much social as you were going to get out of her." Weyenberg recalls that once, when Ana was on vacation,

President Clinton's National Security Council asked the DIA to analyze which base the Cubans would likely use to try to hack into US military aircraft communications systems. Weyenberg helped to prepare the official military response, in consultation with many colleagues. "What we responded, fully coordinated, was if Cuba had done this thing, it would've occurred at either location, A, B, or C in Cuba. That's all it said."

The National Security Council was grateful, and Weyenberg assumed that it was case closed. Until Ana surfaced. "Everybody was happy until Ana came back from vacation. She sent out a blistering email to everybody in the Cuba community that I was new to Cuba, didn't know what I was talking about, didn't fully coordinate the product, and there's no way Cuba did the thing," Weyenberg said.

Ana was held in such high regard that she was allowed to rewrite the response to the NSC. Weyenberg later suspected an ulterior motive. "I couldn't be seen as being a Cuba expert. She needed to make sure people didn't come to me to respond to requests for information about Cuba. People had to go to her so she could put her Ana-the-spy spin on it," Weyenberg said. "It was absolutely to discredit me as a Cuba analyst."

Suzanne Shafford, the former DIA Cuba analyst, was one of the colleagues who used to privately refer to Ana as "La Otra," because her views about Cuba often were outside the mainstream. "She always kind of tended toward whatever the most innocuous explanation would be or, you know, the least threatening explanation of anything," Shafford said. "So she was like the other point of view." Shafford said that she and her coworkers would kiddingly say, "Those nasty Commies, what are they up to today? And [Ana] was always like the other side of the fence. Totally different."

Ana would offer up benign prognostications on how the Cuban government would react after the death of Fidel, suggesting that the island would go through radical economic reform, like Vietnam after the end of its war with the United States, and start to embrace capitalism. But what really rubbed Shafford the wrong way was Ana's calculated euphemisms. "She never wanted to refer to the Cubans as Communists. Even though it's the Communist Party in power, she always called them Socialists," Shafford said. "And to me, Socialists are like, you know, Sweden. Those are Socialists. When the Communist Party is ruling the country, let's just call them Communists. But she always stuck with calling them Socialists."

Former US ambassador to Colombia and career Foreign Service officer Kevin Whitaker also witnessed Ana's winning personality up close. As a Cuba expert at the State Department, he attended a meeting with Ana in 2000 or 2001. During the Bush Administration, Whitaker said, there was a debate over whether the US should improve relations with the Tropas Guarda Fronteras (TGF), Cuba's version of the Coast Guard or Border Patrol. The TGF could potentially keep an eye on the flow of illegal drugs to US shores, not to mention the steady stream of Cuban migrants using rafts and makeshift boats to flee the island nation. The Bush-era State Department argued to keep the relationship as is, since any rapprochement would be seen by conservatives and Miami-based Cubans as a softening of US policy toward Cuba. Ana took the other side of the argument, and was indignant when she didn't get her way.

"She was angry. It sort of took me aback because it sounded personal," Whitaker said. "The sense of it was, you know, this is the kind of pig-ignorant blinkered thinking that I expect of the morons of the State Department." Whitaker said Ana's brash comments "struck me as a little too hot" for a government meeting, and he asked a friend if Ana was always that way. His friend, also a seasoned diplomat, said that Ana "is always convinced that she's right." If you disagree with her, not only are you wrong, but you are "refusing to see the manifest reality of the truth as presented by Ana Montes."

As a new century dawned, La Otra continued to isolate herself. She had been dating less frequently, and the Cubans tried to compensate with some desperate matchmaking. "Montes eventually agreed to meet a Cuban-supplied potential companion in early 2000. After a few days, she deemed him unsuitable and realized she would not be happy with a 'mail order groom,'" the CIA wrote. Ana met her would-be lover, a Cuban intelligence officer, during a trip to a breezy Caribbean island. But he was hairy and not her type. Ana rejected him, but welcomed the effort. "She was 'very appreciative' and viewed the Cubans' gesture as 'chivalrous,' probably further solidifying her desire to help them," the CIA profilers wrote.

Chapter 25.

McCOY

"…we are indeed grateful for your devotion to duty, your personal sacrifices and your constant loyalty to the FBI."

**—LETTER FROM FBI DIRECTOR J. EDGAR HOOVER TO
BILL McCOY, 1965**

Special Agent Steve McCoy was practically FBI royalty. His father, Earl "Bill" McCoy, had been a deputy assistant director, serving under the legendary and tyrannical FBI chief, J. Edgar Hoover. Bill McCoy saw action in World War II in North Africa and Italy as an Army rifleman, and joined the Bureau just a year after VJ Day. He worked counterintelligence cases against the Soviets in New York City at the height of the Cold War, and then rose through the ranks at FBI headquarters. "He was a muckety-muck," his son, Steve, recalled, and "in the top fifteen or twenty people in the Bureau when he retired."

As a boy, Steve McCoy met J. Edgar Hoover at Bureau ceremonies but was rebellious and never imagined a career in law enforcement. McCoy was plenty bright, but found it hard to compete academically with his overachieving twin sister. Once, in his junior year in high school, he ditched school for a week with a friend and took a bus to Florida, worrying and infuriating his parents.

Despite his high school hijinks, McCoy earned admission to Duke University and developed a passion for writing. When he graduated college in 1973, there was an opening at Bureau head-quarters as a clerk in the mail room. It paid a whopping $5,200 a year, or the equivalent of about $35,000 today. "I followed my Dad's tracks, unplanned." Being a mail clerk was leagues below special agent, but the elder McCoy approved. "He had a lot of pride in the FBI and at least I wasn't going to be on the street," Steve said. "I was going to be doing something and it might as well be in the Bureau."

A year after McCoy joined the FBI, coincidentally, his father Bill retired. "People back then said, 'Bill, why are you retiring early?'" Steve recalled. He said his father would reply that Director Hoover had died and the Bureau had hired his son at the same time. "So I realized the organization was going to hell," Bill McCoy used to joke.

His mail room days behind him, McCoy worked as an analyst in the FBI FOIA office. He was tasked with reading the Bureau's raw files on the assassinations of President John F. Kennedy and the Reverend Martin Luther King Jr., and helping to decide which documents could be released to the public. McCoy put himself through law school at night and became an FBI special agent just like his father. It had taken eight long years. "When I graduated from New Agent's Training Class at Quantico in 1981, my Dad presented me with my badge, which was the same badge he had carried throughout his career," McCoy said. His first assignment was at the Cincinnati Field Office, where he worked bank robberies, kidnappings, and drug cases. "It's actually a great place for a new agent to go to because, whether you like it or not, you're going to end up working all kinds of stuff because there's just not that much manpower there."

A few years later, McCoy transferred to the FBI's Washington Field Office. As Ana was being groomed as a spy, McCoy handled counterintelligence cases involving shadowy North Korean, Polish, and Vietnamese figures. He worked on the FBI's investigation of Felix Bloch, a former high-level State Department official suspected of working for the Russians, and of Jonathan Pollard, the US Navy intelligence officer who sold classified materials to the Israelis. In 1989, McCoy got assigned to WFO's Cuban counterintelligence squad. And so it was that Steve McCoy was seated in the room when Elena Valdez and her bosses at NSA first briefed the FBI on a promising Cuban UNSUB case in 1998.[201]

"I was at a meeting with the originating agency and our headquarters personnel," McCoy said, refusing to name NSA or confirm which government agency provided the very first Cuban UNSUB leads. Despite being the "lowest-level person there," McCoy said, "the UNSUB case was assigned to me."

McCoy said that FBI headquarters set the tone for the high-profile case. Work it hard, his bosses told him, but never talk out of school. "One of the clearest recollections I have out of this meeting is 'Keep this damn information sensitive,'" McCoy said. "You're basically being told, 'Pursue this with all vigor, but don't let it get out.'" NSA was even more guarded. McCoy said that the originating agency "was insistent when I got first assigned this investigation that I keep it as close to my chest as possible."

In multiple interviews over the years, McCoy has been reluctant to discuss the initial tips that the "originating agency" and an FBI field office provided. Elena won't divulge them, either. But other sources have been more forthcoming. The leads that the NSA handed off to the FBI pertained to an unidentified US official whom the Cubans referred to in shortwave radio blasts as "Agent S."

The tips from NSA, and other US intelligence sources, included:

1. The unidentified US government official, or "Agent S," had access to highly classified US programs and could even ask CIA officers for the true name of a Cuban "walk-in," or a Cuban who had recently defected to the United States.

2. The unnamed US official was believed to have visited the US military base at Guantanamo Bay, Cuba, within a two-week date range in July 1996.

3. Agent S had purchased a specific Toshiba laptop, as directed by the Cubans, within a narrow time frame.

4. The same US official had access to a safe disk or something involving the word "Safe."

5. The Cubans had helped Agent S, the UNSUB, pay off a college loan.

6. Agent S met with someone important initialed "WD."

Despite the detailed clues, McCoy immediately felt hamstrung. "Remember, I'm a GS-12 or 13 agent at the time. I don't mean to sound defensive, but I'm assigned to this case. If I've got information working counterintelligence against a Cuban target and a primary source of the information is coming from another agency, you can be assured that I have no, I mean zero, nil flexibility or ability unilaterally just to start disseminating that information." McCoy said that the obvious place to start an investigation was with his peers at CIA and other intelligence agencies. But merely discussing the allegations required authorization. "It is commonly known that this kind of information is disseminated solely by our headquarters. It sounds like I'm passing the buck, but that's what I'm doing," he said.

McCoy slowly and methodically worked the case for at least two years, while juggling other unrelated investigations. Based on the leads and historical precedent, he and his unit strongly believed the UNSUB was a man. Americans who have committed espionage-related offenses since 1947 have predominantly been men. From 1947 to 1979, only 5 percent of all American spies caught in the US were women, according to a study by the Defense Personnel and Security Research Center.[202] That figure increased in the 1980s to 12 percent. From 1990 to 2015, just 9 percent of all American spies were women. McCoy had been led to believe that the suspect was a man. In shortwave radio communications decrypted by the NSA, the Cubans had referred to their mystery "Agent S" as a man 70 percent of the time and a woman 30 percent, the sources said.

The DOD Inspector General report leaves clues that McCoy zeroed in on the Guantanamo Bay morsel. The report features a heavily redacted section titled, "Search for Travel Records in Guantanamo," which implies that McCoy and his WFO Cuba Squad had started to hunt for a suspect at CIA. Early on, the IG report states, "judgment was that the unknown subject was most likely employed by CIA. In April 1998, when FBI [and other] officials met to discuss the unidentified subject, the participants agreed that the information on the unknown subject's travel to Guantanamo…was a key investigative lead."[203] But McCoy said that he never had a living, breathing CIA suspect in his sights. "I never got to the point where I was narrowing it down to even an agency. So, no, I never said, 'Oh, it's got to be someone within CIA."

Sources indicate that McCoy reviewed hundreds of xeroxes and paper-based Guantanamo Bay travel records looking for potential suspects who had visited Gitmo in July 1996. The Inspector General noted that flight records to the heavily guarded base had been destroyed. "This effort did not develop any leads."[204] McCoy also chased the Toshiba computer tip, asking the computer manufacturer for sales records for Satellite Pro 405CS laptops sold in the mid-Atlantic. Another dead end.

McCoy's early investigation may have been thorough, but it was plodding. While he "developed analytic matrices to identify possible leads," after two years the FBI still had not considered any suspects at the State Department or within the massive Department of Defense. "As they eliminated a possible lead, they investigated the next lead. Both the DOS and the DOD were on their list; they simply had not yet reached the point of the investigation that included those agencies," the Inspector General chided.

By 2000, back at the NSA, Elena's patience was shot. She had turned over Easter eggs to the FBI, and the Bureau had disappointed her. When she called her FBI counterparts for updates, they stiffed her. "The frustration was that they didn't do anything, they didn't understand it and come back to us, or they didn't even care," she said. "They wouldn't speak. They wouldn't speak to us and tell us what was going on. That's the territoriality of it..."

As an NSA employee, Elena said she was very familiar with spy agencies jealously clutching their cards. "The world of counterintelligence is very weird, and nobody trusts anybody." But the FBI's early silence, she felt, was counterproductive. "I don't know what was going on behind the scenes... There should have been close cooperation but there wasn't." In after-action reports on the case, the Defense Department seemed to agree. "Interagency rivalries and personal rancor persisted through a major portion of the Montes espionage case," it concluded.

For Elena, the final insult was yet to come. She called the FBI yet again for an update and spoke with her assigned point of contact, an intelligence operations specialist who worked on Cuba matters out of FBI headquarters. "I said, 'Well, have you guys moved on this?' And they said, 'The case is closed.'... 'The case is closed and that's it.'" In an interview, the former FBI operations specialist denied it. To this day, it's not clear if the FBI specialist actually thought the matter had been closed (it wasn't), told Elena that to get her off the scent and end her constant haranguing, or if Elena in some way misinterpreted the call. Regardless, Elena's belief that the FBI had ended the inquiry lit a fire.

How could such unusually detailed leads go nowhere? Elena

fumed. "We have worked for years, and it can't end like this." She told her NSA unit to keep digging, trying to find any additional SIGINT analysis that could move the would-be investigation along. "We will figure this out," she told herself, "even if I have to do this on the side."

Chapter 26.

WARMING UP THE ICE QUEEN

"To my deep regret, I realize I invested all that time just out of pure stubbornness at being initially kept out, not with any hope of what I would find on the inside."

—ANA'S FORMER BOYFRIEND ROGER CORNERETTO, 2013

In the summer of 2000, Ana met a guy and fell in love. Still processing the death of her father and reeling from the strategic disappearance of her handlers, she welcomed the newfound distraction. Roger Corneretto was cute, kind of preppy, and just thirty-four when they met—nearly nine years her junior. He also was outgoing, lighthearted, impulsive, and a bit immature—qualities that had not been associated with Ana in decades, if ever. But the new couple did have one trait in common. Roger was an expert on Cuba.

Corneretto was a civilian employee for the US Southern Command, the Department of Defense combatant command that oversees all US military activities in Latin America. SOUTHCOM is the giant military installation in Doral, Florida, that the Wasp Network recently had tried to infiltrate. Not only was Roger a senior intelligence officer at a base that the Cubans were desperate to penetrate, but he helped lead SOUTHCOM's intelligence efforts against the always-plotting Cubans.

The community of US intelligence analysts who study Cuba is small and clubbish, and it was inevitable that Ana and Roger would meet. Ana may have been introverted, but she was a legend in her field. Roger was impressed by her smarts, memory, and toughness. It didn't hurt, he said, that she wore tight skirts. The older woman vibe, he added, was "part of the attraction."

At first, Ana was standoffish, and Roger relished the challenge of breaking down the defenses of what he called DIA's "ice queen."

"As everyone has said, her personality was cold," Corneretto wrote in an email to the author in 2013.[205] "It took a long time for her to finally let me in, and when she did I realized that warmth and niceness were not going to come pouring out in a way to make up for how she was and for her inexplicable hostility to good people and ideas." Corneretto describes those first months as a "long period of persisting headlong through her layers of self-defenses to get in."

Corneretto had the kind of pedigree that would intrigue Ana. His father was the editor of scientific journals and books in New York City, and his stepmother was a longtime dance professor and president of the American Dance Guild, their obituaries reveal. Although Roger lived in Miami, the new couple stayed close by flying to each other's cities, vacationing as often as two demanding jobs allowed. "Remember that for our work we were focused outward in a very hard-charging and insular way," Corneretto said. "Once you were on the team, that was it, now let's get to work and get the bad guys..."

Roger's friends never got the attraction. "They h-a-t-e-d her. Vocally, raucously, comically, remorselessly could not stand her," he said. Roger would defend Ana by saying, "you should see her work," and suggesting that his friends be "more charitable to someone so unfortunately anti-social." But his protestations fell on deaf ears. "These are professionals, intelligence people, PhDs, Latin America specialists and diplomats and they have these bawdy nicknames for her and they are screaming and carrying on and banning her from social events in Coral Gables." In retrospect, Corneretto said he deserves credit for dating Ana at all. In a flash of juvenile anger, he joked that he should earn a "merit badge for swashbuckling the first ever ticket of admission to the fortress of solitude of the tight skirt, fishnet and heels ice queen Super Woman of D.C. spookdom." Being Ana's boyfriend, he adds, "was not easy to do."

Ana's brothers didn't care for Roger, but Lucy said she was relieved that her sister was finally in a committed relationship. "He didn't seem like a great match for her, but she liked him enough to marry him apparently. So I was happy about anybody who made her happy," Lucy said.

Despite the obvious potential Roger embodied as an intelligence target for Cuba, most investigators believe that Ana's affections were sincere. "Did the Cubans know about Roger? Yes, they knew about him," the FBI's McCoy said. "She claims that they never asked her to try to get anything from him or even report anything that might have slipped out. And she would not have done that on her own." McCoy adds that the Cubans realized "they had the golden goose" in Ana and "were not about to try to jack her up" with tasking orders for her new boyfriend.

Hector Pesquera is not so sure. The former special agent in charge of the FBI's Miami Field Office helped to oversee the Wasp case and is a veteran of Cuba's spy wars. He also happened to be Lucy Montes's top boss for years. Pesquera believes the Cubans always had Roger in their sights. "I'm a hundred percent sure he was targeted by Ana." Pesquera said it's possible that Ana legitimately fell for Roger, but that the original assignment was to report back to Havana with what she learned from him. "The Cuban intelligence services, they say, 'Okay, here's this guy, see what you can do with him.' That's basic, that's 101. You don't think that they know everyone that works in SOUTHCOM?"

All Ana's family knows is that her feelings for Roger seemed genuine. Ana confided to her first cousin and loyal supporter, Miriam, that she hoped to marry Roger one day. Ana made a point of telling Miriam that Roger's father's family was from Italy. "So in a way he was Latin. That was important for her. She prefers Latin men to American men," said Miriam, who lives in Puerto Rico. Joan, Ana's then sister-in-law, said that she and her husband, Tito, got to know Roger well. "We went out, I mean, we spent time with them quite a bit because she fell in love with him." Lucy agrees. She met Roger at least three times and said Ana was "very enthused" with him. "I think he was in love with her and wanted to marry her. And she was contemplating marriage to Roger." In a 2022 interview, Roger denied ever wanting to marry Ana or ever discussing marriage with her.

Life was looking up. Roger had swept Ana off her feet and now DIA wanted to congratulate her again. In August 2000, her supervisors handed her a $2,000 performance bonus—just one of the ten awards or special recognitions she received during her much-celebrated career.[206]

Chapter 27.

GRIP AND GRIN

"We need your logic, expertise and ingenuity to protect the Nation from subversive activities like sabotage and espionage. Think this could be you?"

—RECRUITMENT BROCHURE FOR DIA'S COUNTERINTELLIGENCE SPECIALITIES[207]

Elena Valdez was at her office in the NSA's massive Fort Meade, Maryland, complex when a small team from DIA came for a road show. They were giving a presentation to their NSA counterparts on an unrelated Cuban matter. Elena had no idea that DIA even had a Cuban counterintelligence squad, and her mind started racing. It was August or September 2000, and she and her team of Latin American counterintelligence analysts had been waiting years for the FBI to act on the UNSUB case. And now the case was closed? Maybe it's time to expand the circle, Elena thought, and give other agencies a crack. "I was convinced this was an identifiable person and I felt like not enough effort was being put forth."

So she buttonholed the DIA briefers and nonchalantly asked about their counterintelligence resources. "At that point I was exploring, I was investigating." They were happy to talk. "And so they invited me to go and take a little tour."

A week later, Elena was standing inside DIA headquarters, the DIAC, at Bolling Air Force Base. She had been assigned to meet with Chris Simmons, an affable Army paratrooper who had just returned from his second tour of duty in Bosnia. Simmons, whom his former boss described as "more paranoid than the average analyst," had spent the last five years as a DIA counterintelligence analyst specializing in Cuba. Like Elena, Simmons was a student of Cuba's crafty DGI, and a world-weary observer of the brutish Castro regime.

After some pleasantries, Elena requested a secure meeting room. "I said, 'I need to talk to you about something. And I'm going to ask you some questions…and I can't really tell you any detail. But I need your answers.'" Simmons perked up. He had been expecting a boring meet and greet. He led Elena and her NSA colleagues, about five in all, to a secure conference room or Sensitive Compartmented Information Facility (SCIF.) It was a SCIF within a SCIF, since most of the DIAC is shielded to prevent outside surveillance. "We had no sooner sat down than this lady [says], 'We're not here for a grip and grin,'" Simmons recalled.

Elena got right to the point. She confided that the NSA had handed the FBI evidence on a Cuban UNSUB espionage case more than two years ago, and the inquiry apparently had stalled. "The language was pretty colorful," Simmons said. "It was essentially there's no way in hell a good special agent couldn't have found this UNSUB by now. Not her exact words, but it was colorful."

Then Elena dropped some top-secret documents on the table in front of Chris. "I brought a sample and he looked at it and I thought his eyes were going to pop out. There are nebulous kinds of things, but it meant a lot to him," she said.

Multiple sources have revealed that two of the key NSA tips included decrypted shortwave radio transmissions between Cubans providing a date range, between July 4 and July 18, 1996, when the UNSUB had visited the Guantanamo Bay US military base in Cuba. In addition, there was the cryptic tip indicating that the UNSUB had used a "safe" or a "safe" diskette.

Simmons immediately felt he could do some good. "I'm not the smartest guy in the world, but if you're on a military facility [Guantanamo], chances are you're associated with the defense sector." The word "safe" also held special meaning for DIA analysts. Secure Analyst File Environment, or SAFE, was the proprietary name for DIA's classified messaging system, the central database for analyst reports and investigative leads created by officials at the DIA, CIA, and many other US intelligence agencies. "And that's when I was like, 'Holy shit,'" Simmons said. "You've been looking in the wrong place. That person has got to be in this building," he told Elena and her team.

The Defense Department Inspector General's 2005 report on the Montes case inadvertently helps to verify some of the reporting regarding the NSA's initial clues. While heavily redacted, there are paragraphs in the normally boring "Administrative Comments" section at the end that were inexplicably never blacked out. They hint at the information that the NSA parceled out to investigators, and that the FBI had stumbled over. "Delete part of the sentence…and replace with 'the FBI personnel had no reason to equate the case term "safe" with the DIA SAFE message system,'" it states on page 148. It adds: The FBI "had no logical basis for connecting the vague case term ["safe"] to the DIA classified message system."

Simmons had heard enough. He ran down the hall to tell his boss, Lieutenant Colonel Jim Stuteville, a branch chief overseeing DIA counterintelligence analysts. Moments later, Simmons, Elena, and one or two other NSA team members were jammed in Stuteville's secure office. Elena laid out the evidence again. "What the lady showed me indicated we had some kind of a problem in DIA, let's put it that way," said Stuteville, who retired as a full colonel in 2011 after a thirty-year career as an

Army officer. "We didn't know who it was or [had] any idea yet, but we knew that somebody was in DIA that was not working for our side."

Stuteville asked Elena if she had briefed the FBI, and she explained that the Bureau had failed to understand the significance of the leads. That's when Stuteville realized that Elena and her unit had come to DIA out of desperation—and behind the back of the FBI. "We knew that she was doing this without permission. And we knew that she was so frustrated with the Bureau because she told us that," he said. "She thought the Bureau was just a bunch of dweebs. She was not impressed." Simmons was more blunt. He says Elena's NSA squad was furious. "They were pissed off because the UNSUB search...had been going on for three years."

Elena acknowledges that she never requested NSA or FBI permission to speak to Simmons and his DIA peers. But she had already briefed other investigative agencies and had only neglected DIA out of ignorance. Now, she thought, it was time to goose the case along. "I said, somebody has to know who this is." She had to share the leads, she said, but not broadly enough that the UNSUB found out. "I was extremely careful. It's a fine line, to provide information and at the same time protect it."

Chapter 28.

SCOTT AND GATOR

"Gator and I were a team: a Yankee from Wisconsin and a Rebel from
Louisiana."

—SCOTT CARMICHAEL'S MEMOIR, TRUE BELIEVER

As an analyst, Chris Simmons had no power to investigate an
espionage case on his own. So he called Scott Carmichael, the
counterintelligence investigator inside DIA's Security Investigations and Polygraph Branch based in Clarendon, Virginia. He
thought Carmichael would be the logical guy to work over the
newly found clues.

Carmichael could pull off his aw-shucks, farm-boy routine
with ease. He grew up in Fort Atkinson, Wisconsin, home to the
National Dairy Shrine, and had been a small-town cop in Edg-
erton, Wisconsin, population 5,945. He never lost his pinched,
midwestern Dan Akroyd accent, and lately has been traveling
the country in an RV for months at a time. But Carmichael is
no rube, having studied Mandarin at the Defense Language Institute in Monterrey, helping to monitor Chinese communications during the Vietnam War from Navy submarines, and later
working as an agent for the Naval Investigative Service. Car-

michael's partner was Karl "Gator" James, also a former cop. James was a retired special agent of the Air Force's Office of Special Investigations who grew up in Louisiana with a pet alligator and a father who was a game warden. Consequently, to this day, everyone calls him Gator.

Carmichael and James are well-trained in the rules governing disclosure of classified information. But multiple sources have established that they quickly got their own briefing from Elena and NSA's analysis unit and began searching DIA's massive databases. DIA employees surrender a lot of personal information as a condition of employment, so the partners had access to financial records, medical data, and travel histories for all DIA personnel worldwide, just a few clicks away. They had one hot NSA lead, the sources said, and were excited to get started. "Scott and I came back to the office, and we were joking. And I told him, I said, 'I bet I can identify the person first' because the clues were very clear to us," Gator said. They wagered a Coke over who could find the spy first.

In a race with his office mate for a sugary drink, Carmichael focused on the Guantanamo Bay lead. He knew from the NSA leads that the unidentified subject, Agent S, had visited the Cuban naval base in July 1996, so he queried the DIA's mainframes for all military visits to Gitmo in a two-month range. The system spit back about one hundred files. Across the cubicles in their open-layout office, Gator heard a shout. "We'd only been back in the office for less than an hour. From the other side of the room, I heard a real loud, "Oh shit!" And I knew instantly that I had lost the bet."

After opening about twenty digital files, Carmichael saw Ana's name. He had worked all kinds of security cases since their confrontation four years earlier and had nearly forgotten about her. But now "Ana Belén Montes" was flashing on his computer monitor. "I saw her name and I went, 'Damn!' Actually what I said was, 'Oh Shit.' Because I realized, I didn't know what it was, but I knew, I knew, I really knew it's her." Carmichael called Gator over. "He knew right then and there it's her. And then we started comparing the clues and the notes and the previous investigation," Gator said. Over the weeks to come, they would match other NSA clues with their databases and kept running smack into Montes.

Carmichael thought he had likely identified a major Cuban spy working inside his own agency. He wanted to warn the FBI right away, but first had some cleanup to do. He was worried that Chris Simmons and his colleagues might have innocently started sharing the news about an open investigation of a possible Cuban infiltrator. Sure enough, about eight analysts and supervisors already knew. Carmichael, who admits he can be "bullheaded" and has a "freaking volcanic" temper that's hard to trigger, forcefully shut down the leaks. He got his boss to send a cease-and-desist order to everyone who had heard about the FBI's open spy case and had a heart-to-heart with Simmons and his boss.

Colonel Jim Stuteville said that Carmichael "blew such a gasket" and that everyone who knew about the UNSUB investigation had top clearances and were in a position to help. Years later, he's still aggravated. "He treated all my people and even myself kind of like we were just a bunch of minor leaguers." Stuteville explains that counterintelligence agents can wait their whole career to catch a spy. Carmichael overreacted, he said, and assumed the worst about his colleagues. "I think he saw an opportunity with this new information, and he wasn't going to let anybody get close to it." Carmichael said he acted properly. "I didn't overplay my hand. I felt it was a necessary thing to do in order to shut things down so that Ana did not hear about this."

As the year progressed and the Montes case grew, the number of insiders who became aware of the investigation expanded. Later, the Inspector General conducted a forensic analysis of more than three thousand DIA and Defense Department e-mails related to the case. "We found that at least 85 DOD employees had knowledge of the FBI Montes investigation."[208] Based on postarrest interviews with Ana, however, the Inspector General noted that DIA's efforts to ensure that Ana did not learn of the investigation were successful and "...she never heard from anyone at the DIA that there were suspicions about her being a spy."

Chapter 29.

"WE'RE GOING TO WAR"

"...the well-meaning intent of Presidential Decision Directive 24 did not inspire counterintelligence entities to cooperate or coordinate; instead interagency rivalries and personal rancor persisted through major portions of the Montes espionage case."

—DOD INSPECTOR GENERAL REPORT ON THE MONTES CASE, JUNE 2005

It was time to brief the FBI on their own open investigation.

There's a hierarchy in the Intelligence Community, and DIA investigators are nowhere near the top. While Scott Carmichael and "Gator" James had dealt extensively with FBI agents and supervisors in the past, they had never worked with this particular Cuba Squad of the Washington Field Office. They were outsiders from an obscure agency, with ill-fitting clothes and goofy nicknames. At their first meeting with the FBI, they weren't exactly heralded as spy-catching superheroes.

Carmichael reached out to FBI headquarters to break the news. They quickly set up a meeting. As he and Gator were excitedly recounting details of their awesome detective work, an FBI headquarters supervisor interrupted. "How did you find out about our case?" he asked. The integrity of the investigation was paramount, not any potential suspects. After all, DIA had been the recipients of an unauthorized leak about a major national security crisis, in the FBI's view. "They were concerned about their OPSEC more than anything else," Gator recalled. "We were outsiders…"

Carmichael had anticipated the question, and handed off a list of everyone at DIA who knew about the FBI's active search for the UNSUB. It didn't help. "As soon as I told them that much, and I handed over the list of names, the [supervisor] got up and left. So they had told me what the priority was. He didn't give a shit about the rest of what I had."

The meeting only got worse. Carmichael was clutching a fat folder of information on Ana, including her job history, background investigations, and notes from Carmichael's 1996 interview with her. He was starting to roll out his evidence against Montes when, he said, he was interrupted again. "I just barely launched into it when this other guy at the end of the table says, 'Well, I've heard enough. And I've got no reason to believe that the person I'm looking for is a female, no reason to believe this person is in the Department of Defense. So thank you very much.'" It was the lead case agent, Steve McCoy, from the Washington Field Office. Carmichael claims that McCoy knocked down his investigative theory brick by brick and then abruptly walked out of the room. "He just got up and left! And so I'm sitting here looking at the female Supervisory Special Agent." Carmichael said he awkwardly pushed his foot-high folder toward the last remaining FBI staffer in the room and left.

Out on the street, the perceived snub fueled Carmichael's demons. "Gator and I left, they escorted us out, and we got onto that sidewalk. And I remember it to this day, and I told Gator, 'That's it. We're going to war.'" Carmichael was standing outside FBI headquarters, fuming. "I can remember looking off in the direction of the DIAC and being so freaking pissed off, because I knew that as we were standing there in that corner on Pennsylvania Avenue, that bitch was in my building over there," Carmichael said. "I said, 'We're getting rid of that damn woman. And these guys don't know it yet, but they're opening a case on her.'"

McCoy retired in 2004 and emphatically denied in multiple interviews that he ever walked out of a meeting in his entire FBI career. "That's a flat out dramatic lie." He also doubts that he would have so casually dismissed a fellow investigator, especially with his superiors watching. "I did not storm out of the meeting, walk out of the meeting, crawl out of the meeting. Nothing." Gator, who was also at the meeting, said that he can't recall all these years later if McCoy walked out. But he does confirm that the FBI completely dismissed their early evidence of Ana's involvement.

The dispute reflects the sore feelings that remain to this day between the FBI and DIA over the early stages of the case.[209] Carmichael researched and wrote parts of his memoir, *True Believer*, while the Montes case was active and he was still employed at DIA, infuriating the FBI. Even though Carmichael had permission from DIA to write a book, the FBI's lead case agents were shocked at the breach of law-enforcement custom. And they worried that Scott's writing project might jeopardize the investigation. Ana learned about the book during her debriefings, McCoy said, and was so angry that the FBI thought she might stop cooperating. Mostly, though, the FBI agents thought Carmichael embellished DIA's role in the investigation. "His book was so self-aggrandizing," McCoy said, adding that it was "unreadable" with "a lot of falsehoods."

True Believer had to pass DIA and FBI prepublication review, and Carmichael clearly wrote some sections to try to smooth over tensions with the Bureau. In describing his initial meeting with the FBI, Carmichael writes that Agent McCoy "politely interrupted my discourse" and "made several good points that seemed to rebut my case." The FBI "were professionals, after all, who were trained to review information objectively..." the book gushes.

In reality, Carmichael was seething. He wanted the FBI to embrace his theory and open a proper criminal investigation. He retreated to his Clarendon DIA office to strengthen his case and address the deficiencies that McCoy had highlighted. He needed more evidence and additional decrypted conversations, and the NSA's Elena Valdez would be crucial to the new strategy. (Carmichael only refers to Elena as "Big Mouth" in *True Believer* and never mentions that she worked for the NSA. He downplays her crucial role in the case, referencing "Big Mouth" in only four paragraphs and omitting how he repeatedly sought her out to provide fresh clues to fuel his investigation.)

But there was a problem with Carmichael's new plan. So few people knew about the NSA leads that the FBI had already fingered Elena as the leaker. "Oh yeah, they got to her real quick, got to her real quick. They figured it out," Carmichael said. Elena was in trouble for sharing classified information out of school with a competing intelligence agency. An FBI supervisor reamed her out for passing secrets without the Bureau's knowledge or approval. "I was getting slapped around and being threatened [with] being arrested and investigated," she said. "It was scary. I said, 'God that's all I need, for doing my job they're going to arrest me and put me in jail.'"

Elena used her trump card to defend herself. "I was told there was no case," she replied to the angry FBI supervisor. "So how can I get in trouble for sharing case information when I was told there was no case?" She also claimed that she had the legal authority and clearances to brief the DIA unilaterally. "We have a charter, we have a mission that tells me who to share, what to share." The NSA's public affairs office declined to comment on Elena Valdez, now retired, or any aspect of the Montes case.

Chris Simmons marveled at Elena's backbone. She was a Cuban-American woman standing up to the FBI, with only her tiny NSA unit backing her. "Brave as hell. She knew they could get fired for what they did, but they did it anyway. Because she was convinced that it was right. She and her whole team were convinced it was the right thing to do."

Carmichael needed Elena's continued help, but she was petrified. Her bosses at NSA were taking the FBI's side and threatening to discipline her. "The Bureau had her scared to death," Carmichael said. With all the heat, he couldn't reveal to McCoy how he kept improving his case. "I didn't want him to know that my source was still providing information to me, because they had already threatened her," Carmichael said. "So I'm on the phone with her all the time and begging her for just one more tidbit of information, pulling it out of her like teeth."

A week after their initial dustup, Carmichael called McCoy to check in. McCoy said he had not yet read Carmichael's report but hoped to get to it soon. When nearly another week had come and gone, Carmichael made a phony excuse to visit a second FBI squad he knew at the Washington Field Office. "Once I got in the building, I called Steve. I said, 'Hey Steve I'm in the building. Can I come up?'" Carmichael said. "And when I got there, that's when I found my stack of stuff on his desk. And the top folder was folded back, but he hadn't touched the damn thing. And I even asked him. He said, 'Well, I haven't had the chance to get around to it yet.'"

Carmichael wouldn't relent. He kept calling Elena, and each new fact she divulged continued to match the UNSUB to Ana. Like an annoying little brother, Carmichael faxed McCoy memos several times a week, saying, "Take a look at this," with his latest findings. He even figured out how McCoy had missed signs that Ana had visited Guantanamo Bay in 1996. Carmichael said that McCoy obtained a list of everyone who had overnighted in July 1996 at Gitmo's main housing unit for officers and civilians. The list had about one hundred names, but not Ana's. When McCoy sought similar records for a US Navy–run hotel on the base called the Navy Lodge, those papers records had been destroyed. For McCoy, it was a dead lead. "Ana's name was not on the list, so he never would've gotten to Ana Montes. Ever," Carmichael claims. By contrast, from the comfort of his office, Carmichael was able to search DOD computerized records for all visits to Guantanamo in July 1996. He instantly produced a more comprehensive list and found, hidden within military travel vouchers, Ana's receipts at the Navy Lodge. Ana had been to Guantanamo Bay in July 1996—just like the UNSUB.

After nearly a month of feeding the FBI corroboration, with no results, Carmichael asked to speak to McCoy's squad supervisor, Diane Krzemien. He realized that going over McCoy's head was a self-destructive move in a top-down military culture like the FBI. "That was the kiss of death for me. I mean, as soon as the other FBI agents would find that Scott actually went and asked for a supervisor, that would be, professionally, it's like you can't trust Carmichael. But did I care? Fuck no! You know why? Because [Montes] was still working in my building." The reckless gambit failed. Krzemien politely raised a solid new objection with Carmichael, a new reason why the UNSUB couldn't be Ana. The FBI knew when the Cubans had communicated by shortwave radio with the UNSUB, and Havana had sent coded messages even when Montes appeared to be out of the country and not in a position to receive them. Krzemien thanked Carmichael for his time but threw her support behind McCoy, her experienced case agent.[210]

McCoy recalls that he had every right to be skeptical. Carmichael had made mistakes. "Even though the information they provided about Montes at the time seemed to match some of the things from the original source information, at that time, there were a couple of things that did not match." And he felt that Carmichael and Gator had a simplistic understanding of the FBI's rules for opening a full criminal investigation. "I think they thought that, well, 'Here, we're giving you a name, go for it.' But that's not how we operate."

Carmichael decided he had to go all in. With Elena scared

to fully cooperate, he made her an offer. "I tell her, 'Look, the Bureau isn't telling you shit. I'll tell you what. I'm going to be your best friend. Here's what I'm going to do. You give me a tidbit of information and you are going to be the first person I call. I'm going to match this up. If it matches up on Ana, you are the first person I'm going to call. I'm not going to call the FBI and tell them. I'm going to tell you.'"

And that's what he did. He kept his secure phone line to Elena open and shared his notebook in a way the FBI never had. "I would call and I would call and I would call. Then she would finally give up one more little tidbit. I'd match that up and then I'd call her back and I'd say, 'Here's what I've got.'" One day, he even visited Elena and her team of Latin American experts at NSA, and sat with them as they patiently read through their raw Spanish-language translations of high-frequency broadcasts. Carmichael kept at it for weeks until he wore Elena down. "It's like a waterfall at the end. She finally says, 'What the hell? If they're going to throw me in jail or whatever, I might as well give you everything.' And she did."

Chapter 30.

FULL FIELD

"Full investigations may be initiated to detect, obtain information about, or prevent or protect against federal crimes or threats to the national security or to collect foreign intelligence."

—FBI DOMESTIC INVESTIGATIONS AND OPERATIONS GUIDE, 2008

Carmichael was the lucky recipient of one more lead that he couldn't believe. The NSA had picked up high-frequency chatter mentioning that Agent S had met someone with the initials "WD." The DIA investigator said he raced back to the typed notes of his 1996 interview with Ana. And there it was in black and white—Ana's repeated boasts about working closely in the US Hard Target group with William Doherty, the chief of the FBI's counterintelligence section.[211] The initials, WD, were a perfect match. "It took me about two-tenths of a second to put that together."

Carmichael said he immediately nudged McCoy again. "I faxed him a copy of my 1996 written report about my interview with Ana and I highlighted in yellow William Doherty's name," Carmichael said. "And that is what turned him around." McCoy began to warm up, Carmichael said, even providing his home phone number and pager to his DIA counterpart.

In an interview in 2022, Doherty said he was unaware that Ana ever invoked his name to Carmichael to profess her innocence, or that the initials "WD" were meaningful to the case. He recalled working with Ana when she was a Cuba analyst. "We went to meetings, some meetings together, and I'll be honest with you. I had no real impression of her other than she seemed serious about her business," Doherty said. McCoy also doesn't recall that the "WD" initials had any bearing on his decision to move forward on the case. He said that the "major sticking point for me" was that the same "originating agency which Scott relied on for profile info on the UNSUB," meaning the NSA, "was also the same agency which originally said that the UNSUB was more likely than not to be a male. We had to overcome that apparent inconsistency and later did." McCoy said he moved ahead with the Montes investigation based on other evidence he had gathered and Scott had presented. "Any link between Ana and 'WD' was not necessary to do so," McCoy added.

McCoy opened a preliminary investigation of Ana Montes on October 16, 2000, and a full field investigation about six weeks later. Carmichael had been frustrated with the FBI's methodical pace, but it took McCoy less than a month to open the preliminary investigation. "Scott did not have to 'convince me' to open a PI," or preliminary investigation, McCoy said. "We open them routinely and with little predication." He added that Carmichael has invented the controversy. "Scott has been beating this dead horse about what he alleges to have been my recalcitrance to push the investigation along. It really is becoming tiresome."

Carmichael insists his version of the story is accurate. Regardless, he concedes that, once McCoy opened a full-field investigation, the Montes case was in good hands. "Right then I knew it was going to be okay. Because I had great confidence in the FBI, they're a frigging machine. And once they decide to go after something, okay, I'm on easy street at that point," Carmichael said.

The FBI knew that Montes had close family members in the Bureau. Lucy, of course, could not learn that her sister was under investigation for espionage. Joan and Tito, special agents in Atlanta, also had to remain in the dark.

Meanwhile, Ana made plans to advance her career. In September 2000, she applied to be a Research Fellow with the National Intelligence Council, a senior advisory board that conducted research for the Director of Central Intelligence (DCI), who was still George Tenet. "Drawing on the best available expertise inside and outside Government, it provides the DCI and Government policy makers with an authoritative voice on the complex international issues of today and those that lie ahead," the Defense Department explained. In November 2000, the same month that the FBI opened its full criminal investigation of Ana, the National Intelligence Council approved her application. Ana was the first DIA employee ever named to the prestigious fellowship. The fully committed Cuban spy was making plans to move offices to the CIA's headquarters in Langley, Virginia.

The FBI had its work cut out. It had to build an airtight case against a highly respected military analyst that would stand up in court and, in the meantime, stop her from burrowing deep into the CIA.

In an interview, McCoy reflected candidly on the early stages of his investigation. "Is it fair to say that it was a 'fruitless' two-year search? Well sure, in retrospect, because obviously we didn't come up with the ID of the agent." He said he's willing to look honestly in the mirror. "I don't mind if I'm portrayed in a fashion like, 'Hey, for the first two years Steve McCoy had this case and basically worked real hard on it, but nothing was accomplished." But in his defense, he added that he had a very real fear that the well-connected UNSUB would learn about the investigation. And he had to play by the rules. "Had I been the provider of the information who passed it without authorization onto DIA... I would have been investigated for it within my own organization."

Today, despite their many hard feelings with the DIA, the FBI case agents credit Scott Carmichael for his tenacity. "The Bureau got really lucky when the DIA came to us with Montes as a suspect," said Pete Lapp, who became McCoy's partner on the Montes case in January 2001. McCoy added that Carmichael gave the FBI "a huge break at the beginning." Scott "broke the case. He gave us our subject." But then McCoy added, pointedly: "From that point on, the FBI made the case."

Cooperation between the feuding agencies started slowly. Elena recalls that she invited both McCoy and Carmichael to the NSA to review the evidence. Finally, the FBI and DIA would be working as a team. "They were both sitting around the table, and I made a stack for McCoy and a stack for Scott. Scott was devouring the information. McCoy sat with his hands folded over the stack," Elena said. "I said, 'Steve, aren't you going to read this stuff?' And he's like, 'Oh I've seen this before.' He was disinterested completely, like he was being forced to be there." Meanwhile, she said Carmichael's "face turned red like a tomato" in anger. Twenty years later, Elena offers a harsh opinion of the FBI's lead agent. "He was like checked out," she said.

Carmichael remembers that same awkward meeting. He had just met Elena and her team at NSA, but couldn't acknowledge to McCoy that he had recently been at the spy agency, scooping up valuable tips from his secret source. "I had to pretend like I'd never met these people before," Carmichael said. "But I had just met with them like two weeks earlier. I don't know if it fooled Steve, probably not, but I had to play the game." In a recent interview, McCoy said he didn't work closely with the analyst and said their relationship was "never antagonistic." He suggested that any criticism she may have had of him should probably be directed to the FBI at large. "If she felt that way, it could only have been by guilt by association."

Under FBI rules, the Bureau has to satisfy all kinds of legal predicates before opening a full field investigation on a suspect. The burden is high because the potential intrusion of privacy is even higher. "A full investigation gives you access to all kinds of all the goodies and bells and whistles," McCoy said. While initially cautious, the FBI caught up quickly, assigning more than fifty people to work the high-priority full-field investigation and professionally building a solid case. Undercover operatives tailed Ana by car and on foot and filmed her making suspicious calls on pay phones—even though she had a cell phone in her purse. The Bureau even intercepted her mail and inspected Ana's trash. Gretchen Gusich, a young philosophy graduate student who was friendly with Ana and lived in the unit above her on Macomb Street, learned after the arrest that the FBI had seized the contents of her dumpster. "They would go through all of the trash from the entire building," she said. McCoy confirmed that the Bureau worked in cahoots with the trash company that regularly picked up garbage from Ana's building. After a trash run, WFO employees would be waiting back at the dump. "We had some poor bastard on our squad" who picked through the entire building's trash looking just for Ana's portion, McCoy said, to "see if there was anything interesting."

For months, FBI sleuths with the Special Surveillance Group recorded Ana's every move. The SSG, or "Gs" as they sometimes are called, are FBI civil servants trained in surveillance and deception who look like ordinary citizens. Their ability to blend in is legendary. "A young mother with a baby in a stroller, joggers, street repair crews in hard hats, an old man with a cane, telephone linemen, white-haired grandmothers with shopping bags, young lovers necking in the park—all may be Gs on the job," espionage author David Wise once described them.[212]

As recorded by the Gs, Ana's tradecraft is a walk down memory lane—in and out of Borders Books and other DC-area retailers long since out of business. "Montes left her residence and drove to the Hecht's on Wisconsin Avenue, in Chevy Chase, Maryland," the FBI reported. "She entered the store at 1:07 p.m. and exited by the rear entrance at 1:27 p.m. She then sat down on a stone wall outside the rear entrance and waited for approximately two minutes. At 1:30 p.m., the FBI observed her walk to a pay phone approximately 20 feet from where she was sitting. She placed a one minute call to a pager number using a prepaid calling card. At 1:45 p.m. she drove out of the Hecht's lot and headed north on Wisconsin Avenue toward Bethesda, Maryland. At 1:52 p.m. she parked her car in a lot and went into Modell's Sporting Goods store."[213]

By late November 2000, the list of US government officials aware of the sensitive investigation had grown. DIA brass briefed the military's Joint Counterintelligence Evaluation Office and the assistant secretary of defense, who in turn briefed Secretary of Defense William Cohen. The FBI began providing twice monthly briefings to the DIA director, Vice Admiral Thomas Wilson.[214] The circle was expanding.

Adding urgency was Ana's pending transfer to CIA. Carmichael and the FBI needed to quietly stall the National Intelligence Council assignment without alerting their suspect. While Ana had near carte-blanche access to classified intelligence at DIA, working inside the CIA would have opened all kinds of new doors.

Vice Admiral Thomas Wilson was the thirteenth director in DIA history, and ran the agency from 1999 to 2002. In an interview in 2022, he said he let Montes stay in place at DIA while the investigation was hot, to help the FBI catch her red-handed. "It wasn't my favorite thing for us to do," he conceded. "I was willing to look at the big picture and understand that they were trying to catch bigger fish." But letting Ana work at CIA was a nonstarter, said Wilson, who previously had served at CIA as Associate Director of Central Intelligence for Military Support. "I think everybody was concerned about her going... I didn't want to allow her to increase her scope of knowledge to share with the Cubans. And I think CIA certainly felt the same way."

But one of Ana's former top contacts at the National Intelligence Council claims that Ana's access to state secrets actually would have plummeted inside CIA. Fulton Armstrong was a senior CIA analyst on Cuba who in 2000 was promoted to National Intelligence Officer for Latin America, the US Intelligence Community's senior expert on the region. He helped to vet Ana to work at the National Intelligence Council, which he described as "the premier analytical body of the entire Intelligence Community" and a collection of "senior people who had very good access to the policy world, to the operational world, to the collection world." Anyone accepted as a fellow to the NIC, Armstrong said, would be seriously plugged in. "They had juice, basically Washington juice."

Nevertheless, Armstrong labels it "disinformation" to claim that Ana would have become more dangerous inside the halls of the CIA. The project she intended to work on at the NIC was an anodyne evaluation of the billions in aid that the US government was spending in Colombia, Armstrong said. "She wasn't coming to work on Cuba." Armstrong accuses the DIA of hyping the supposed uber-access Ana would have had at CIA, while downplaying the agency's own sixteen-year failure to stop her. "The speculation and conspiracy theories are that she was coming to the NIC and that it was going to be some gold mine for her as a spy for the Cubans," Armstrong said. "She had more access to things over at DIA than she would have on the NIC… she had access to shit that we analysts didn't have. And I think that's probably pretty sloppy of DIA…"

While it's plausible that the Colombia project Ana hoped to work on would not have been a treasure trove for the Cubans, there's no doubt that the prestige of working at the NIC and possibly getting face time with the CIA director and his senior staff would have elevated Ana's status. And made her a better spy. It seems disingenuous for Armstrong to claim that the NIC fellowship amounted to a "practically routine rotation." Admiral Wilson concurs, saying that he, the FBI, and CIA agreed Ana had to be stopped. "We just did not want to put her in a more advantageous spot to spy."

To stop the fellowship in its track, Wilson and his team concocted a simple ruse. At the next big staff meeting that Director Wilson chaired, a staffer casually mentioned that a large number of DIA employees were on loan to outside agencies. It was a true statement and a common practice at DIA at the time. On cue, Wilson exploded. "I just kind of had a fake tantrum and said, 'I'm tired of this! Our people are always walking out to do temporary duty at some other agency and other agencies aren't responding. I want to put a freeze on all that effective immediately.'"

The theatrics worked. Ana never knew that DIA's new agency-wide moratorium was designed just for her. "We did it primarily to prevent her from going and not be able to ferret out that it was aimed at her, but it was a general freeze," Wilson said. Dozens of supervisors at other Washington agencies called their DIA counterparts to complain, but Director Wilson held tough. Ana never worked inside the CIA, and a mandatory polygraph examination that Ana had planned to take to gain admittance to the NIC was put on ice.

Chapter 31.

CONFIDING IN ROBERT HANSSEN

"Hanssen was the most damaging spy in FBI history, and he betrayed some of this nation's most important counterintelligence and military secrets, including the identities of dozens of human assets, at least three of whom were executed."

—FROM THE JUSTICE DEPARTMENT INSPECTOR GENERAL'S REPORT ON ROBERT HANSSEN, 2003

Shortly after opening its investigation of Ana, the FBI made an embarrassing blunder that could have torpedoed everything. It provided a classified briefing on the Montes espionage case to the biggest traitor in FBI history, Robert Hanssen.

Before November 2000, the FBI had no idea that Hanssen was a turncoat using Russia as his cash machine. They just thought of Bob as the "The Mortician" or "Dr. Doom," the dour oddball who was FBI liaison to the State Department's Office of Foreign Missions.[215] Known as OFM, the Office of Foreign Missions served as Washington's watchdog over foreign embassies. For a Russia expert who had been an FBI agent for nearly a quarter century, OFM was a backwater. Hanssen monitored travel by foreign diplomats and oversaw plans by foreign nations to build new embassies. A glorified paper pusher.[216]

Hanssen ended up in the State Department boonies after the FBI "involuntarily removed" him from a much more important role as Chief of the National Security Threat List Unit at FBI headquarters. He got caught breaking into the FBI's computer system and accessing highly sensitive Soviet counterintelligence documents located on the hard drives of his supervisors—a security breach that he later claimed was a white-hat hack to reveal an obvious security vulnerability. In the same post, Hanssen also came under investigation for a "physical altercation" with a female FBI support employee. The FBI censured Hanssen, then a Unit Chief, and gave him a five-day suspension.[217] "Hanssen's FBI superiors saw the OFM liaison position as a good 'out of the mainstream' job for Hanssen, a supervisory agent who had proven incapable of supervising others," the Justice Department's Inspector General reported.

Hanssen was indeed out of the mainstream. But in his State Department office in room 2510-C, complete with a crucifix and picture of the Blessed Mother on the wall, the already disgraced FBI manager kept his hand in sensitive matters. Despite his abysmal record as a steward of classified information, Hanssen remained on an interagency counterintelligence group while at OFM. The FBI routinely briefed him on delicate matters involving foreign diplomats and other cases that might ruffle international feathers.

Just as the Montes investigation was building steam, the Chief of the Cuba Unit at FBI headquarters did just that. FBI Unit Chief Terry Holstad said he provided Hanssen with a detailed briefing of the Montes investigation via secure telephone. "I had shared with him extremely delicate information about this case," Holstad admitted in 2022, in the first interview he's ever granted. "These were oral briefings. I don't recall putting anything on paper to send to him, because I didn't want a paper trail where somebody at State Department might accidentally see something."

Holstad believed that he needed to inform Hanssen about the Cuban spy case since Hanssen was the FBI's senior rep at

OFM. When the Bureau initiated an intelligence investigation that might upset a foreign government, Holstad said, the FBI frequently would seek a "No Foreign Policy Objection" from the State Department. "To the extent that it could prove potentially an embarrassment to the US government, or it could affect diplomatic relations overseas with that country, we are required to go to the State Department." Hanssen "certainly would've been aware of some of the sensitivities" of the Montes case after the FBI asked him to obtain the No Foreign Policy Objection, Holstad said.

Holstad can't recall if he provided Ana's name to Hanssen or just described the UNSUB in detail. Either way, the inadvertent admission to an FBI colleague who, just weeks later, would be unearthed as a craven Russian agent sparked fear in Holstad.

By 2000, Hanssen was nudging the SVR, Russia's external intelligence service, to deposit his illicit earnings into a Swiss bank account. He chided them for failing to respond to his latest signal at a Virginia dead drop location. "Giving up on me is a mistake. I have proven inveterately loyal and willing to take grave risks which even could cause my death, only remaining quiet in times of extreme uncertainty."[218] The FBI, meanwhile, had stopped supervising Hanssen at State. "The job carried no significant operational or managerial responsibilities, and once Hanssen was at OFM, FBI management largely forgot about him. No one checked on him or his work—or even ensured that he was at work," the Justice Department Inspector General reported. Left to his own devices, Hanssen was dangerous. He convinced the Bureau to provide him with a desktop computer at OFM connected to the FBI's ACS computer system, giving him ready access to thousands of internal FBI classified documents.

As he trolled the database for secrets worth selling, Hanssen was unaware that a former Russian intelligence agent had just sold the FBI a KGB file on an unidentified American mole. The FBI had paid $7 million for the file, and it contained a dynamite tape recording of a conversation between the unknown mole (posing as "Ramon Garcia") and a KGB officer in July 1986. The FBI played the recording multiple times and, in November 2000, heard a familiar voice. "We went back and listened to the tape again and this time I realized it was Hanssen. I said, 'My god, that's him,'" Michael Waguespack, a senior FBI counterspy, told author David Wise.[219] Other letters in the purloined KGB file tracked back to Hanssen, along with a black plastic trash bag used to protect the classified documents Hanssen frequently left for the Russians in Virginia parks. The FBI forensic lab found two latent fingerprints on the trash bag that clearly belonged to Hanssen.

The FBI placed Hanssen under surveillance and got approval from the Foreign Intelligence Surveillance Court to search his home, office, computers, and car. Even though he feared he was being watched, telling the Russians "I believe I have detected repeated bursting radio signal emanations from my vehicle," he didn't flee. On February 18, 2001, Hanssen drove to Foxstone Park in Vienna, Virginia, and quietly slipped a plastic bag under a wooden footbridge. The trash bag contained seven classified documents, but nothing involving Montes. As he emerged from the woods, FBI agents with MP-5 automatic weapons swarmed him. "You're under arrest! Put your hands in the air," they shouted.

Two days later at a press conference, FBI director Louis Freeh put a punctuation mark on the humiliating saga of the FBI supervisory agent who had spied for nearly twenty-two years for a sworn enemy. "The criminal conduct alleged represents the most traitorous actions imaginable against a country governed by the rule of law," Freeh said. "I stand here today both saddened and outraged."

When the FBI's Terry Holstad learned about Hanssen's shocking treachery, his emotions turned to dread. Holstad had briefed Dr. Doom on the Cuban UNSUB case just weeks before his takedown in the woods. "That was a concern I had because I knew I had briefed him. I told my boss, I said, 'If he's passed any of this to the Soviets, we could be dead in the water because they would pass it to the Cubans.'"

Holstad said that, even if he had not used Ana's name in his briefing with Hanssen, the Cubans would quickly realize their top spy was in danger. Once the Russians "had passed it to the Cubans—which are an excellent intelligence service—they probably could've figured out [Ana's identity] and they would've broken off contact for a period of time. And that would've stymied the investigation. So that was my concern with him." Holstad said the months after Hanssen's arrest were excruciating because Ana still was walking free. "Once it surfaced that he had spied… I wanted to get things moving a little bit faster."

Upon retirement and after Ana's arrest, Holstad got the opportunity to ask his former colleague, face-to-face, if he had revealed the FBI's Cuba investigation to his Russian handlers. As a contractor assigned to the CIA's Robert Hanssen damage assessment team, Holstad grilled Hanssen in jail in Virginia and at the Supermax federal prison in Colorado. Hanssen flatly denied it. "He was only interested in giving them for the most part Russian intel. He claims he never passed anything Cuban," Holstad said. But Hanssen frequently lied, Holstad stated, and today he wonders if the Russians knew about the UNSUB case before Ana's arrest made the news. "I don't believe him… He never admitted to passing anything" about Montes or other Cuban matters. If that's the case, it's unclear if the Russians ran out of time or decided it was too risky to tip off their Cuban friends. For the time being, Ana was in the clear.

Chapter 32.

SNUCK IN LIKE NINJAS

"FISA, as amended, establishes procedures for the authorization of electronic surveillance, use of pen registers and trap and trace devices, physical searches, and business records for the purpose of gathering foreign intelligence."

—THE FOREIGN INTELLIGENCE SURVEILLANCE ACT OF 1978 (FISA)

As 2000 came to a close, Lucy invited Ana to join her in Florida for Christmas. She hoped that Ana's relationship with Roger had mellowed her. It was not to be. Ana was "uncomfortable" the whole time, Lucy said, and "was really starting to get on my nerves." On Christmas morning, moments after the kids had ripped open their presents, Ana's cleaning compulsion kicked in. "It was five minutes later and she was picking up all the wrapping paper to throw it away. And I said, 'Ana, it's Christmas. You know, kids open their presents. They play, you leave the wrapping paper out and clean it up tonight or whatever,'" Lucy said. "You know, she never seemed to be able to just relax and be part of the family."

Roger was in Miami and wanted to see Ana, but she wanted to stay with her niece and nephew. They argued, Lucy said, and Roger "got all hurt."

"She always seemed tense," Lucy said.

After New Year's, however, the budding relationship took off. A few weeks after George W. Bush was inaugurated as president, Roger flew to Washington to be with Ana.[220] They spent holidays and vacations together and headed to Cape Cod for a special weekend. "She was enthused with the guy and was serious enough to introduce him to us, her family," Lucy said.

More recently, Roger has gone to pains to minimize his feelings for Ana. "Despite the time elapsed, our relationship did not amount to much. We lived in different cities and saw each other once a month at best and I was focused entirely on work as she was obviously," he wrote to the author in 2013.

Ana never saw it that way. She fantasized about starting a family and ditching her espionage career. She couldn't exactly fire up her shortwave radio with a man around. But the closer she got to Roger, the more the Cubans pushed back. They were not about to let Castro's top producer just walk away. "Montes considered ending her espionage because she wanted a life with Roger," the CIA reported. "She naively believed that they would thank her for her assistance and allow her to stop spying for them." Ana was devastated and had a hard time grasping that her friends could be so transactional. "I'm a human being with needs that I couldn't deny. I thought the Cubans would understand," she said.

The showdown had a predictable outcome. Ana raced to her psychiatrist with "a resurgence of anxiety, panic attacks, and insomnia." She continued bimonthly sessions with Dr. Tarantolo and privately began to realize that she "did not feel having a significant relationship and engaging in espionage were compatible," she later told the government behavioralists. The CIA's psychology team diagnosed Ana with "obsessive-compulsive traits" that she used to mitigate anxiety. Quoting her brother, Tito, the CIA said Ana became "very compulsive about cleanliness" and would "remain in the shower for hours, repeatedly cleaning herself with different soaps." Ana adopted "draconian" diets and started eating "Spartan sorts of meals, such as boiled potatoes with no condiments or seasoning." She regularly wore gloves when driving her car, Joan said, supposedly to protect her hands from the sun.

Behind the granite and concrete walls at WFO, Ana's problems were deepening. In the nearly four months since the FBI opened its preliminary investigation, the evidence it had collected was sparse. No one had witnessed Ana meeting a Cuban agent, typing coded messages, or visiting a dead drop. Admiral Wilson was growing impatient, and the investigators were starting to wonder if their suspect had gone dormant. McCoy and his new partner, Pete Lapp, a former police officer from Pennsylvania who had been an FBI special agent for three years, needed a boost. They prepared an application with the Foreign Intelligence Surveillance Court, Washington's shadowy wiretap panel, to place Ana under intense scrutiny. The FBI's lawyers carefully reviewed the application before sending it to DOJ's Office of Intelligence Policy and Review, where another set of lawyers put McCoy through the paces. "We had a lengthy, skeptical audience at DOJ," he said. Investigators close to the Blue Wren investigation admit it was a highly circumstantial case, focusing on Ana's travel to Gitmo at the same time as Agent S, her unparalleled access to classified information, and Ana's presence in the DC area when high-frequency broadcasts were being sent to the UNSUB agent.

In 2000, the Justice Department submitted 1,005 applications to the Foreign Intelligence Surveillance Court for electronic surveillance and physical searches and got approval for them all.[221] In 2001, the Justice Department submitted 932 applications; again all 932 were approved. Despite DOJ's perfect track record with Foreign Intelligence Surveillance Act requests, or FISAs, McCoy said he sweated the Montes application. "The FISA was not a slam dunk," he said. "It's supposed to be hard to do because it's so intrusive."

Intrusive it was. On February 16, 2001, the Foreign Intelligence Surveillance Court granted the FBI permission to monitor Ana's every keystroke and wiretap practically every conversation. The Bureau could now legally read her emails, listen to her phone calls, and surreptitiously search her apartment, office, car, and Riggs Bank safe-deposit box. The decision, which was subject to review every ninety days, also gave the FBI the power to install hidden cameras and microphones in her office and home—which they did. "I seem to recall some discussion we had not only about the microphone, but about a video surveillance camera, which we did have in the apartment. Because [there] was concern about, 'Can we put it in the bedroom?'" McCoy recalled. "And the reason people wanted to put it in the bedroom was we thought that might be where her radio is," alluding to the shortwave radio the FBI believed that Ana used to listen to Cuban high-frequency broadcasts. "I think with the FISA authority, we would have been able to probably put the video and microphone anywhere we wanted."

In April, FBI agent Lapp used a National Security Letter, a form of administrative subpoena, to dig deep into Ana's credit records. Although Lapp wouldn't discuss classified details of the case, one of the decrypted messages had mentioned that "Agent S" had bought a specific Toshiba laptop. Lapp used the National Security Letter to pull old paper sales records from DC-area computer stores. One of his most gratifying moments in the case came when he learned that Ana had applied for a line of credit in 1996 at a CompUSA store in Alexandria, Virginia. Her purchase? The same model of Toshiba laptop that the NSA had told the FBI about years earlier. A solid match. "A hunch is a theory. I wanted proof, and a sales slip is proof," Lapp said. "It was awesome," he adds. "This was regular old detective work." McCoy was at Lapp's side when they found the sales slip in a storage trailer behind the CompUSA. "We took the original and Pete and I drove back to the office. We were almost screaming out the windows, and we were pretty excited about it," McCoy said. Finally, there was some positive news to share with the FISA judge and to quiet the critics.

Weeks later, McCoy and Lapp got ready for their first sneak-and-peek of Ana's Cleveland Park home. There was so much riding on it, and the odd-couple partners were nervous. "An apartment building? Everybody there is a potential 911 call," McCoy said. They researched the layout of the building and all the exits. Before the search, McCoy even posed as an interested apartment buyer to do some recon and get a closer look. To his surprise, he ran into Ana at an open house and briefly chatted with her. "The apartments are small, the building is small, everybody knows everybody else there," McCoy said. "Although [Ana] was not a social animal, when she was out of town, people knew it. If they hear noise in her apartment or they see lights, it's going to be like Watergate, a minor version," where the police are notified of an apparent burglary.

McCoy would be on the street during the operation, listening over police radio to DC's Metropolitan Police and ready to create a distraction if the cops spotted the break-in team. Lapp would be on the inside. "There's no bigger stress that I've had professionally than being in someone's apartment, legally, with them not knowing it and having a chance to get caught," he said. "You're being a cat burglar, legally, but you can get caught, and the entire case is blown."

On Friday, May 25, 2001, Lapp and a small team of FBI black-bag specialists tiptoed up the stairs to the second floor of 3039 Macomb Street and slipped inside apartment 20. Ana was out of town with Roger for the Memorial Day weekend. FBI techs in gloves and protective clothing began methodically searching the closets and any potential hiding places. The break-in team leafed through shelves of Ana's neatly stacked books and quietly photographed her personal papers. In the bedroom, under Ana's window, they spotted a cardboard box. Inside was a Sony ICF-

2010 shortwave radio. That's promising, Lapp thought. Then the techs found the same Toshiba laptop that the FBI knew Ana had purchased from CompUSA in October 1996. Bingo. They copied the hard drive, shut down the computer, and were gone. Ana's nosy neighbors never suspected a thing.

Lapp and the FBI techs would repeat the performance a few more times, including at night. "They're going through an apartment at night looking for stuff, trying to leave the dust undisturbed," McCoy said. "In the dark. That is tough to do, that's drama." The searches often went on for hours. "This was a true black bag job. We snuck in," McCoy said. "There was no ruse, it's the middle of the night. Snuck in like ninjas."

Several days after the initial search, an FBI computer unit faxed the translated contents of Ana's hard drive to WFO. Lapp and McCoy couldn't believe it. There were eleven pages of incriminating documents, including direct messages to and from Ana and her Cuban spymasters.

The recovered text included directions on how to translate Cuban numbers station broadcasts and then ditch the evidence. "…destroy that file according to the steps which we discussed during the contact," the Cubans warned. Ana had ignored or failed to complete the steps needed to delete the files from her hard drive. The documents also included basic tech assistance— like a Cuban version of a Genius Bar. "I learned that you entered the code communicating that you were having problems with radio reception. The code alone covers a lot, meaning that we do not know specifically what types of difficulty you are having," Havana's geek squad wrote. "I'm going to repeat the necessary steps to take in order to retrieve a message." There were notes on communicating safely by beeper ("…this beeper is public, in other words it is known to belong to the Cuban Mission at the UN and we assume there is some control over it" by the FBI). There were tasking orders for Ana to attend a war games exercise conducted by the US Atlantic Command (ACOM) in

Norfolk, Virginia. "We think the opportunity you will have to participate in the ACOM exercise in December is very good. Practically, everything that takes place there will be of intelligence value," the home office instructed; Montes attended the classified exercise in 1996 and reported back to Havana. There were messages from Ana giving the Cubans critical details on NRO's MISTY satellite, the costly and highly sensitive Special Access Program she got briefed on in May 1997, several sources said. Perhaps most damningly, though, there were passages using the true last name of a US intelligence officer who had been operating undercover in Cuba. The hard drive records confirmed that Montes had turned over the agent's secret identity to her handlers.

Lapp and McCoy were massively relieved. After months of frustration and doubt, the eleven faxed pages would seal Ana's fate. "That was kind of our Eureka moment," Lapp said. "Finding that whole computer with that stuff on it, that brought us to probable cause," McCoy added. "We basically had a green light from that point. We knew we had enough to arrest her... What was on her computer convicted her." The FBI had solved the main mystery of the Blue Wren investigation.[222]

Chapter 33.

A MANATÍ FAREWELL

"I hope it will help you understand me better. I hope you will enjoy it, and I hope that as you read through it, you grasp its central message—that when one enjoys learning, which leads to enjoying work, the world is full of opportunities and happiness."

—LETTER FROM DR. ALBERTO MONTES TO HIS CHILDREN, 1995

On June 8, 2001, a federal jury in Miami convicted five Wasp Network conspirators on twenty-three spy-related charges. "Cuban Spies Convicted of Sweeping Espionage," the *Miami Herald* headlines screamed. "Guilty on All Charges." The news would affect the Montes sisters differently. Ana privately wept in her apartment, as hidden FBI cameras watched, and no doubt worried that her turn might be next. Meanwhile, Lucy won another award for her contributions to the Wasp case, a plaque from the Miami Police Department handed out to FBI investigators and federal prosecutors at the Latin Chamber of Commerce. "We feel humble, and we feel extremely proud," her boss, the FBI's Hector Pesquera, told reporters.[223]

For Ana, the stress was becoming overwhelming. Her handlers had practically disappeared since the Wasp fiasco. Ana was about ready to quit and wanted to marry Roger. It all came to a head in July, when the Montes family gathered in Puerto Rico to spread Alberto's ashes. "My former husband asked to be cremated and have his ashes deposited in the Manatí River, a large creek that runs close to his hometown," Emilia wrote. The four Montes children were together again—Ana, Lucy, Tito, and Carlos. Tito's wife, Joan, joined cousin Miriam and other Montes and Badillo relatives to bid a final farewell to Alberto. There were solemn moments and fun family dinners, but Ana's mother immediately noticed that her eldest child was more on edge than usual. "Ana shared her hotel room with me and it was pleasant to be together but I noticed her as being very tense, upset, anxious, with her phone in her hand waiting for calls from I do not know whom," Emilia wrote. "She did not tell me, but she went out of the room to the open hall to wait and talk."

Ana and Miriam had always been close. During a car ride during the trip, Ana confided to her first cousin that she had fallen in love with Roger. Their marriage was on hold, Ana claimed, because Roger's father was ill. "She said that his father was sick with cancer, and he won't marry because of that. And I said, 'Well, but what's the point? I don't get it,'" Miriam said. Ana, of course, didn't mention the real reason the marriage was impossible. "She shrugged, like, 'Well, I don't know either.'"

McCoy and Lapp continued to build their case, but wanted more. They needed the floppy disks that Ana used to decrypt high-frequency numbers broadcasts. The Wasp defendants in Miami had been foolish enough to leave their decryption programs sitting around, and the NSA had been feasting on the intelligence bounty for years. During the surreptitious entry of Ana's apartment, in May, the FBI did find sixteen diskettes—but none contained a crypto code. So Carmichael and his DIA confederates devised a stunt to get Ana out of town, to allow the FBI to search again. They concocted a reason why Ana absolutely needed to attend a last-minute conference happening at the Missiles and Space Intelligence Center in Huntsville, Alabama. When she resisted, her boss's boss, Dave Curtin, stroked

Ana's ego and made it clear he needed her expertise. (Carmichael had previously shared details of the investigation with Curtin and a few other top supervisors.) On August 7, twenty unsuspecting DIA analysts got on a plane to Huntsville. Ana begrudgingly joined them.[224]

The next night, the FBI broke into Ana's apartment again. This time, they discovered an additional forty-one floppy disks. All were blank. Admiral Wilson's patience was about shot. He had allowed a traitorous spy to stay in his building, hoovering up classified information, for nearly a year. It was time for the FBI to wrap it up. "I was occasionally bugging them about getting her arrested, and they were always wanting more time," Wilson said.

There was one last place to look. Ana's pocketbook. She was inseparable from it. It seemed completely illogical that someone as paranoid as Ana would carry the decryption programs with her, in and out of the DIAC and past the armed security guards. "We were not anticipating finding disks. That would have been a real bonanza," McCoy said. But they had to try. It fell to the DIA's Scott Carmichael to design a plan so Ana would abandon her pocketbook and purse in her office.

Dave Curtin again was in on the con. He sent Ana and a dozen other analysts an email inviting them to an urgent DIAC meeting regarding Venezuela. Left-leaning officials there had abruptly stopped allowing US Army personnel to embed inside Venezuelan military headquarters. There was a legit Cuba hook, and Curtin asked Ana to give prepared remarks on Havana's reaction to the Venezuelan–US showdown. Carmichael selected a conference room just one floor away from her cubicle. His goal was to pick a location close enough that Ana might not bring her pocketbook, with a meeting short enough that she wouldn't need her purse to buy lunch afterward.

On August 16, as the Venezuela meeting kicked off, two IT geeks huddled by Ana's cubicle to investigate an annoying new computer malfunction. One of them happened to be the FBI's own Steve McCoy. When Ana's office mates weren't looking, McCoy nonchalantly tossed Montes's pocketbook into his toolbox. "I knew where to look for her purse. I grabbed it and I walked out." Analyst Steve Smith missed all the action. Just before McCoy entered his workspace, Smith was called to the DIA parking lot. Some jerk had bumped his van and kept driving. It was another distraction. Working with a retired DC cop, Carmichael had ginned up the bogus accident to get Smith out of the way for an hour.

Inside a nearby command post, McCoy and Lapp began carefully emptying out the pocketbook. "Our only concern at that time was if we would have enough time to go through her purse and put everything back exactly how it was and copy anything that we might have interest in before she got out of this conference," McCoy said. There were no encrypted disks, and in fact the FBI never found any. But the search still proved useful. Tucked inside Ana's wallet were the prepaid calling cards Ana used when dialing on pay phones, a New York pager number (area code 917) later traced to Cuban intelligence, and a set of digits that comprised codes Ana used when dialing her handler's pager. "After contacting the pager, she keys in a code to be sent to the pager which communicates a particular pre-established message," McCoy explained.[225]

McCoy returned the pocketbook without incident, and Ana was none the wiser. Director Wilson was now ready to pull the plug. He booked time with the Office of the Secretary of Defense to discuss an exit strategy. They needed to convince the FBI to arrest Montes or let the DIA immediately fire her. The meeting was scheduled to take place on September 21.

Chapter 34.

OUT OF TIME

"As no other event in U.S. history, not even Pearl Harbor, the deadly assaults on New York and Washington that took the lives of almost 3,000 people on 11 September 2001 shattered the nation's sense of security."

—FROM THE PENTAGON'S OFFICIAL HISTORY OF THE 9/11 TERROR ATTACKS[226]

DIA director Thomas Wilson was leading a routine meeting in his Pentagon office on the morning of September 11, 2001, when he was interrupted. "An aide walked in and said, 'Admiral a plane has flown into the World Trade Center,'" Wilson recalled. He and his staff turned on a television in time to see a second plane, United Airlines Flight 175, crash into the World Trade Center's South Tower. Phones everywhere began ringing, and the threat was getting closer. "I was actually on the secure line with Admiral Jacoby, who was the J-2, and I heard the plane fly past my window, then felt the shudder as it hit the building."

American Airlines Flight 77 had left Dulles International Airport for Los Angeles at 8:25 a.m. Five Al Qaeda hijackers were onboard, including Hani Hanjour, a Saudi citizen who had trained as a commercial pilot in Arizona. A half hour into the flight, the terrorists overpowered the crew and turned the plane eastward, back to Virginia. Arlington County police motorcycle officer Richard Cox recalls driving near the Pentagon that morning when he saw the Boeing 757 "flying so close to the ground that the polished underside of its fuselage reflected the images of the buildings it passed on its flight." The ninety-ton airliner deliberately accelerated to 530 miles per hour as it slammed into the first floor of the Pentagon's west side.[227] "I said, 'Good God, they got us,'" Admiral Wilson said. "Smoke soon filled our office, very quickly making it uninhabitable." He made sure his staff was accounted for, then ordered everyone to secure classified materials and evacuate.

The 9/11 attack killed 125 civilian and military personnel inside the Pentagon, and all 64 on the hijacked plane. The DIA's Program and Budget Office on the first floor took a direct hit. Christine Morrison was working with about seventy of her colleagues in DIA's Office of the Comptroller when Flight 77's burning fuselage cut through the Pentagon and stopped at her office, #1C535. "From the back of the room there was a heat wave-like haze extending from the back of the room up to the ceiling," Morrison said. "You could see through it. It was moving. Before I could register or complete that thought, this force hit the room, instantly turning the office into an inferno hell. Everything was falling, flying, and on fire, and there was no escaping it."[228]

Morrison said she was "slam-dunked" into an office cubicle and trapped. The lights went out and "my lungs felt like they were burning and collapsing." Barefoot, Morrison managed to crawl to safety.

She was one of the fortunate ones. Seven DIA employees died inside the Pentagon that day. They were the accountants, budget managers, and office assistants who keep the agency running. Another seventeen were badly injured. It was the largest single loss of life in the history of the DIA, and shifted Admiral Wilson's priorities in a flash. "The next few weeks became the most diversely challenging period of my 34-year Navy career," Wilson wrote in an 9/11 remembrance in 2021.[229] Not only did the DIA chief have to tend to the wounded and comfort the families of the fallen, but now he was in charge of gathering intelligence to take the country to war. "The deliberate and deadly attacks which were carried out yesterday against our country were more than acts of terror," President Bush told the nation on September 12. "They were acts of war. This will require our country to unite in steadfast determination and resolve. Freedom and democracy are under attack."[230]

DIA would play an integral role in launching Operation "Enduring Freedom," helping to wipe out Al Qaeda command-and-control and batter the Taliban regime in Afghanistan. Babysitting an accused Cuban spy suddenly seemed a low priority.

The horrific attacks shook the Montes family. Joan Montes worried about her sister-in-law Ana in Washington and immediately gave her a call. Joan had been taking a class at Quantico to learn how to conduct surreptitious entries and other skills, prior to joining the FBI's tech squad in Atlanta. "I called her when I got home and I was crying and I was really upset and I remember she was crying," Joan said. "And I was like, 'We need to go after them bastards,' and stuff like that. And I was very upset. I thought she was crying too."

But Ana's mother got an entirely different reaction. On 9/11, an emotional Emilia called Ana at work and asked who was behind the terrorist acts. Ana's cynical response stunned her mother. "She said these words more or less, 'We have done some people so much wrong I can't guess which one is doing this today,'" Emilia recalled. "At that very moment she was watching the burning of the Pentagon from the DIA offices. Why would she say such a thing at that moment?"[231] Ana was blaming America's own foreign policy for triggering the deadly attacks, in a candid moment with her role model and greatest supporter. In an email after 9/11 to her close friend and college roommate, Lisa Huber, Ana again couldn't help but criticize the

US after the attacks. "I could see the Pentagon burning from my office... Dark days ahead," Ana wrote. "So much hate and self-righteousness on all sides." [232]

Marty Scheina, Ana's boss and another longtime fan of hers, also found her reaction to 9/11 off-putting. On that tragic day, he and a senior DIA analyst were in Ana's cubicle discussing the horrors of the previous hours. Would the White House or Capitol be next? "Everybody was wondering if the next plane was coming down our window," Scheina said. But Ana's main preoccupation seemed to be Cuba. "So here we are just a few hours after the planes had crashed and Ana said to [the analyst], 'Do you think they're going to go after the Cubans?' And he said, 'Oh yeah, for sure.' And she took it seriously. And I'm thinking, bullshit, they're not going to go after the Cubans on this. This is not a Cuban-directed thing. This is coming from the Middle East someplace," Scheina said. "It was meant as a joke and she didn't understand it," he said. "She didn't really seem upset about what happened on 9/11, but she really took seriously the thought that we were going to retaliate against the Cubans."

Ana's immediate concern for Cuba's safety helps to explain the flurry of calls she placed on the weekend after 9/11. On Friday, September 14, Ana left the DIAC and drove home. Still in her work clothes, she walked to the National Zoo and paused for thirty seconds in the "Prairie Land" overlook. The FBI's Special Surveillance Group was on her tail. Ana walked farther into the zoo and then doubled backward, a classic surveillance-detection technique. By the zoo's pedestrian entrance on Connecticut Avenue, she pulled a piece of paper out of her wallet and made two calls on a public pay phone to a pager number. The next day, Ana made another call to the same pager, lasting one minute. And on Sunday, September 16, she rode the Metro one stop north to the Van Ness/UDC station and called the same pager number, using a pay phone in the station. [233]

Back at work, Ana was in the 9/11 mix. DIA had made her

part of the team preparing to go to war. Just three days after the terrorist attacks, Ana's branch chief got reassigned to the Army. Ana got an instant promotion to branch chief and acting division chief and "was selected to serve as one of several analytic team leaders who would process target information from the operations staff in the Pentagon."[234] Incredibly, DIA supervisors who were ignorant of the spy accusations picked Ana to process target lists for Afghanistan. An accused traitor was about to get her hands on America's highly classified war plans.

Admiral Wilson was not about to let that happen. He recalls reading a memo shortly after the attacks "which was nominating people to go and serve on a battle damage assessment team and Ana's name was on it." The DIA director was not amused. "I told my exec, I said, 'We're not going to go to war with a spy in our organization.'" Wilson said there was a "legitimate concern" that the Cubans could share or sell America's bombing targets and classified war plans with the Taliban or the terrorists. "I'm not aware of any specific relationship between Cuba and Al Qaeda. But in that world of bad-actor intelligence services, who knows?" he said. Michelle Van Cleave, who headed up the Montes damage assessment effort, said that she wouldn't put anything past Cuba. "The damage to the United States from the loss of sensitive national security information to Cuban espionage is not bounded by the national security threat presented by Cuba alone, but also by its value to potentially more dangerous adversaries."

For Ana, the only upside was that she got to spend more time with Roger. He had come to DC and was stuck there now, with all US flights grounded. He camped out at a hotel near Ana's apartment. After the arrest, Corneretto claimed that he was about to break up with Ana when 9/11 happened. "One thing that gives me comfort is that... I had already started to date someone else," he wrote. "She didn't know it only because

I was not looking forward to what she would be like hearing the news, she was wound very tightly."

The Montes investigators wondered if, in all the chaos, the Bureau might catch Ana passing battlefield plans to the Cubans. No jury would forgive her for that. But they knew they couldn't keep waiting. Once Admiral Wilson learned that Ana would gain access to bombing targets over the upcoming weekend, he issued an ultimatum. "I called the FBI and said, 'It's time to arrest her. I don't care where your investigation is, I want her out of here.' And to their credit they said, 'Yes, sir.'" The FBI's Blue Wren investigation had run out of time.

Chapter 35.

THE IMMACULATE CONFESSION

"Interrogators steer the subject toward a confession by offering a face-saving alternative. This process is called 'minimization'—downplaying the moral consequences of the crime without mentioning the legal ones."

—FROM "CURRENT STATE OF INTERVIEW AND INTERROGATION," IN THE FBI LAW ENFORCEMENT BULLETIN, 2019

On Friday morning, September 21, Ana drove her trusty red Toyota to work and was seated punctually at her desk when the phone rang. It was Dave Curtin. By now the second-highest-ranking official in the Directorate of Intelligence, he oversaw thousands of DIA analysts who suddenly were focused on bringing the fight to Al Qaeda. Now that Ana was an acting division chief, Curtin would surely be calling more frequently. This morning, however, he was not in a chatty mood.

"Ana, I just haven't got time. You know, we're in the middle of this, getting ready for the war, and I get a call from the IG's office that says that there's a problem with one of your employees and their time cards," Curtin said. "Would you please go to the IG office and square this away? I just haven't got time."

Ana marched straight down to the fourth floor of the DIAC, to the Inspector General's corner office suite, to handle the time-card snafu. A receptionist welcomed her and ushered her toward Leroy Elfmann, DIA's Assistant Inspector General for Administration. Elfmann nonchalantly walked Ana to a conference room. And there, as he opened the door, were Steve McCoy and Pete Lapp. Alert and waiting.

It was Carmichael's final deception. There wasn't an employee time-card issue. Carmichael had asked Dave Curtin to call Ana and get her quietly down to the IG's office to avoid making a scene. In fact, Curtin was sitting now in a makeshift FBI command post just a few feet away. Carmichael had commandeered the IG's offices, and FBI agents and DIA security officials lurked behind nearly every door.

As Ana took a seat, McCoy and Lapp introduced themselves as FBI special agents assigned to the Washington Field Office's Cuba Squad. McCoy had prepared a monologue. "I spent like two days setting up a briefing book of how we're going to... obtain this miraculous confession from her," he said. He began with a bluff. "I started off with a lengthy bullshit story to the extent that the US Intelligence Community had acquired over time information from a variety of, and I emphasized a variety of, sensitive sources. And I told her that they involved HUMINT as well as technical sources... I did try to implant in her mind, to some extent, the fact that some of this information may have come from either a defector source and or a human penetration of the intelligence service."

McCoy kept talking. "I also told her that this information, per usual from these myriad of intelligence sources, was at times contradictory and whatnot, so that it was possible that there were some exculpatory explanations for why she might've had contact" with Cubans.

McCoy hid from Ana that the FBI was sitting on eleven pages of intercepted communications and had videotaped her calling suspicious pagers from public pay phones. He was hoping that she would volunteer to clear up the "contradictory" intelligence and incriminate herself in the process. "We were basically offering her the opportunity to try to clarify." He implied that his tips had come in part from human sources. In case Ana later alerted her handlers, he wanted the Cubans looking over their shoulders. "I mean, as far as we were concerned, if they had done a purge of their entire intelligence service it would have been the best thing for us."

Ana didn't speak. She was staring straight ahead with a blank expression. She was pale, and a rash broke out on her neck. Finally, McCoy dangled Ana's many family members working for the FBI. "At some point during that whole bullshit dialogue, I also said that obviously we were aware of the fact that she had siblings that were employed with the FBI, that she was dating somebody that had clearances with the US Intelligence Community and in the military, and we want to make sure and confirm that they had no involvement in it."

McCoy insists that he never implied that Lucy, Tito, or Roger were mixed up with Cuban intelligence. "It certainly was not more aggressive like suggesting that they are involved. No, absolutely not. Even though we're allowed to lie outrageously, no, there's no way I would have said that. It would have been counterproductive," McCoy said. But his FBI partner doesn't quite recall it that way. In interviews, Lapp said that their plan all along was to use Lucy and Tito as bait. Paraphrasing what McCoy told Ana that day, Lapp said, "'We have suspicions about Tito, we've got suspicions about Lucy. We've got suspicions about Roger, and we're just going to fucking turn their world upside down. We're going to start talking to the neighbors…because we think they're all in on it.' And our hope was she said something just minimal like, 'Leave them alone, they were not a part of this.' Something just as small as that would be an admission."

Regardless of precisely how McCoy phrased it, Ana was unimpressed. She knew her family was not involved and saw right through the bluff. "She had no response for my whole little song and dance," McCoy said. Lapp agreed. "We had a little skit planned, if you will, and it failed miserably." McCoy's briefing book full of photos and laptop evidence sat untouched.

When Ana asked if she was under investigation, the charade quickly fell apart. "I basically said, 'I'm sorry to tell you but you're under arrest for conspiracy to commit espionage,'" McCoy said. Lapp slapped on the handcuffs. Ana barely reacted.

Positioned nearby in the IG's office was FBI Special Agent Molly Flynn, another member of McCoy's Cuba Squad. Flynn already had a stellar résumé at the Bureau. She was the first FBI investigator to connect an angry twenty-three-page essay written in 1971 by a Harvard-educated loner to the bitter anti-technology manifesto penned in 1995 by the Unabomber.[235] A lawyer who represented the brother of the essay writer had provided it to Flynn, worried that perhaps there was a connection to the deadly bombings. The Unabomber had killed three people and injured twenty-three others in a nationwide bombing campaign, and was the subject of a massive FBI manhunt when the FBI's Flynn first read the essay. "I started reading it, and all of a sudden, it was 'Bing! bing! bing!' all over the place, and so I went to the manifesto and started comparing it, paragraph by paragraph, back and forth," Flynn said.[236] Even after Flynn showed the twenty-five-year-old essay to the FBI crime lab and they determined that it had not been typed on the typewriter that produced the anonymous thirty-five-thousand-word manifesto from 1995, she would not give up. She faxed the essay to the FBI's UNABOM task force in San Francisco and encouraged agents there to take a close look. "She just didn't want to let it go," a former UNABOM supervisor recalled. "It was the most significant document I had ever seen." Flynn had solved a riddle that had perplexed the FBI for nearly two decades. The FBI UNABOM task force arrested Harvard loner Ted Kaczynski at his remote Montana cabin just two months later, in April 1996, and he subsequently pleaded guilty to all charges.

On the day of Ana's arrest, Flynn's role was more prosaic. She patted Montes down for weapons and then joined McCoy and Lapp as they escorted Ana out of DIA for the last time. "We did essentially a perp walk, but it wasn't really obviously a perp walk, if you will, right down the halls of the DIA. She was very quiet and stoic," Flynn said.

Carmichael had positioned a nurse, oxygen tanks, and a wheelchair in the wings. He recalled how Ana had nearly fainted when Dave Curtin had surprised her with a big promotion. But the Queen of Cuba didn't need any help. "We figured she would just kind of collapse, be a wreck," Lapp said. "And I think she could have just carried both of us out on her back. She walked out that calm—I won't say proud—but with that kind of composure."

Chapter 36.

YOUR SISTER IS A SPY

"A cryptanalysis examination seeks to identify and 'reverse engineer' manual codes and ciphers used by inmates, gangs, terrorists, and other criminals to protect communications and/or conceal information."

—FBI'S HANDBOOK OF FORENSIC SERVICES, 2019

On the car ride to the Washington Field Office to be photographed and fingerprinted, Ana took one last look at the scene of the crime. She glanced back deliberately at the DIA headquarters where she had worked for the past sixteen years. "I remember Ana looking out the window and looking that way," Flynn said. "I just looked at her looking and [was] thinking, 'Oh, she's kissing that life goodbye.'"

Over on Macomb Street, FBI evidence teams immediately began a comprehensive search. Their discoveries further sealed Ana's fate. In a closet, they found what appeared to be her getaway bag, a red leather tote with maps of Paris, Spain, and other locales, and four crisp $100 bills. In another part of Ana's closet, the FBI found a large leather notepad holder with several strange flaps. Inside the linings were five white slips of paper. One was the handwritten cipher that Ana used three days a week to decrypt Cuba's numbers station broadcasts by hand. Cryptology experts call the primitive cheat sheet a "straddling checkerboard" cipher that she used, after the Wasp arrests and without the aid of her Toshiba laptop, to convert the decrypted messages back into plain text. "A" = 4, "T" = 3 and so on, and agents are meant to use "one-time pads" in combination with the checkerboard cipher to decode the messages sent by the home office.

The FBI also found scribbled shortwave radio frequencies and emergency pager codes: "111" meant "I don't hear the radio;" "333" meant "I'm Okay;" "444" meant "Danger," and "777" meant "I left the country."

On one of the white pieces of paper, Ana had written the name of a small museum in Puerto Vallarta, Mexico. If she had fled the country quickly in an emergency, she would have met her Cuban rescuers at the Museo del Cuale. All of the handwritten evidence could be easily destroyed. The crib sheets would vanish if exposed to water.

Inexplicably, Ana's red leather go-bag contained an old Smith Corona typewriter cartridge. Ana hadn't used a typewriter in ages. The FBI examined the ribbon and found unencrypted messages to the Cubans that were a decade old. "There was absolutely no reason for her to keep that," Lapp said. "It was classified, the information she passed was secret. It was national defense information."

In the days after the terrorist attacks, the FBI's Miami Field Office was on high alert. Most of the hijackers had spent time in South Florida, and FBI investigators were desperate to learn whether any more had lingered behind. So when the Miami office's chief clerical officer showed up at Lucy's desk on Friday September 21 and asked her to follow her, Lucy didn't flinch. "I thought, 'Oh, this must have something to do with 9/11. Maybe they have a special assignment for me or something.'"

Lucy was ushered to the SAC's large private office. Waiting for her was the Miami Field Office's assistant special agent in charge, and Richard "Gino" Giannotti, supervisor of Miami's Cuban counterintelligence squad. Lucy had worked with Giannotti on the Wasp Cuban spy case just a few years earlier. The assistant special agent in charge started off. "I need to tell you something that's going to be difficult. It's going to be difficult for your family." Lucy was puzzled. "That's when I started to get a little nervous."

Giannotti had made his bones in the FBI by spending years infiltrating the Weather Underground, the radical militant group active in the '60s and '70s. The veteran lawman turned to face her. "Lucy, your sister has been arrested for espionage," he said. "Your sister has been arrested for spying for Cuba." What? Lucy needed to hear that again. "I asked him, 'Is it true?' That was my first reaction. You know, because they say when you're in shock, you don't believe what people tell you. I said, 'Is it true?' And he said, 'Yes.'"

Lucy didn't stand up in protest, didn't run out in stunned disbelief. Instead, she found the news oddly reassuring. "I believed it right away." She cried for a minute in front of the men but then caught herself. The revelation that her sister was a spy, a traitor working for a broken, repressive regime, actually provided answers. Yes, it was horrifying and terribly embarrassing, but at last Lucy could begin to fathom the root cause for Ana's decades of hostility, distance, and calculated silence. "I knew it had to be true because the FBI doesn't make stuff up. And I thought, 'Yeah, that kind of makes sense because she's been so odd for such a long time. That would explain a lot of things.'"

Lucy offered to take a polygraph and volunteered to her colleagues that Ana's boyfriend, Roger, worked in a classified position in the Pentagon. "Yes. We know he works there. He's being interviewed right now," Giannotti said. He told Lucy that a polygraph would not be necessary, but that the Bureau wanted to interview her. "They were more nervous than I was because I think they were worried about how I would react."

A couple of FBI agents drove Lucy home, where they pressed her for hours about Ana's travels, her DIA-approved visits to

Cuba, and her life story. Lucy informed them of Ana's relationship with leftists Ricardo and Eduardo, and Ana's inordinately
close friendship with former SAIS student Marta Velázquez.
"I told them about Marta because, at the time that Ana was
friends with Marta, I noticed something off, something odd
about them." Lucy never asked for a lawyer. "I knew immediately I would cooperate. I would help them," she said. She
gathered up photos of Ana and her friends, anything that might
aid the FBI in its investigation, and just turned them over. "I
wasn't going to try to defend my sister or hide anything that she
did. She committed espionage." Lucy also realized that her job
could be on the line if she wasn't truthful. "It wasn't a hostile
interview. I was just filling in some blanks for them. I think I
was very helpful. And by the end of the interview, I was pretty
sure I still had a job."

Hector Pesquera was Lucy's ultimate boss in Miami, the special agent in charge of more than seven hundred employees in
the Miami Field Office. When he first learned about the Montes investigation, he had obvious questions about Lucy and Tito.
"Well, it's, basically, 'Okay, what do we have here? Could they
potentially be involved? Is it a family affair? What is it?' Well,
I mean, the thought does occur." But as the investigation advanced, and especially once the FBI had legal authority to eavesdrop on Ana's phone calls and intercept every email, Pesquera
realized Lucy was innocent. "You're able to ascertain whether
there are communications, were there trips, were there all other
sorts of things that may potentially involve any of the other two
[siblings]. In our case, there wasn't," Pesquera said. "Anything
and everything that could have been done to establish the absence of Lucy's involvement was done. And we didn't have any
problem with her at all. And neither did Headquarters." When
asked if his agents separately monitored Lucy's calls and emails,
Pesquera demurred.

His one disagreement with Headquarters was over its decision to not require Lucy to sit for a fresh polygraph. "I actually inquired about it, and I don't remember if I ever got a straight-through answer. To me, I would've, and I said we should, but the powers that be said it's not necessary." Once he learned that Lucy was cooperating and not party to Ana's treachery, Pesquera laid down the law. He refused to transfer Lucy to another field office or find innocuous busywork for her in Miami. "You don't want to damage someone's reputation for life just because of guilt by association." Anyone at the Miami Field Office who treated Lucy like damaged goods would have to deal with Pesquera's wrath. "We wanted to treat her like she deserved to be treated, like a good employee." He told all her coworkers that Lucy was not to be stigmatized for Ana's crimes. "I'm very particular and very straightforward, sometimes too straightforward. But I'll say it bluntly, including flowery language: Back off."

In Atlanta, Tito and Joan also got summoned to a private office on the morning of the twenty-first. The supervisor of their foreign counterintelligence squad wanted to see them together. "And we're like, 'Okay. This is weird,'" Joan recalled. "And then he said, 'Tito, your sister Ana at this moment is getting arrested for espionage.' And we're like, 'What? Is this a joke?' You know? And he says, 'No, this is not a joke. They've had an investigation on her for a while, but due to 9/11 and all the things going on, they had to speed [it] up."

Joan said the news was hard to fathom. "I went through all the emotions after she got arrested." Her first instinct was denial. "First, we were a little angry at the Bureau, like, 'What? You're lying.'" But as she and Tito thought more about it, they began to accept the truth. "After that, it was like, 'Well, we're in the Bureau. We know that they wouldn't do this unless they had a whole bunch of evidence, especially for something like this.' So it was a realization that was just surreal."

Emilia was not so accepting. Tito called his mother and advised her to sit down. "He told me that he was calling from the office of the FBI chief of the Atlanta office and that Ana had been arrested and charged with espionage at her office in DC. I felt as if I had been hit over the head with a brick." Joan said Emilia was inconsolable for months. "She would have bouts of, 'My baby!' and cry. She couldn't believe it. I mean, who would want to think their child would do such a thing?" Lucy drove to Emilia's apartment as soon as her FBI interview was over, to console her mother. "We were stunned," Lucy said. For Emilia, the news wouldn't compute. "I do not recall what happened for many days; I just survived," she said. "I could not sleep for days. I tried to recall all the prayers I had memorized in my youth and found them one at a time somewhere in my brain." She refused to believe that her beloved daughter had made such a horrible life choice. "I could not reconcile my idea of my smart daughter with that of a spy."

Roger's reaction was instant, volcanic. He had been intimate with Ana, trusting, even discussing marriage. And all the while she was playing him for a fool. He was supposed to be helping SOUTHCOM fend off the Cubans, yet had been sleeping with Castro's greatest operator. "As a close community we were all fooled, but on top of that, I was even dating her so [my] sense of shame and guilt and failure and personal responsibility was indescribable," he wrote. "The anguish, interestingly, was focused on the loss to the mission and didn't derive at all from loss of her, of any fondness I had for her. The exception to that I guess being that as my life's work went up like a bonfire set from within, the fact that I dated her was like a gasoline accelerant for the professional guilt."

Finally, it was time to inform Ana's colleagues. Dave Curtin and Drew Winneberger, DIA's chief of security, gathered all of Ana's coworkers in an upstairs conference room for an emergency meeting. They had no idea why. "Ana Montes was arrested by the FBI a short while ago," Winneberger announced.

"The FBI arrested Ana under suspicion that she engaged in a conspiracy to commit espionage against the United States."[237]

Some in the crowd gasped. "When it was announced, one colleague actually had to ask what name they said, because it didn't even register," said Lourdes Talbot, who worked closely with Ana and had looked up to her. Steve Smith, Ana's longtime cubicle mate, sobbed. "I actually broke down. It wasn't even an issue of disbelief. It was...sort of being told someone had died, suddenly someone that you hadn't expected to die." Talbot later cried, too. "I was more analytic in my thought process when it was announced. But then as the days went on... I was definitely sad. I did cry. I was upset and eventually it turned to anger. And mostly now it's anger. And when I do hear her name, I cringe, because I did work with her so closely and I did admire her." Ana's boss, Marty Scheina, said the staff went into mourning. "Ana's arrest was something that was very devastating to the office. We actually saw the grief counselors the next week to try to understand and accept, understand what was going on, but it was very tough for us."[238]

Ana's fellow analysts began rewinding in their heads conversations that had likely been shared with the enemy. "Every time we discovered something I turned around and I said, 'Hey, Ana, guess what we just figured out, or guess what we just learned?' So it was as good as just turning around and sending Fidel Castro a letter, although it probably got there faster than a letter did," Steve Smith said. Reg Brown, whose early but imprecise suspicions about Ana had helped target her, was left in a dark place. "The greatest success that I have as a counterintelligence analyst and now a Section Analyst is the arrest and incarceration of Ana. That's my sole success because all the other things that I did in those areas, she compromised."

For the NSA's Elena Valdez, news of Ana's arrest was overwhelming. "My emotion was, honestly I felt like crying," she said. It had taken a Cuban American, forced to flee her home-land at age six, to help expose Fidel Castro's most successful spy. "I thought, wow, it's all been worth it."

Chapter 37.

"ALL THE WORLD IS ONE COUNTRY"

"Your honor, I engaged in the activity that brought me before you because I obeyed my conscience rather than the law."

—STATEMENT READ BY ANA MONTES IN FEDERAL COURT ON THE DAY OF HER SENTENCING, OCTOBER 16, 2002

About three weeks after the arrest, Ana's closest relatives gathered in Washington for a dismal family reunion. For some, it was a chance to offer grace at Ana's lowest moment. For others, there were scores to be settled.

Ana was locked up in a jail in rural Orange, Virginia, nearly ninety miles southwest of her Cleveland Park home. During a visit, Emilia clung to hope. "[We] were able to see her behind a glass window. I could tell she was scared, looked fragile; she seemed much smaller than her actual size; she tried to smile," Emilia wrote. "I was sure she was innocent, maybe she was a 'double agent' like in the movies," Emilia fantasized, hoping her daughter really was feeding bogus secrets to the Cubans while helping the Americans behind Castro's back.

One by one, Ana's family addressed her on a jail telephone, desperate for answers. When it was Lucy's turn, she held her fire. "I thought it was better to be a sister and not a judge and jury," she said. The only question Lucy posed was, "What made you think you wouldn't get caught?" Ana, locked in solitary and dressed in a black-and-white-striped jumpsuit, refused to engage in detail with her sister.

Tito and Joan were next. "Why, why? Did you really do this? Why?" Joan recalled that she and her husband asked Ana. Tito was "really, really angry."

"I do remember him saying, 'You need to talk to the Bureau and whatever they need to know, you need to tell them.'" Ana didn't deny anything, but wouldn't come clean, either, aware that an FBI agent was sitting just feet away, always listening. "She didn't really address it. She just cried a lot," Joan recalled.

Roger had his own plan. He visited Ana in the Orange jail months after the arrest and tried to bait her into talking. "So the idea was to start an information flow using the emotional channel that existed" between them. "I gave her the opportunity to at least admit what she did and I said, 'I know you're innocent.' Nothing." Ana didn't claim she was being framed and didn't magically confess to the man she hoped to marry. "She wouldn't admit it in my presence." All she offered were "endless musings about life, the universe and everything. Just filler." The Ice Queen lived up to her name again. "I was emotional as hell," Roger said. "The way this piece played out still causes me tremendous anger to this day."[239]

The Montes family needed money to mount a criminal defense, and made arrangements to sell Ana's co-op, car, and, later, the Bluebeard's Castle time-share. While emptying out the Macomb Street apartment, her relatives found more clues of a troubled mind.

Emilia was cleaning out Ana's desk when she stumbled upon a British police report. Ana had been on vacation in England and was driving when a child "crossed her path unexpectedly and she bumped him with the car," Emilia wrote. Ana stopped to make sure the boy was okay, but he ran away and, local police reported, "the boy was never found." Ana started having "an uncontrollable crying fit," and an elderly British couple comforted her and invited her for tea. Weeks later, the accident stayed with her. "When she returned to the USA, she apparently was very nervous and depressed but she did not share this with me until years later," Ana's mother said. "I regret not having paid more attention to her emotional state; I fooled myself thinking she had overcome whatever was stressing her and that she would always be the strong girl I imagined her to be."

Sister-in-law Joan Montes made her own discovery about Ana at 3039 Macomb Street, in a tidy linen closet. "She had bars and bars of soap. And I found out that she was obsessively cleaning her hands or taking long, long, hot showers." Joan couldn't help analyzing the neatly arranged soap bars. "To me, psychologically, that tells me she's trying to clean something off of her... She might think spying is for a reason that she justified, but maybe part of her didn't like it and was cleaning herself of it."

Ana was facing a possible death sentence and needed proper criminal representation.[240] The family reached out to a Washington law legend, Plato Cacheris. Born in Pittsburgh where his Greek-immigrant father ran a chain of hamburger and waffle shops, Cacheris graduated from Georgetown University Law School and formed a private criminal defense practice in 1965 after several years as a federal prosecutor. "I like the battle against the government," Cacheris once told the *Washington Post*. "And I never really liked seeing people go to jail."[241]

The practice grew along with Plato's reputation and, by the time Ana's family came calling, Cacheris was one of the country's elite defense lawyers. His clients often were ripped from the headlines, players in the biggest scandals of the day. He represented former Nixon attorney general John Mitchell in the Watergate break-in and cover-up, defended a congressman caught taking bribes in the Abscam sting operation, and helped Fawn Hall, the glamorous paper shredder who was secretary to Lieutenant Colonel Oliver North in the Iran-Contra scandal, dodge prison time. When President Clinton had an affair with White House intern Monica Lewinsky, she initially denied the relationship to law-enforcement authorities and faced felony charges. Cacheris kept Lewinsky out of prison, too, obtaining transactional immunity from prosecution in exchange for Monica's truthful testimony against the president. Cacheris even defended the two most important spies of their era, Robert Hanssen and Aldrich Ames, when they were caught selling US secrets to Russia. Reflecting on his infamous slate of clients, Cacheris said he tried never to moralize. "I don't lecture them on what they've done; I don't believe in that," he once told a reporter. "What's done is done; now the question is 'How can we come out of it the best way possible?'" [242]

Ana's legal team of Plato Cacheris, Preston Burton, and John Hundley found the best way out of it for their new client. On March 19, 2002, they convinced Ana to plead guilty to one count of conspiracy to commit espionage. It would mean coming clean on her Cuban friends. In exchange for testifying fully about her long career as a Cuban agent, Ana, then forty-five, would likely be sentenced to twenty-five years in federal prison. With good behavior, she would be out well before her seventieth birthday. She took the deal. "In or around September 1985, the defendant, Ana Belén Montes, willfully, surreptitiously, and without authorization began to provide classified information, lawfully available to her through her assigned duties as a United States government employee, to the government of Cuba," Ana stated in her factual proffer to the court.

With Ana's admission of guilt came daily road trips from the Orange, Virginia, prison to the Washington Field Office of the FBI for extensive debriefing sessions. "She was driven almost every day to DC to be debriefed and she was touched that the driver ([who] called her Ma'am) asked her what music she would like to listen to," Emilia said. Ana preferred classical music and

National Public Radio. Once delivered to WFO, McCoy treated Ana with respect. He would buy her green salads and fresh fruit, since she had complained that she was repulsed by the bologna sandwiches and other fare served in her Virginia prison. Anything to warm her up and keep her talking.

McCoy led the debriefings for the FBI and got along with Ana much better than Lapp, who struggled to find common ground. "Her version of rapport was turning on the tape machine and saying, 'Ask me the first question,'" Lapp said. "It was like she was angry, just, 'Okay, I'm yours, what's the first question?'" Ana had agreed to the plea and was being forced to cooperate, but that didn't mean she had to like her captors. They spent hours together with her nearly every day for months, with downtime during lunch and breaks. "I would sit there and read the paper. It was really awkward and difficult," Lapp said. "She didn't want to have any kind of small talk whatsoever."

McCoy asked Ana endless questions, focusing on the classified programs she compromised and deepening the FBI's understanding of how the DGI runs operations in the United States. The priorities were identifying her handlers and finding Ana's encryption disks (unsuccessful), learning whether Cuba had any imminent military plans against the US or had successfully targeted any high-level US officials, and establishing if the Castro regime had partnered with Al Qaeda or other terrorist groups, McCoy said. He found his quarry to be difficult, and skilled at shifting blame. "Ana was an extremely intelligent and complicated individual, possessing a subtle arrogance with which she attempted to rationalize (at least to herself) behavior that everyone else instinctively recognized as irrational," McCoy wrote in an email to the author.

The CIA and NSA also got a crack at Ana, and then the DIA took its turn. They had months of questions on how Ana had pulled off her ruse for so long, right under DIA's nose. Lisa Connors, Mark Ritter, and Cheryl Ruiz did the honors, with DIA counterintelligence expert John Kavanagh supervising the action in a separate WFO room, live via video link. Ritter, the DIA counterintelligence officer and trained interrogator, recalls that Ana at first sat at the table "arms folded, chin tucked in, legs crossed under her chair and just sitting, staring at me, brows knitted." He said that before he could get cooperation, he had to pass muster with the confessed criminal. "I had to essentially intellectually prove that I knew what I was doing and that I was worthy of sitting across from her." Connors, a US Army master sargeant, said Ana was "closed mouth" during debriefings and wouldn't volunteer anything useful. "She was super evasive with me when it came to anything that might cause that sentence to go up."

One day, the DIA allowed a special visitor to sit in on the debriefings. It was the NSA's Elena Valdez. Elena sat in a separate room in the FBI's Washington Field Office, watching Ana live on a video feed. "I wanted to see her persona," Elena said. "For me as a counterintelligence analyst, what is inside the mind and the heart and the soul of somebody who would betray the country so nonchalantly, and believe in their head that they were doing something good for an evil [intelligence] service?" Elena came away offended by Ana's blasé, business-as-usual mindset. "What I remember most was her attitude when they were asking her things. It was like she wasn't afraid. She had no remorse. It was like, 'Yup, yup. I did that.'"

The DIA debriefers told Elena that she could come back and watch any day, but she was so disgusted that she never did. "It was hard for me to watch that. Because, you know, she was working to support why I'm here, why I had to leave [Cuba.] And she's helping that regime continue."

After seven months, the US Intelligence Community had mostly exhausted its curiosity. Ana had several convenient memory lapses during her debriefings, but never enough for McCoy and the prosecutors to challenge her veracity or cooperation.

The Department of Justice's main prosecutor on the case, Assistant US Attorney Ronald Walutes Jr., concluded that Ana had "fully cooperated with the government and understands that her obligation of cooperation is a lifelong commitment."

Montes revealed the names of Ernesto and her other DGI contacts in the US and Havana. The most useful morsel that Ana shared concerned her old SAIS girlfriend Marta Velázquez. Ana revealed how Marta had helped recruit her in graduate school, introduced her to a Cuban intelligence officer in New York, and then joined her on their operational trip to Cuba. The FBI would open a second espionage investigation into Velázquez.

On October 16, 2002, Ana sat before US District Court Judge Ricardo Urbina, awaiting judgment. The first Latino appointed to DC's Superior Court, Urbina's thoughtful and incisive manner convinced President Clinton to nominate him to the federal bench in 1994. When most clients are about to be sentenced for serious crimes, their attorneys will advise them to be contrite and to humbly seek the mercy of the court. Ana would have none of that. She refused to apologize, instead spinning a fairy tale for Judge Urbina that skirted personal responsibility.

Dressed in a black-and-white striped prison jumpsuit, she began innocently enough. "An Italian proverb perhaps best describes the fundamental truth I believe in: 'All the world is one country.' In such a world-country, the principle of loving one's neighbor as much as one's self seems, to me, to be the essential guide to harmonious relations between all of our nations' neighborhoods… It is a principle that, tragically, I believe we have never applied to Cuba."

Ana then explained her idealistic rationale for spying. Looking at Judge Urbina, she said: "I believe our government's policy towards Cuba is cruel and unfair; profoundly unneighborly. And I felt morally obligated to help the island defend itself from our efforts to impose our values and our political system on it." She was forced to equal the playing field, she argued. "My way of responding to our Cuban policy may have been morally wrong. Perhaps Cuba's right to exist free of political and economic coercion did not justify giving the island classified information to help it defend itself. I can only say that I did what I thought right, to help counter a grave injustice."

She then fantasized that her traitorous behavior might somehow bring the two nations closer. "I hope my case in some way will encourage our government to abandon its hostility toward Cuba and to work with Havana in a spirit of tolerance, mutual respect, and understanding." She ended by expressing a gullible worldview of Cuba that ignored the Castro brothers' more than forty-year history of political repression, their campaign to export Communism far and wide, and the many armed conflicts that Cuba has supported around the globe. "I hope for U.S. policy that it's based, instead, on neighborly love, a policy that recognizes that Cuba, like any nation, wants to be treated with dignity and respect..." Ana told the judge. "It would enable Cuba to drop its defensive measures and experiment more easily with changes. And it would permit the two neighbors to work together and with other nations to promote tolerance and cooperation in our one-world country, in our one and only world homeland."[243]

Ana's mother was worried she had blown it. Emilia fretted that her daughter "insisted in telling the Judge her beliefs, and this did not make that man have any sympathies for her." Lucy was in court that day and was equally blunt in her assessment of Ana's statement. "I didn't think it was good at all for her or her case, but that's the way she is," Lucy said. "I thought it was really stupid."

Prosecutor Ron Walutes was not swayed, either. In a court filing to Judge Urbina, he rejected Ana's sugarcoated rationalizations.[244] "Unlike most of the criminal defendants who appear before this Court for imposition of sentence, this defendant is totally unapologetic for her conduct...in an act of incredible arrogance and ultimate selfishness, she stands before this Court unwilling to repudiate her betrayal of the United States. Although she wishes she had never been caught, she in no measure apologizes for her betrayal of the United States to the Cuban Intelligence Service."

Walutes explained how Ana put US intelligence officers abroad in danger. "In the end, she is the ultimate hypocrite. She condones a life of deceit and turns a blind eye to the risk she placed others in by compromising sensitive and highly classified military and intelligence information." Her disloyalty cast a wide shadow. "Ana Belen Montes is a spy who has betrayed her family as much as she betrayed her country. She brings shame to a family of hardworking, loyal American citizens." Finally, the prosecutor highlighted the options Ana had, in a country that values free speech, to legally promote Cuba's cause. "Ana Belen Montes did not devote her life to an organization such as the Peace Corps. She did not join in organized public protest against this country's foreign policy." The prosecutor concluded by urging the Court to sentence Ana to twenty-five years behind bars. "This defendant richly deserves to spend her life in a prison with others who have harmed the community."

Next it was Ricardo Urbina's turn. The federal judge resisted editorializing on Ana's unusual monologue. Instead, he focused on the harm she caused. "Today is a very sad day," he said, addressing the defendant. "It's a very sad day for you, Ms. Montes, for your family, for your loved ones, and for every American who suffers the betrayal of a fellow countryman." Judge Urbina didn't mention it, but he shared some characteristics with Ana. His mother was from Puerto Rico, too, and the judge had overcome hardscrabble beginnings in a Spanish Harlem four-story walk-up to attend Georgetown University on a full scholarship. The United States had given the Urbina family many opportunities.[245] Judge Urbina couldn't help lecturing Ana on her disloyalty. "In my mind, if you cannot love your country then, at the very least, you should do it no harm. Instead, you decided, with deliberation, to put your fellow Americans, specific individuals, and the nation as a whole in harm's way. For this you must pay the penalty." Judge Urbina sentenced Ana to twenty-five years. "Pursuant to the Sentencing Reform Act of 1984, it is the judgment of the Court that the defendant, Ana Belén Montes, is hereby committed to the custody of the Bureau of Prisons for 300 months." The hearing was over in minutes. Ana was handcuffed and led away.

In Havana, the Cubans could finally take a victory lap. In a surprise move, two days after Ana was sentenced, Cuba saluted their prized asset. Felipe Pérez Roque, then Cuba's Minister of Foreign Affairs, wrote on a government website that he felt "profound respect and admiration for Ms. Ana Belén Montes." Cuba's top foreign official praised Ana's "moral stature" and devotion. "Her actions were motivated by ethics and by an admirable sense of justice," Pérez Roque added.[246]

Chapter 38.

ESCAPE TO SWEDEN

"Rising from many islands linked by bridges and with water everywhere, Stockholm is one of the most ideally situated of all national capitals."

—FROM THE 1950s PROMOTIONAL TRAVEL FILM, PICTURESQUE SWEDEN[247]

In 2021, an exciting new candidate applied for an opening as a teacher of law and Spanish at one of Sweden's most prestigious high schools. "As can be seen from my resume, I have degrees from top universities in the United States as well as a Master's in Education from the University of Stockholm," the applicant wrote. She had recent experience instructing Swedish high school students, but her résumé ran so much deeper. "Before becoming a teacher I worked as a lawyer and economist, and my experiences working and living overseas bring a great depth to my work in education," she boasted. "I believe that my extensive knowledge of living conditions within and outside Sweden, as well as my academic studies in law and international relations will prove of benefit to your students and can be an asset to your program."

What's more, the job seeker insisted, she was a real team player. "I have good working relationships with my colleagues and am used to working in a team." The aspiring teacher seemed perfect for the job. Her impressive three-page résumé checked every box a discerning principal might want to see.

But the job candidate had failed to mention one final credential. She had left out the part about being an international fugitive from justice.

In 2002, shortly after Ana pleaded guilty and began openly confessing her crimes to federal investigators, Marta Velázquez magically decided it was time to quit her $96,000 a year US government job.[248] She abruptly retired as director of the US-AID's Regional Office of Trade and Economic Analysis, based at the US Embassy in Guatemala. She moved to Sweden with her husband, Anders Kviele, a Swedish diplomat, and their two young children.

On February 6, 2003, just months after fleeing Guatemala, Marta became a Swedish citizen.[249] She already had general immunity from prosecution afforded the spouses of most foreign diplomats. Now she was a citizen of Sweden, too, a country that refuses to extradite residents accused of espionage. Marta Velázquez has remained outside the United States, and out of the FBI's clutches, since 2002.

She left a lot behind. From a prosperous Puerto Rican family of eight children, her siblings attended top universities, just like Marta. Her Princeton-educated sister is a successful pediatrician in Norfolk, Virginia. Her brother is a lawyer in Puerto Rico with degrees from Stanford, Northwestern, and Cornell. Marta can't visit them anymore, at least not on their turf. When her beloved father, Don Miguel, a well-regarded judge and law school professor, died in Puerto Rico in 2006, Marta stayed away from the funeral. They had been close, and no one understood her absence. "The family said they could not find her," said a fellow law school professor and friend who eulogized Don Miguel. "It was an extraordinary situation. Nobody knew why. I thought there was some break between the family. It was not that," the professor told the author of *Spy Schools*, published in 2017.[250]

After graduating from SAIS and taking Ana to Cuba in 1985 to receive operational training, Marta kicked off her own duplicitous US government career. She worked for the Department of Transportation and then spent a dozen years as a lawyer with the State Department's US Agency for International Development, or USAID, which works to reduce poverty, promote democracy, and provide disaster assistance abroad. As a USAID lawyer, Velázquez held a top-secret security clearance and was posted to the US Embassy in Nicaragua from 1990 to 1994. She moved to Managua, the war-torn Nicaraguan capital, at a sensitive time for Cuba. Voters had just kicked the Cuban-backed Sandinistas out of office and Violeta Chamorro was elected president. Marta was in a perfect place to inform the Castros about American activities in the region and Chamorro's moves during the post-war transition. From her base at the US Embassy, Marta also would have overlapped with Ana when DIA sent her to brief President Chamorro on Nicaragua's military capabilities. It's unclear if Marta and Ana secretly reunited and shared notes in Managua. One person whom Marta did socialize with was Anders Kviele, a diplomat at the Swedish Embassy in Nicaragua who was listed as the "2nd Embassy Secretary" and, in one newspaper account, its chargé d'affaires.[251] Velázquez and Kviele fell in love in Managua and married in 1996 at the Second Union Church in Puerto Rico, celebrating with family from San Juan and Sweden.[252]

Marta moved from Managua to Washington, where she worked as an assistant general counsel for USAID's Asia Near East Bureau.[253] She supervised lawyers in DC and abroad and received a promotion.[254] She gave birth to son Ingmar in 1997 and daughter Ingrid in 1999, and relocated to Sweden with her growing family when the children were infants. By 2000, Marta was back in action. She moved with her kids from Stockholm to Guatemala City, where she worked out of the US Embassy on economic issues for USAID. Conveniently, her husband, Anders, got assigned as an aide to the Swedish ambassador in Guatemala, so they could all be together.

Like Ana, Marta always had a side hustle. She routinely exchanged encrypted messages with Cuban operatives while at USAID and traveled to Panama for operational meetings with her handlers, the DOJ said. Velázquez used her cover as a State Department lawyer to work as an agent in place for Cuba, the Justice Department concluded.

The FBI began formally building its case on Velázquez after Ana revealed in debriefings who had helped recruit her as a Cuban agent. The Bureau already had doubts about Marta after Lucy provided the FBI with Marta's name on Ana's arrest day. On February 6, 2004, precisely one year after Velázquez became a Swedish citizen, a grand jury in Washington indicted Marta for conspiracy to commit espionage. The FBI's Steve McCoy testified before the then-secret panel. The indictment, which remained sealed until 2013, alleges that Marta "would and did maintain clandestine contacts with Cuban Intelligence Service officers and agents for the purpose of receiving instructions regarding her operational activities in support of the Cuban Intelligence Service's activities against the United States." Marta has deliberately dodged the FBI for two decades. "Defendant Velázquez is well aware that she is subject to arrest if she places herself within the jurisdiction of the United States," Justice Department prosecutors revealed. "She has studiously avoided doing so since at least 2002."

Today, it's clear that Marta has made the most of her freedom. With the help of a Swedish investigative journalist, I tracked Marta down at her home outside Stockholm.[255] The accused spy lives with her husband, Anders, and their adult children in a well-kept villa in Solhöjden, the "Sunny Heights" neighborhood of Spånga, a quaint upper-middle-class suburb. The couple bought their yellow two-story home a decade ago for nearly $450,000, just months after Marta's indictment was unsealed and her case became public. It is now valued at close to $800,000, according to local property records.[256] The detached prewar home with balconies sits on a quiet street surrounded by fruit trees, a pleasant garden, and mature evergreens. A silver Volvo V70 station wagon waits in the driveway. The tidy Spånga town center is a short walk away, with commuter trains whisking passengers to Stockholm in just fifteen minutes, plus handsome cafés, charcuteries, florists, beauty salons, and other essentials for a comfortable life. When Spånga gets tiresome, Marta and her family can dash off to their rustic cabin near Hjorted, in southern Sweden, for swims in Lake Slissjön and quiet picnics in the country.

It's doubtful that Marta's neighbors have any clue that she is a suspected spy. Few Swedes do. Swedish custom prohibits the local media from identifying criminal suspects who have not been fully adjudicated, so Swedish newspapers didn't print Velázquez's name when the Justice Department unsealed her indictment in 2013 and when foreign media outlets ran detailed stories about her. "Between 1989 and 2002, the Swedish woman worked for the American aid agency USAID in Washington," Sweden's *Expressen* newspaper reported in 2013, describing Marta only as "the Swedish woman" or "Barbara," her Cuban code name. No Swedish newspaper has used Marta's actual name in any articles to this day.

Despite her status as a wanted fugitive, Marta applied for and was accepted in 2021 as a Swedish public school teacher making about $50,000 a year. Today she teaches Spanish, law, economics, and social studies at Kungsholmen's Gymnasium, one of the country's finest high schools. (Swedish gymnasiums are similar to high schools, teaching students who are typically sixteen to nineteen years old and bound for university.) Lesley Brunnman was the Kungsholmen's Gymnasium coprincipal who hired Marta. In a recent interview, she told the author she had no idea that Marta was an accused Cuban spy when she was applying for the teaching position. "No, I wasn't aware of anything like that," she said. "I have not heard of anything like this spy business." She said the only clue that Marta gave off, in retrospect, was when she mentioned during job interviews that she would not be interested in traveling internationally with her students.

Kungsholmen's Gymnasium, or "KG," is housed in a magnificent red-brick and white-plaster building constructed in the early 1900s and is conveniently located on Kungsholmen, or King's Island, in the Swedish capital. KG's thirteen hundred students test among the highest in Sweden and can specialize in fields of study including music, rhetoric, drama, international relations, criminology, philosophy, and computer programming. "My education gave me a lot. Especially critical thinking and analysis, weighing pros and cons, that everything is not black or white," one student says of KG in a promotional video. "Studying in English opens a lot of doors internationally. Me and many of my classmates feel that we have plenty of space to leave Sweden after school and study abroad," another student notes.

Marta's workplace has a cosmopolitan, cultivated air about it and boasts of progressive values that must make her proud. "We are a school characterized by diversity and tolerance. We develop your knowledge and foster your readiness to meet future challenges. You are meant to take responsibility for and influence societal development," the KG website states. Students can take classes in human rights, "Power and Empowerment," global health, and African development—taught in collaboration with sister schools in Zambia and Rwanda.

Marta began her teaching career shortly after quitting USAID. While evading the law, she refused to just sit home. She followed Anders to Austria and taught English at a private vocational school in Vienna. When the Swedes assigned her husband to Lisbon, she pulled up roots and taught Spanish to Portuguese high school students and English to British Petroleum engineers. In 2009, she even worked for the British Council, the UK's international organization for cultural relations, teaching the Queen's English to young Portuguese up-and-comers.[257] Austria and Portugal do not extradite residents for espionage. Like Sweden, both countries consider spying to be a political matter. Starting in 2012, Marta taught Spanish, English, and law for nearly a decade at Stockholm's Thorildsplans Gymnasium, a large technical high school known for its diverse student body.

Marta's globetrotting and refusal to surrender infuriated the FBI. Remarkably, some investigators even contemplated a rendition, or a forcible abduction of Marta overseas, with a secret transfer back to the United States for prosecution. During the early stages of the War on Terror, the Bush Administration frequently used "extraordinary renditions" to kidnap accused terrorists and other illegal combatants and move them to CIA black sites. FBI agents involved with Marta's case discussed the option. "Could you have grabbed her and stuck her on a plane and flown out and just said, 'Screw you Guatemala, screw you Sweden, screw you, whoever'? Sure," one of the FBI agents assigned to the Velázquez case said. Cooler heads prevailed, and Marta was left in place.

Some observers think the FBI blew it and could have grabbed Velázquez immediately following Ana's 2001 arrest. "The FBI dropped the ball," said Chris Simmons, the former DIA expert on Cuban intelligence. "They had plenty of time to arrest her while she was still working for USAID." Even one FBI special agent agrees, and remains frustrated that the Bureau didn't trick Marta and apprehend her when she was still working for the US government. "The bottom line is, let's just say the element of surprise was lost between September 2001 and whenever Ana started talking," said now-retired agent Molly Flynn, who worked extensively on Marta's case.

But that's in the past. On May 19, 2022, a Swedish reporter and a photographer spotted Marta Velázquez and her daughter, Ingrid, smiling and chatting while walking home on the peaceful streets of Sunny Heights. Marta, now sixty-five, was using two collapsible hiking poles on the return trip from the town center. She was dressed in a green jacket and sneakers and toting a black KG school backpack. The reporter identified himself and asked Marta if the US charges against her were fair. "Excuse me, this is private [property]," she replied, as she opened her mailbox next to her driveway and tried to ignore him. "If you come in here, I will call the police," Ingrid added. (Marta and Anders declined to respond to multiple emails seeking comment.)

The Swedish reporter tried one final question. "What do you want to say to Ana Montes?" he shouted. Marta didn't reply, simply closing the door to her snug suburban home behind her.

Chapter 39.

"A PSYCHOLOGICAL HELL"

"The population of the Administrative Housing Unit includes inmates on death row, or inmates who have escaped or attempted escape, exhibited predatory/assaultive behavior, have chronic behavioral problems, are national security risks, are high danger (terroristic threats), and high profile inmates."

—DESCRIPTION OF CARSWELL PRISON'S ADMIN UNIT BY AN OUTSIDE AUDITOR, 2018[258]

For more than twenty years, Ana's home has been one of the most isolated women's prisons in America. The Administrative Housing Unit sits on the grounds of the Federal Medical Center Carswell outside Fort Worth, Texas, on the site of a former Air Force base. Carswell's massive prison campus features three main facilities—a medical and psychiatric hospital that treats women inmates throughout the federal system, a one-thousand-bed general correctional unit, and a minimum-security prison camp. Carswell's fourth and smallest facility, the bloodlessly named Admin Unit, houses the nation's most threatening women.

Ana's family still doesn't know how she got there. After her sentencing, Judge Urbina and Ana's defense counsel recommended that she be confined to one of the low-security federal prisons in Tallahassee, Florida, or Danbury, Connecticut. But because of her strict communications restrictions, Ana didn't get the Martha Stewart treatment.

Psychologists working inside the Admin Unit describe it as a

SuperMax for "female inmates with histories of escapes, chronic behavior problems, repeated incidents of assaultive and predatory behavior, or other special management concerns."[259] The Bureau of Prisons built it as an impregnable island for violent misfits, Carswell's very own Hannibal Lecter Wing. Dentists and priests make house calls, instead of letting the inmates venture outside and risking escape. There's no mess hall, so individual meals are wheeled in and out three times a day on carts. The Admin Unit's khaki-clad inmates almost never mix with Carswell's general population—the everyday drug dealers, fraudsters, and thieves who will, on average, do five to seven years behind bars.[260] By contrast, the Admin Unit has lifers and even the occasional death row case. There are rarely more than two dozen women inside the barbed-wire confines at a time, their movements closely monitored and heavily scripted.

Carswell has been the recurring subject of disturbing allegations. In May 2022, a former correctional officer admitted to sexually abusing at least three female inmates at the prison complex in the previous year (not in the Admin Unit.)[261] In a 2022 Prison Rape Elimination Act audit, federal investigators concluded that thirty-six inmates had reported sexual abuse at Carswell, among the total population of some 1,300 women prisoners.[262] The COVID-19 virus hit the facility hard, and eight inmates have died of COVID at Carswell since March 2020, the Bureau of Prisons reports.[263] One prisoner who was in the third trimester of pregnancy was flown to Carswell at the height of the pandemic. She was placed in quarantine in a six-by-eight-foot cell with three other women and contracted COVID and died, according to a lawsuit filed by the late inmate's family. "The prison did not implement modified COVID-19 procedures, such as requiring staff to wear masks, until April 2020," a local newspaper reported.[264] Inmates were given just one mask per person per week during the pandemic, according to a separate lawsuit filed against Carswell by seventy-three convicts, who called the prison a "house of horror."[265] In a handwritten two-hundred-page complaint, the women give accounts of rotten food, negligent medical care, and malicious treatment. That tracks with what investigative reporters have found for years. "Accusations of gross medical neglect, rape by prison guards, and toxic exposure for prison workers…continue to pile up," the *Fort Worth Weekly* reported in 2005.[266]

Prison reform advocates have been sounding off about Carswell, and specifically about the Admin Unit, for decades. "The prisoners are only allowed to exercise in a small, fenced-in, concrete, outdoor area topped by double-coiled razor wire where there is little room for physical activity," a group called Campaign to Close Carswell writes of the Admin Unit where Ana is housed. "The unit is frequently and unpredictably locked down for hours on end due to violence and suicide attempts resulting from the claustrophobic and oppressive conditions."[267]

Ana can bear witness. In handwritten letters from inside the concrete walls, she chronicled her *One Flew Over the Cuckoo's Nest* isolation. "Well, I'll tell you a little about my stay here," she wrote to her old friend Mimi Colon in 2013, when they were briefly and fruitlessly trying to reconcile. "I do everything I can possibly do to not be here mentally in what is, lamentably, a hell. Mentally distancing myself is my way of surviving."

After more than a decade at Carswell, inmate 25037016 took stock of her surroundings. She described her maximum-security prison as "pretty decent," with a private shower and toilet in a cell she has all to herself. She complimented the prison food and said that she easily keeps warm and "I can do some semblance of exercise." Ana wrote that the "medical attention is better than what a lot of Americans get," and lauded the prison staff for treating "prisoners in a humane way."

But her fellow inmates are another story. "Lamentably, this place—on top of the severe deprivations that any maximum-security prison imposes—is a psychological hell because almost

all the inmates here are either very or extremely unhinged and
those that are verbally or physically violent make the place a torture chamber. These constitute about half," Ana writes. "The
violence, in one form or another, and the screaming are constant." Ana has stayed safe by rarely engaging with anyone. In-
voking the historically neutral country where her friend and
fellow traveler Marta Velázquez found safe haven, Ana explains
her prison-coping strategy. "I act like I'm neutral like Sweden
or a rock in the corner," she writes.[268] She describes living in the
Admin Unit as being a "non-combatant" in a "continuous war
amongst the insane." The Admin Unit is "a place that is almost
designed to bring out the worst in everyone," Ana adds. "From
what I can judge, at least half of the inmates here should be in
a psychiatric hospital prison…"

She may have a point. In twenty years in the specialty lockup,
Ana has shared intimate quarters with the kinds of neighbors
she never could have imagined back in Charlottesville or Upper
Northwest DC. Besides Charles Manson devotee Squeaky
Fromme, Ana has lived for years with Aafia Siddiqui, the accused Al Qaeda operative who was convicted in New York in
2010 of trying to kill American soldiers and FBI agents with
an assault rifle while detained in Afghanistan. A Pakistani neu-
roscientist who graduated from MIT and received a PhD from
Brandeis University, Siddiqui was arrested in 2008. The FBI
said she was carrying instructions on making dirty bombs and
had handwritten notes on US landmarks that could be targeted
in a "mass casualty attack." Her lawyers argued at trial that she
was mentally ill, which Siddiqui denied.[269] A federal judge sentenced her to eighty-six years in prison.

In recent years, Siddiqui has argued that it's the Admin Unit,
not her, that's truly dangerous. In 2021, she filed a lawsuit against
the Bureau of Prisons claiming that a fellow inmate attacked
her inside her cell, unprompted. Prisoner Barbara McCarty
barged into her Admin Unit cell in July 2021 and "brutally as-

saulted Ms. Siddiqui," the complaint alleges, adding that Mc-Carty "smashed a coffee mug filled with scalding hot liquid" into Siddiqui's face and then punched and kicked her.

McCarty, who was released from Carswell in January 2022 and did not respond to requests for comment, has a violent past and a long history of mental illness. In 2008, already in prison for bank robbery, the Texas native pushed, kicked, and spat on a correctional officer in Florida. During a sentencing hearing, her father explained that Barbara's mother suffered from schizophrenia and killed herself with a gun when his daughter was only ten. Barbara herself became suicidal with a "schizo-affective" disorder. "When Barbara's medications are working, she is a very likeable and affable sort of person," father Bob McCarty told the court in 2009. "However, in her moments of mania or depression, she is very, very hard to like or love."

The Admin Unit's other characters can be equally menacing. One of Ana's longtime housemates was Kristen Gilbert, the veterans' hospital nurse from Massachusetts who killed four patients with massive injections of adrenaline and tried to snuff out two others in her care. "Her patients were weakened soldiers who had marched against Hitler, battled Tojo in the South Pacific, or risked the terror of bamboo prisons along the Ho Chi Minh Trail," the *Boston Globe* wrote in 2000. "Gilbert, thirty-two, is a calculating predator, nothing less than a serial murderer in a white lab coat who attacked her victims at the Department of Veterans Affairs Medical Center here with needles of poison." A federal prosecutor agreed, calling her a "shell of a human being" who dispatched her victims with overdoses of epinephrine, making their hearts race out of control to the point of failure.[270]

Ana's cellmates also have included Emma Coronel Aispuro, the former beauty queen who helped her husband, Mexican drug lord Joaquin "El Chapo" Guzmán, escape from prison and smuggle at least 450 kilograms of cocaine and 90 kilograms of heroin into the United States; Lynne Stewart, the disgraced lawyer who willfully passed messages from terrorist Sheikh Omar Abdel-Rahman, the "Blind Sheikh," to his violent followers in Egypt; and Marius Mason, formerly known as Marie Mason, the Earth Liberation Front anarchist and convicted arsonist.

Robert Danage is an expert on the Admin Unit. He was a supervisory chaplain at the Carswell prison and was in and out of the maximum-security cells several times a week from 2006 to 2015. Admin time, he said, is hard time. "In prison period, but specifically in that Unit, it's very dehumanizing, very drab, very mundane, very dark and depressive and lonely and fearful. Prisons are very predatory, especially in [the] Admin Unit," Danage said. "You can seriously get hurt if you make one misstep and cross the line on any given day by another inmate."

Danage knew Ana and found her to be quiet and respectful. "She went about her business. And did her time." Ana occasionally would seek out a Catholic priest for counseling and spent her free time reading nonfiction, exercising in the outdoor pen, and translating her mother Emilia's historical novel about her grandfather into English. "I have started to learn relaxation techniques with the prison psychologists," Ana wrote in 2013. "The techniques have helped me be less heavy with myself and others, and helped me mentally separate from my environment. The psychologists here are really good and truthfully so are the chaplains."

The Admin Unit is so compact, just twenty or so cells around common rooms with TVs and tables and board games, that it's impossible to completely disappear. "There are no secrets in prison. There are too many cameras and too many busybodies. Everybody knows what's going on with everybody," Pastor Danage said. The inmates are forced to interact. "The Unit is so confined, you're going to see them in the cafeteria. You're going to see them in the TV room. You're going to hear about things that happen to them if they do something and the officers have to come in and lock them up." And in the fishbowl, life's small moments take on greater significance. "You knew about whether or not somebody got a letter, or somebody got money on their commissary [account]," the chaplain added. "There are no secrets in prison, trust me."

Pastor Danage has worked in prison ministry nearly his entire adult life and has an avuncular, forgiving bedside manner. There's no sinner he's met who isn't deserving of redemption. "Some of the most decent people I know on the face of the earth are locked up in jail," he said. "I've always kind of felt like God had a love and a grace for broken people who happened to have broken the law. I, myself, was a lawbreaker at one point. And so I believe in mercy and grace and redemption, no matter how heinous the crime may have been."

There's arguably no one in Admin Unit history who has committed a more heinous crime than Lisa Montgomery. In 2004, the mother of four drove from her Kansas farm to Missouri ostensibly to buy a puppy from Bobbie Jo Stinnett, a twenty-three-year-old dog breeder who was eight months pregnant. What Montgomery did next is unthinkable. She strangled Stinnett with a rope and then cut her living fetus from her womb with a knife. The baby girl survived and Montgomery took her away, drove home, and attempted to pass the child off as her own.

Lisa Montgomery was caught and easily convicted. Her defense attorney claimed at trial that Montgomery was delusional and had a rare mental condition that causes a woman to falsely believe she is pregnant. The legal strategy failed, and Montgomery was sentenced to death. Her lawyer had underplayed the serious sexual trauma and mental abuse Lisa endured as a child. Jurors never heard how Montgomery's alcoholic stepfather began to rape her when she was around thirteen, even bringing friends to join in.

Awaiting execution at the Admin Unit, Montgomery opened up to Pastor Danage. "Lisa was very active in the chapel program. She made a faith commitment and a faith confession" about her gruesome crime, he said. "She talked to me about it. She felt remorseful about it. She knew it was wrong, evil, and wicked and she would cry about it. She asked me to pray for her."

Remarkably, Lisa Montgomery was the only real friend Ana made in prison in over twenty years, three sources confirmed. Ana bonded with one of the Admin Unit's most broken of the broken. "Now her and Lisa were very close and that's not uncommon," Danage said. "I mean, you will find someone that you can enjoy or confide in or be around that was nonthreatening. And so I think Lisa was that person for her."

Pastor Danage said that Ana must have uncovered Lisa's humanity, like he did, and stopped focusing on her crime. "What Lisa did, what Ana did, what other ladies did that got them there, they no longer had the opportunity to do that. So if you did something heinous and stupid and sinister and evil, Lisa couldn't do that in the Admin Unit. So you saw a part of Lisa that was quite different from what she did." The Admin Unit, Danage added, has an equalizing effect. "One thing about being in prison, everybody wears khakis, everybody gets counted at the same time, everybody gets treated the same way. So ain't no sense in you pointing your finger at me for what I did, because you're here too."

In letters home, Ana confided that she had made a friend—a friend who happened to be on death row. Consequently, their time together was short. On January 13, 2021, Lisa Montgomery was executed by lethal injection at the federal prison complex in Terre Haute, Indiana. Her death marked the first federal execution of a woman in nearly seventy years. Ana's only prison friend was fifty two years old.[271]

Chapter 40.

"YOU ARE A COWARD"

"Isn't that what you wanted? To punish this country? Or maybe secretly you had to punish Mom, too, because she is the one who really suffered."

—LUCY MONTES LETTER TO ANA, NOVEMBER 2010

For nine years after Ana's arrest, Lucy held her tongue. Out of pity. "My role at that point in her life was to be a sister to her and not an FBI employee." She was furious with Ana, of course, but what would be the point of reaming out someone locked in a dungeon? So Lucy quietly carried on, raising Matthew and Emily as a single Mom, translating drug-dealer chatter for the Bureau, and doing her best to boost Emilia's spirits with a daughter behind bars. That last task wasn't always easy. Lucy had often felt that her mother ignored her and showed an obvious preference for Ana. Sometimes they clashed, as mothers and daughters can do. Lucy was struggling trying to raise kids on her own, and Emilia was despondent over her daughter's imprisonment. "We were both going through a very difficult time and my mother couldn't be there for me when I needed her," Lucy said.

One day, during her regular weekly phone call with Ana, Emilia mentioned that she and Lucy had been fighting. Ana grew upset and decided to jump to her mother's defense. She dashed off an angry letter to Lucy, advising her to see a psychologist to treat "the rage that she still held" against their mother.

Lucy couldn't believe the gall and lack of self-awareness. She was not about to allow a traitor with her own closet full of unresolved issues judge her. Lucy fired off a typewritten retort dripping with vengeance and bilious indignation.

"What a cruel letter. It was extremely harsh, even for you," Lucy's November 6, 2010, letter began. "I thought now would be a good time for me to tell you exactly what I think about you, too..."

Lucy saw or talked to Emilia practically every day in Florida, so she began by educating her jailed sister on the hidden impact of her arrest. "You should know you ruined Mom's life. Every morning she wakes up devastated by what you did and where you are. Every night she goes to bed thinking the same thing. She thinks about it all the time." She added a line that must have hit home. "I've heard her cry because of you." Lucy then reminded Ana of their mother's already tough lot in life. "It's not enough that her parents and only brother all died before she was 30... Or that she was married to a violent man for 16 years and raised four children by herself. No, you had to ruin her final years she should be living in peace and contentment."

Then, Lucy enumerated Ana's countless sins. "You have no loyalty towards any of us. You betrayed your family, you betrayed all your friends. Everyone who loves you was betrayed by you, including the man who wanted to marry you. Tito and Carlos don't want to talk to you, and I don't blame them. There is no forgiveness for what you did." What's more, she wrote, Ana's reckless actions didn't only harm her inner circle. "You betrayed your co-workers and your employer, and you betrayed your nation. You worked for an evil megalomaniac who shares or sells our secrets to our enemies. You helped our enemies."

Next, Lucy chopped down Ana's rationalizations. "You are a

coward. You could have stood up for your principles openly and acted on your beliefs in a public way, because in this country you have the freedom to do so. But you hid, like a coward, to punish them in secret." Finally, Lucy laid bare her sister's true motivations. "Why did you really do what you did? Because it made you feel powerful. Yes, Ana, you wanted to feel powerful. You're no altruist, it wasn't the 'greater good' you were concerned for, it was yourself."

Lucy signed off with a flourish. "Just don't ever tell me *I* need to see a psychologist for rage. Your rage has ruined your life..."

For Emilia, Ana's arrest continues to cause deep pain. "Ana Belén, you were misguided," Emilia wrote to Ana in prison in 2002. "You have no idea of our disappointment."[272]

Despite her family's disapproval, prison hasn't mellowed or rehabilitated Ana. "...I am a person who is extremely rigid, compulsive, tied to stupid habits, and if I forgot to mention RIGID, characteristics that have only gotten worse with age and makes my stay here more difficult..." she once wrote.[273] If anything, arrest and conviction only intensified her self-righteousness.

In a remarkable letter to Lucy's then seventeen-year-old son, Matthew, Ana openly embraced her zealotry. She seemed to have few regrets about her duplicitous life as a spy. "Prison is one of the last places I would have ever chosen to be in, but some things in life are worth going to prison for—or worth doing and then killing yourself before you have to spend too much time in prison, which is my personal preference." Quite a sentiment to share with a high schooler.

The 2010 letter to Matthew is a fourteen-page, single-spaced word bomb. In it, Ana can be loving and even light with her teenaged nephew ("...when you are a millionaire I won't ever ask you for money.") But mostly the letter is a disjointed justification of Ana's criminality peppered with lengthy diatribes on US atrocities from 1898 to the present. Why did she spy? "I believed in the early 1980s that US policies toward Latin America were very unfair…it was my responsibility, my duty, as a human being to help the Nicaraguans and later the Cubans." Why not use conventional means to help bullied nations? "US policies towards these two countries were impossible to change legally…"[274]

Ana crammed every inch of her precious prison notepaper with factoids to win over her nephew. While noting that "overall the US is an admirable country," she then packs page after page with examples of inexcusable US behavior around the globe. It's a survey course on American interventionism taught by an old-school leftist. "During WWII the US deliberately killed hundreds of thousands of German and Japanese civilian citizens," she writes. And: "Before 1979 the US had spent decades supporting dictators in Nicaragua…" And: "I also suggest that you read about the sea mines that the US put in a Nicaraguan harbor…" And: "I personally witnessed certain (not all) State Department officials being extremely rude to Cuban officials…"

There are footnotes to young Matthew ("See P.S.2 on p. 12"), homework assignments ("Look up the subject 'Iran-Contra Scandal'"), and obscure asides ("In the 1980s the US supported Jonas Savimbi and his UNITA organization that attacked the Angolan government…") But the truest sentiments come close to the end, when Ana comments that a small percentage of Americans are doing all the fighting and dying in Iraq and Afghanistan. "Do you plan to do anything to help your country (or the world) also?" she goads Lucy's son. "Is it fair to make a few Americans sacrifice so much so that other Americans can live an easy (comparatively) life and overeat? I'm confused about what it means to be a patriotic American. Maybe you can explain it to me."

Chapter 41:

RELEASE

"Upon release from imprisonment, the defendant shall be on supervised release for a term of five (5) years with conditions."

—ANA MONTES SENTENCING TERMS, OCTOBER 16, 2002

On January 6, 2023, Ana is scheduled to walk free. She will have spent twenty-one years, three months, and seventeen days behind bars. That's a generous reduction of her twenty-five-year sentence, nearly four years off for good behavior.

Once freed, Ana will live under strict conditions for five years, not allowed to use a computer with online access without the written approval of her probation officer, and barred from having contact with Cuban officials or any foreign government or agents. She'll be subjected to drug tests, unannounced computer searches, and frequent check-ins with her probation officer. She's forfeited her government retirement pay and will have to find a job. She is prohibited from discussing classified materials for life.

Ana still refuses to apologize and has made her loyalties clear. "I owe allegiance to principles and not to any one country or government or person," she wrote from prison. "I don't owe allegiance to the US or to Cuba…or to the Castro brothers or even to God."

Lucy Montes knows all about allegiance, too. After Ana's arrest, she struggled with how, or even if, to support her sister. "I didn't know if I should talk to her. I didn't know if I should write to her. I didn't know if I should find her a lawyer," Lucy said. She asked Gino Giannotti, supervisor of Miami's Cuban counterintelligence squad, for guidance. "His response to me was, 'Be a sister to her, we'll handle the rest.' So that's what I've tried to do the last, what, twenty-one years. I've tried to be a sister to her."

Lucy has almost always lived up to that tenet—and not piled on. "The investigation was not my job; that was the job of the FBI. Her prosecution was not my job; that was the job of the attorneys at DOJ. And it's not my job to punish her because that was the job of the Bureau of Prisons." And now that Ana is so close to freedom, Lucy is trying to only look forward. "She's completed her sentence and she's been punished enough in my mind," Lucy said. "She did her time and now it's her chance to start life over again."

When Ana leaves the Admin Unit and walks out of Carswell for good, Lucy is hoping she'll get the first call. Ana will likely fly immediately to Puerto Rico with her cousin, Miriam. While there's "nothing acceptable" about Ana's actions, Lucy said she'll help her sister reunite with Emilia. Lucy has even contemplated letting Ana live with her for a short while, if she truly needs the help and asks for it.

Making peace with Ana will be incredibly difficult. But Lucy is willing to try. "I'm her family. I'm her sister," she said, almost trying to convince herself. "I can't turn my back on her."

EPILOGUE

There's a temptation to discount Cuba as a besotted old tiger, eager to harm the United States but lacking the fangs and fury to pull off the job. The KGB is gone and the Cuban Missile Crisis is a vague memory now, a cautionary tale that grandparents like to tell. For many Americans, if they still think of Cuba at all, the island nation is just another sunny locale, a clichéd fantasyland of vintage Chevys, cheap Cohibas, and sugary mojitos by the pool.

But as Ana Montes is released from prison, emerging back in society after two decades in a Bush-era time capsule, she'll be a walking reminder of the other Cuba. The Cuba that to this day operates a totalitarian regime that spies on its people and stifles dissent. A Cuba that covets the information that the United States holds dear and runs a scrappy spy agency capable of prying those classified secrets loose. Trained by the Soviet spy services and run by hard-line Communist party members, the DGI remains hungry. And mercenary. "They're good, and they don't have any restraint," said Hector Pesquera, former FBI special agent in charge of the Miami Field Office. "They can do whatever they want. They can do [it] to whoever they want. It doesn't matter. There's no law... There's no policy, there's no manuals. There's nothing. You do what you have to do to get the information."

Michelle Van Cleave was for years the National Counterintelligence Executive, the head of all US counterintelligence, in a position established by Congress in the wake of the Aldrich

Ames spy scandal. She also ran the Montes damage assessment team and is well versed in the harm Cuba poses. "I think most Americans would be astonished by the extent to which foreign intelligence services have been able to steal our Nation's national security secrets, often with impunity," she told Congress. The DGI is Russia's "star pupil," Van Cleave said, ensuring that Cuban intelligence operations in the United States are "painfully successful." As Cuba vacuums up American intelligence, it often trades it to the highest bidder. "There is a continuing market for such stolen U.S. secrets, which can be sold or bartered to third party states or terrorist organizations that have their own uses for the information," she said.

As we reflect on the Montes saga, the casualty count runs long. Yes, there's the unauthorized disclosure of costly collection systems and mounds of top-secret data. There's the unmasking of American operatives hidden deep within Havana. And, highly likely, there's the violent death of a US Green Beret father of two, plus forty-three Salvadoran soldiers who fought alongside him in the jungle. Ana is responsible for all of that and more. As she conceded: "Espionage always hurts someone."

In her own letters from prison, Ana once played amateur media critic. She mocked the *Washington Post Magazine* cover story I wrote about her in 2013, suggesting it might have been better suited to *People Magazine* given the article's focus on personality and the "diametrically opposite" way Lucy and Ana conducted their lives.[275] Ana wrote that she would much have preferred a clinical analysis of *why* she spied, with a history lesson for readers on the US attempt's to "unjustly overthrow the government of Nicaragua in the 1980s," and other examples of what American administrations have done to foreign countries from the nineteenth century to today. In Ana's recounting, gone would be any personal accountability, replaced by fact-laden stories of American hostility and imperialism worldwide.

Which of course misses the point. For the sake of argument,

let's concede that the United States has acted as a bully where and when it could. Let's even assume that American behavior against Cuba has been counterproductive, cruel, and unjustified. Many reasonable people feel that way. But the point is that the politics, the *why*, ultimately don't matter. Ana's behavior was dangerous, immoral, and traitorous. She's not more virtuous than Hanssen or Ames because she was motivated by ideology instead of cash. Illegal is illegal and wrong is wrong. Ana had countless other legal ways to protest, condemn, and shape American foreign policy. Spying wasn't her only option, it was simply her most expedient one. And one that placed her at the center of attention. It was a cowardly shortcut for someone who, as Lucy wrote, became obsessed with power. "You're no altruist," Lucy told her sister, you were concerned for yourself.

Beyond the Pentagon and the halls of Washington, Ana's spying produced many victims. There's Emilia, Ana's mother, who has spent her golden years haunted by her daughter's imprisonment and infamy. There's Roger, the ex-boyfriend, who was thoroughly humiliated. For years, Ana sent him letter after letter—prison musings which Roger studiously ignored. There's Mimi, the college friend, who feared for years that she had somehow offended Ana and caused a break. There's Tito and Joan and Carlos, and Ana's nieces and nephews, who have all but lost a family member.

And then there's Lucy, who began imagining that maybe she was to blame for the broken relationship with her only sister. Ana's decision in 1985 to work for a hostile nation continues to reverberate today, dividing and devastating a uniquely American family in ways she could never have imagined.

★ ★ ★ ★ ★

AUTHOR'S NOTE

I first learned about Ana Montes on the day she was arrested, September 21, 2001. At the time, I was a producer and off-air reporter for NBC News, based in the network's Washington Bureau. Teamed with NBC's Justice Correspondent Pete Williams, I had been covering the FBI and Justice Department for years when the arrest of a Defense Department analyst on espionage charges hit the wires. But in the chaos after the 9/11 terror attacks on New York and Washington, there simply was no time to chase a story on an American woman caught spying for Cuba. Pete and I were reporting nonstop on the FBI's massive investigation of the 9/11 terrorists for the NBC *Nightly News,* the *TODAY Show*, and MSNBC. The spy tale would have to wait.

About a week or so later, I learned that I had a connection to the accused Cuban agent. Ana Montes had purchased her apartment on Macomb Street from my college roommate and dear friend John Bredar, a talented documentary filmmaker. I had spent countless hours with John and his wife inside Apartment 20 at 3039 Macomb Street, NW. As I read the FBI's criminal complaint, with details on how Ana used to crank up a shortwave radio in her apartment to get the latest coded messages from Havana, I could imagine the look of her living room and kitchen on the second floor of her redbrick apartment building, first door on the left. My good buddy used to live in Ana's apartment, and I had hung out there. The coincidence stayed with me.

I also happened to know one of Ana's longtime friends. Journalist Gideon Gil and I worked together as young reporters for the *Trenton Times* in New Jersey in the 1980s. It was a small, tight-knit newsroom at 500 Perry Street, and Gideon and I were friendly back in the day. Ana Montes attended Gideon's wedding and had become his friend. Gideon's wife, Lisa, was Ana's college roommate at UVa.

These connections, while small, have propelled my interest in the Ana Montes story for nearly two decades. So many people have helped me along the way, graciously sharing their time and memories to chronicle one of the most remarkable, yet least known, spy sagas in American history.

Under the terms of Ana's plea bargain with the government, she has been barred from speaking to reporters and authors. I couldn't have interviewed her even if she had wanted to. Fortunately, her family, friends, coworkers, and the investigators who debriefed her have shared their first-hand accounts. To research this book, I conducted more than three hundred interviews with at least a hundred and twenty-five people. Some sources were interviewed more than a dozen times. Wherever possible, all sources are identified by name. I also drew on court records and transcripts, the classified CIA behavioral analysis of Ana I obtained, congressional testimony, the DOD Inspector General's report, and many other primary documents. *Code Name Blue Wren* was made richer by exclusive access to the unpublished autobiographies penned by Ana's parents, Alberto and Emilia; by handwritten letters from Ana, Lucy, Emilia, and others; and by hundreds of photographs, slides, and old paper records documenting generations of the Montes and Badillo families.

It all starts with Lucy. I first interviewed Lucy Montes in 2007 and she has patiently humored my endless questions ever since. She let me quote her extensively for a cover article I wrote for the *Washington Post Magazine* in 2013, has indulged my Sisyphean quest to develop this story into a dramatic television series, and never flinched in assisting me write this book. Whether in

Washington, in Lucy's kitchen in Florida, or over the phone, she has been kind, honest, and understanding in dealing with a writer who is probing a sister's treachery and a family's most difficult moments. I will be forever grateful to Lucy for trusting me to tell her family's story. And I hope Ana will be understanding of why Lucy felt compelled to speak out so forcefully.

I also met Scott Carmichael in 2007, and he has never hesitated to share his side of the story and answer every last question. Scott has a great laugh and a self-deprecating manner, and it's been a pleasure to interview him in Maryland, Wisconsin, or parts unknown. Lately, he's been driving around the country in a forty-two-foot-long "fifth wheel," whatever that is. I appreciate Scott's help, especially from his Forest River Cedar Creek Hathaway Edition traveling home.

From the earliest days, the FBI has helped me understand the nuances of its Blue Wren investigation. Mike Kortan and Bill Carter, previous leaders in the FBI's public affairs office, made early and important introductions. Steve McCoy, the lead case agent of the Montes investigation, has faithfully endured my curiosity for fifteen years. Steve has proved to be a reliable and even-tempered chronicler of the Montes case, and I can't thank him enough. Pete Lapp also provided crucial help from the very beginning. More than a dozen FBI supervisors, special agents, and analysts spoke to me, some on the record and some only on background. I thank the Society of Former Special Agents of the FBI for connecting me with several Bureau officials who otherwise might never have shared their contributions to the Montes case.

The DIA's help was equally important. Vice Admiral Thomas Wilson, the former DIA director, sat for a long interview and explained why he kept Montes on staff even after he knew she was working for the other side. Chris Simmons filled in blanks on the earliest days of the investigation, and his knowledge of Cuba's intelligence agencies proved invaluable. Karl "Gator"

James shared memorable insights on the case, as did DIA Counterintelligence Officer Mark Ritter and his colleagues on the Montes debrief team. Many of Ana's coworkers and fellow analysts were eager to explain the anger and betrayal they felt, as were Ana's bosses, Marty Scheina and Dave Curtin. I am in their debt. I especially would like to thank DIA historian Orlando Pacheco and Amanda Schuler Zepp of DIA's Office of Corporate Communications, for assisting with this project. (As the DIA lawyers helpfully reminded me: "The opinions and stories shared by Defense Intelligence Agency employees were provided solely in their personal capacities and their views on Ana Montes do not reflect those of DIA or the US Government.")

I couldn't have fully pieced together *Code Name Blue Wren* without Ana's friends and relatives. Ana "Mimi" Colon shared letters and photographs and stories, and laughing with her eased the tension of completing such an ambitious project. Horace Jennings, who dated Marta Velázquez and was friends with Ana, was a valued source. Roberto Álvarez, who dated Ana at SAIS and today serves as Minister of Foreign Affairs for the Dominican Republic, didn't complain once when I insisted on keeping him in the book after he became his country's foreign affairs chief. A gentleman.

Joan Andrzejewski, Ana's former sister-in-law, helped me better understand Ana and the complicated dynamics of the Montes family—and greatly expanded my pathetic knowledge of all things *Star Trek*. Michelle Manthey, Ana's stepsister, bravely recounted how Dr. Alberto Montes physically and emotionally abused her family. I will always appreciate Michelle's honesty and the trust she placed in me.

For me, the most surprising revelation in my reporting for *Code Name Blue Wren* was the discovery of the former NSA analyst whom I call Elena Valdez. Elena put herself at risk twice during the Ana Montes case. First, she was threatened with arrest and termination for going behind the back of the FBI to let

DIA investigators know about the Cuban UNSUB case. Her tenacity broke the case wide-open. More recently, she took a second risk in speaking to an author about the Blue Wren investigation and her struggles with the FBI and her own agency. It's incredibly rare for officials of the National Security Agency to talk to the media; Elena had never even met a reporter before. I'm honored that she decided to tell me her story, and in the process revealed the fabrications that the Montes investigators have been peddling for years to protect the NSA's role in the investigation. I look forward to learning Ana's reaction when she finds out that it was a Cuban-born woman, who despises the Castro regime, who helped take Ana down.

Outside the United States, two talented investigative reporters helped me advance the story in their home countries. In Sweden, Ola Westerberg tracked down Marta Velázquez and is the first reporter to ever question her about the active espionage charges against her. Ola is an award-winning journalist and editor based in Stockholm. A member of the International Consortium of Investigative Journalists (ICIJ), he has worked on projects such as the Paradise Papers and Pandora Papers, exposing top-level financial crime. With photographer Lina Nydahl, he assisted in obtaining the first photos of Marta enjoying her freedom just outside of Stockholm.

In Argentina, the enterprising journalist Candela Ini conducted the first interview with Eduardo Fernández, Ana's old friend and early political mentor. Candela also ran the traps on Ana's former boyfriend, Ricardo, the Argentinian leftist whom Ana fell for during her junior year abroad in Spain. Candela is an industrious and connected reporter at La Nacion in Buenos Aires, and I thank her and Ola for their help.

Behind the scenes, there was a small army propping me up while I was simultaneously reporting and writing. Special thanks to "R.J." Gardella, my friend and former NBC News colleague, who tracked down many of the infamous prisoners who became

Ana's neighbors at the Carswell prison's tiny Admin Unit. My
interns at Seven Oaks Media Group ran down countless factoids.
The indefatigable Kevin Bohn has offered guidance and will
soon be badgering TV bookers and others until they relent. I
had additional research assistance from the archivists at the Topeka & Shawnee County Public Library in Kansas and at SAIS's
Mason Library in Washington. Historian Margaret Power, who
is writing a biography of Ana's radical relative, "Don Juan" Corretjer Montes, provided helpful background on Puerto Rican
nationalist movements.

I'm a first-time book author and couldn't have had a better
editor to guide me than Peter Joseph at Hanover Square Press.
He kept the trains moving with good cheer and made countless edits to the manuscript that sharpened the writing and improved the flow. Peter and Eden Railsback make for a talented
team and I'm grateful for their help. I've been equally fortunate
to work with the clever agents at the Javelin literary agency.
Robin Sproul is an old friend from our days at competing TV
news networks, and immediately understood the news value and
drama inherent in *Code Name Blue Wren*. She teamed me with
Javelin founders Keith Urbahn and Matt Latimer, who have
been invaluable partners.

But mostly I am indebted to my friends for encouraging me
throughout the creation of *Code Name Blue Wren*. Mark Upde-
grove, the presidential historian and bestselling author, reviewed
the manuscript and made it better. I remain sorry that I stole
most of Mark's shoes from his bedroom when we were fifteen.
His mother never forgave me, but Mark stayed loyal. College
buddy Mike O'Shea made several insightful improvements to
the manuscript and encouraged the parallel construction of the
Ana and Lucy timelines. His long and successful career as a lawyer clearly hasn't hampered his narrative abilities. High school
friend and former journalist Kevin Murphy weighed in with
keen suggestions from Myanmar. He is not to be blamed for any

campy phrases that survived the final edit. Dave McKenna, Bill Rademaekers, John Bredar, Mike Cantor, Tom Hardart, Gary Cohen, Grant Cooper, and so many others are always there for me. What a gift my friends are. I'd also like to thank my fellow Jersey pal and producing partner Anthony Mastromauro of Identity Media for supporting our project through thick and thin. Aaron Sterling and Rob Hopson kept me healthy during this long slog.

Finally, some love for my family. My brothers Danny and Andy were with me every step of the way, and their loyalty these past few months has been remarkable. My mother, who taught me my love for writing and my disdain for magic, has been lobbying me for a mention in the book. Mission accomplished. Love you, Moms.

I dedicate this book to my children, Zach, Phoebe, and Ben. I hope that at some point in your promising careers that you'll love something so much that you'll gladly devote every weekend and evening to it. If you're lucky, you'll get stuck working on the same damn project for fifteen years. Mom and I are so proud of you and can't wait to see what you have to offer the world.

—*Jim Popkin*
Washington, DC
September 2022

AFTERWORD

On January 6, 2023, just three days after the publication of *Code Name Blue Wren*, Ana Montes was released from federal prison. She flew to Puerto Rico, her parents' homeland and Ana's refuge during countless family vacations. Within days, she quickly dispelled the notion that two decades of prison had cowed her or softened her worldview.

In a written statement released to the media, the convicted Cuban spy was unrepentant. She began with a personal observation. "I am more than happy to touch Puerto Rican soil again," Ana wrote in Spanish. "After two quite exhausting decades and faced with the need to earn a living again, I would like to dedicate myself to a quiet and private existence." Therefore, Montes pledged, she would decline all "media activities."

But Ana couldn't stop there. True to form, she used the spotlight of her homecoming to denigrate American foreign policy. She encouraged people to focus on "important issues" confronting the Puerto Rican people and the longstanding United States economic embargo against Cuba. "Who in the last 60 years has asked the Cuban people if they want the United States to impose a suffocating embargo that makes them suffer?" she implored. She went on, casting herself as a unique moral authority and asking for attention to be paid to the "pressing need for global cooperation to stop and reverse our destruction of our environment."

With no hint of self-awareness, Ana closed her public statement with an unfortunate turn of phrase. She stated that while she was irrelevant, "there are serious problems in our global homeland that demand attention and a demonstration of brotherly love." Brotherly love. Left unsaid in her coming-home statement was any demonstration of love or concern for her brother, Tito, or sister, Lucy, stalwart FBI employees who were devastated by Ana's epic deceits. Like an out-of-touch Hollywood actor on Oscar night, Ana exited stage right without so much as an acknowledgment of her family, who had suffered so much.

In early January, Ana and her legal team also released a fresh photograph for publication. Shot from above, Ana is smiling, hands folded in her lap. Pink lipstick, concealer, and black eyeliner help blunt the ravages of twenty-one years of isolation and fluorescent lighting. Like her iconic FBI mug shot, Ana poses again for the camera in a blue sleeveless blouse. Yet the images are markedly different. Patches of gray now streak her hair, and crow's-feet feather out from her eyes. But this transformation runs deeper. Ana looks happy, healthy, even confident in the new headshot. The subtext seems to be "I'm back. You threw prison at me and it didn't change me."

The defiant messaging makes sense considering Ana's fiery new legal adviser. The defense lawyer who distributed Ana's statement and photo to the world is Linda Backiel. Born in Wilmington, Delaware, Backiel now works in San Juan, Puerto Rico, as a lawyer representing criminals, death-row clients, and militant Puerto Ricans seeking independence from the United States. Backiel writes articles and poems for a self-described Socialist magazine[276] and once told the *New York Times* that the US embargo of Cuba is "a fossilized Cold War fiasco" that has caused "universal condemnation."[277] The *Times* also reports that she previously represented three Cuban intelligence agents, part of the Wasp Network, who were convicted of espionage in 2001 for spying on Cuban American exile leaders and gathering intelligence on US military bases in Florida. Backiel once publicly defended the Wasp members by writing they "were working with the Cuban Government to protect Cuba from invasion and terrorism organized, funded and launched from Miami…"[278]

Another of Backiel's notorious clients was Kathy Boudin, the militant Weather Underground member who served twenty-three years in prison for murder[279]; Boudin played a role in the 1981 robbery of a Brink's armored truck that resulted in the killing of two police officers and a security guard. As a criminal defense lawyer, Backiel fiercely advocates for her clients. "But especially the guilty. The reviled. The obstreperous and the incorrigible," she wrote in 2014.[280]

Backiel's uncompromising advocacy once went too far. Three decades ago, Backiel was imprisoned in Pennsylvania "because she refuses to testify before a Federal grand jury investigating a client who the authorities say jumped bail," the *New York Times* reported in 1991.[281] Backiel had been helping to represent Elizabeth Ann Duke, a member of a revolutionary group that was storing a cache of arms and explosives in a shed in Doylestown, PA. The FBI arrested Duke, but Backiel got Duke out on bail. After Duke escaped and penned a note for reporters describing her reasons for fleeing, prosecutors asked Backiel to provide access to her client's original note or verify a copy. Backiel refused. "I can't be turned into a witness for the prosecution," the *New York Times* quoted her as saying at the time. "That's not my job." Backiel's defiant stand landed the lawyer in prison for six months on a contempt of court charge.

Ana Montes is Backiel's kind of client. In Puerto Rico, she has helped position Ana as a returning hero. With assistance from cousin Miriam Montes Mosk, Ana sent a letter of thanks to her closest fans. "I never imagined that people would respond in such a way, and you have my profound gratitude," she wrote in February 2023. "I would love to meet you all personally but after consulting with my lawyer, I have decided reluctantly that I should not meet with people outside of the family, in general for now. The limitations that my parole imposes on me are very strict."

Ana reveals in her letter, posted on Facebook, that local allies have been assisting her since her release from prison. She writes that her fans' supportive messages "have mitigated the difficulties that accompany my return to normal life." Ana adds that, "thanks to the support of all of you I have been able to respond to basic needs, such as going to medical and dental appointments, and acquiring the much needed phone."[282]

Online, support for Montes is even stronger. There are multiple Montes affinity groups on Facebook, including Solidaridad con Ana Belén Montes, which has 7,600 followers, and gushing Reddit threads with headlines such as "This Absolute Queen Is Getting Freed." There are Montes fans from nearly every corner. On Ana's birthday in February, about four hundred Facebook devotees left warm greetings. "You are our guide to a world of peace. Congratulations to this faithful and fighting warrior," one commenter said. "Have a great birthday, we love you Ana," another wrote. "Take care of yourself. A kiss and an eternal hug." After Ana's new portrait was released, the compliments flew in. "That is the look and smile of someone who has complied with her conscience and has emerged unscathed from everything she suffered for it," another Facebook booster wrote.

At sixty-six, and with less than five years to go before her probation ends, Ana Montes has a full life ahead of her. Writing and public speaking seem like natural next steps. How long will it be before Montes is invited to American universities with a long history of embracing radical views, or perhaps even to Havana itself, to rail about the injustices of American foreign policy? She'll likely have rapt audiences. As one of Ana's most devoted Havana-based followers once wrote to her on a public forum, "Congratulations sister combatant, patriotic friend, role model, come soon, we miss you."

ENDNOTES

---

1 "candidly, neither is Lynette." The author conducted interviews with Lynette "Squeaky" Fromme in March and April 2022

2 "It didn't go off." The quote comes from *Squeaky: The Life and Times of Lynette Alice Fromme,* by Jess Bravin, 1997, St. Martin's Press, as reported by witnesses. In an interview with the *Code Name Blue Wren* author, Fromme claims she never intended to kill President Ford, but was merely trying to raise awareness of environmental issues. She said: "I knew how to put the bullet in the chamber, but it [firing the gun] wasn't something I wanted to do"

3 "my husband, my brother, my father, my son." Sourcing for Fromme's long prison career includes court records and contemporaneous newspaper articles. "My husband, my brother…" is from Bravin's excellent *Squeaky*

4 "in late 2002…" In a "Secret" psychological profile of Montes obtained by the author, the CIA reported that Montes was "jailed in Texas in late 2002." The behavioral profile was written by the CIA's Counterintelligence Center Analysis Group, in 2005, and titled *Ana Montes's Espionage: Understanding the Interrelationship Between Ideology and Personality Development*

5 "as far as the sixth grade…" Details of Alberto's early life are included in his unpublished autobiography written in May 1995, and from author interviews with Lucy Montes

6 "I had a lovely childhood…" *Baltimore Sun,* June 16, 1976

7 "I spent my first 18 years." From Emilia Montes's unpublished autobiography, "San Vicente Memories: Childhood in a Sugar Hacienda"

8 "Census takers…" In 1960, the US Census Bureau reported Topeka's population as 91.8% White and 7.7% Black. The Census didn't even track Hispanic population then

9 "The United States has had trouble…" *Wichita Eagle,* September 3, 1958

10 "between Mexican-American boys and White girls." *Americano: My Journey to the Dream*, by Thomas Rodriguez, Amigos Publishing Co., 2004

11 "a big dog…" Emilia Montes email, 2017

12 "General Omar Bradley…" Background on Menninger comes from *A Psychiatrist's World: The Selected Papers of Karl Menninger, M.D.*, Viking Press, 1959; and *Menninger: The Family & the Clinic*, University Press of Kansas, 1990

13 "An early ad…" *Menninger: The Family & the Clinic*, illustration

14 "A 'total environment' for its clinic patients…" *New York Times*, July 19, 1990

15 "In childhood parents…" From *The Human Mind*, by Karl A. Menninger, Alfred A. Knopf. Originally published in 1930

16 "It is much easier…" *New York Times* obituary, July 19, 1990

17 "almost unbelievable cruelties…" From *A Psychiatrist's World*. This is a reprint of an article by Dr. Karl Menninger in *The Atlantic Monthly* in February 1939 called "Women, Men, and Hate."

18 Author interview with Dr. Walter Menninger at his Topeka home, February 23, 2022

19 Dr. Herbert Modlin obituary, 2007

20 "The paper was read…" From "Narcotics Addiction in Physicians," in the *American Journal of Psychiatry*, October 1964

21 "Just two years later…" From the Emilia Montes unpublished autobiography, "San Vicente Memories: Childhood in a Sugar Hacienda"

22 "radical" nationalist youth group…" From *Puerto Rico in the American Century: A History Since 1898*, by Cesar Ayala, 2009. For "radical" description, see *Rebeldes al poder: los grupos y la lucha ideológica (1959-2000)*, by José Carlos Arroyo Muñoz 2003. "Among the popular youth, these were the most radical…"

23 "Sheppard stipulated…" From the hospital's website.

24 "He was a very strict disciplinarian,… *Miami Herald*, June 16, 2002

25 "six people were killed…" *Baltimore Magazine* feature story on the 1968 riots

26 "You may think…" Alberto Montes unpublished autobiography, May 1995

27 "Just one month..." Michelle Monthey, Alberto's stepdaughter, says her mother married Alberto July 9, 1977

28 "Nancy and Alberto stayed married..." The divorce took place in 1995, according to court records the author accessed in Hawaii

29 "gregarious Puerto Rican..." *Baltimore Sun*, August 15, 1975

30 *Miami Herald*, June 16, 2002

31 *Baltimore Sun*, August 15, 1975

32 "barriers of prejudice..." *Baltimore Sun*, "Growing Spanish-speaking community here feels miffed," June 16, 1976

33 "government hat-tipping..." *The Evening Sun* (Baltimore), November 25, 1975

34 "Hereford dug in his heels..." *New York Times*, February 11, 1976

35 "Minority Affairs Office..." *Cavalier Daily* retrospective article, November 17, 2006; and "Four Years in Review" article in the UVa 1979 yearbook, *The Corks And Curls*

36 "bastion of upper class whites..." *Cavalier Daily*, August 31, 1976

37 "There must be a terrible mistake..." Journalist Gideon Gil is married to Ana's college roommate, Lisa Huber. On Sept. 30, 2001, Gil wrote a column on Montes for the *Courier-Journal* (Louisville, KY), where he was regional editor. It was titled: "Spy or Not, A Friend's Arrest Evokes Sadness." Full disclosure: The author worked in the early 1980s with Gideon Gil at the *Trenton Times*, where they were both reporters

38 "didn't have a sorority..." From the "Four Years in Review" article, in the UVa 1979 yearbook, *The Corks And Curls*

39 "stalking her..." CIA Secret behavioral report

40 "She smoked weed..." From *True Believer: Inside the Investigation and Capture of Ana Montes, Cuba's Master Spy*, by Scott W. Carmichael, Naval Institute Press, 2007, and the CIA report

41 "She signed up..." The name of the Madrid study-abroad program comes from *True Believer*. Carmichael had access to Montes's security file. The Institute of European Studies is now known as IES Abroad

42 "She took classes..." The Ohio State University professor Richard Gunther tells the author that he interviewed Spanish politicians during this

time period and hired student typists through a local vendor in Spain. He doesn't recall Montes. His name is mentioned in *True Believer*

43 "kidnapped by right-wing squads..." *New York Times*, September 12, 1977 and January 2, 1977

44 "Most of the victims..." Author Raymond Bonner, *The Nation*, April 15, 2016

45 "attracted to the social Communist parties..." The Department of Defense Inspector General report, "Review of the Actions Taken to Deter, Detect and Investigate the Espionage Activities of Ana Belen Montes (Redacted)," June 16, 2005

46 At her Florida home, Lucy Montes maintains Ana's library. In 1991, Ricardo gave Ana the book *La Revolución es un Sueño Eterno* by Andrés Rivera, according to an inscription

47 "Yankee imperialism..." The Corretjer Montes speech appears on page 38 of a once-secret FBI memorandum on the Nationalist Party, published through the Freedom of Information Act (FOIA) and available on the FBI's "Vault" FOIA Library. Corretjer Montes delivered the speech on the day that National Party leader Pedro Albizu Campos returned to Puerto Rico after having served ten years in prison for sedition against the United States

48 "A president has to expect..." *New York Times*, November 2, 1950

49 "The messianic Albizu Campos..." *The New Yorker*, "The Dream of Puerto Rican Independence, and the Story of Heriberto Marín," by Jon Lee Anderson, December 27, 2017

50 "he wrote a letter advocating independence..." From *Spy Schools: How the CIA, FBI, and Foreign Intelligence Secretly Exploit America's Universities*, by Daniel Golden, Henry Holt, 2017

51 "Alberto's second cousin..." The grandfather of Juan Antonio Corretjer Montes was brothers with the grandfather of Alberto Montes, the grocer, explains a Montes family relative and genealogist named Dr. Nydia Hanna

52 "the voice of the armed clandestine movement..." Corretjer Montes was eulogized in *Breakthrough*, the political journal of the Prairie Fire Organizing Committee in its Spring/Summer edition of 1985. *Breakthrough* was a publication dedicated to "the Politics of Revolutionary

Anti-Imperialism," and was written by followers of the Weather Underground Organization

53 *Making the Revolution: Histories of the Latin American Left*, Cambridge University Press, 2019

54 "sentenced to ten years…" The *Breakthrough* obituary, FBI FOIA files, and *A Century of Colonialism: One Hundred Years of Puerto Rican Resistance*, by Oscar Lòpez Rivera, Duke University Press, 2007

55 "at least three arrests for Don Juan…" Corretjer Montes biographer, Margaret Power

56 "friendship with Che Guevara…" Marxists.org article

57 "armed clandestine organizations…" Ibid

58 "Sacred Heart University…" *True Believer*

59 "an opening as a clerk-typist…" The CIA report states that a friend told Montes about DOJ job openings

60 "It couldn't be that bad…" The author reached out in 2022 for comment to Eduardo's wife, Silvia Farnocchia, but she did not respond

61 Scott Carmichael book, *True Believer*. As a DIA investigator, Carmichael had access to Montes's complete job history and the government's many background investigations of her

62 "first ventured…" DOD Inspector General report

63 "GS-9 pay grade…" *True Believer*

64 A GS-4 (Government-Schedule 4 pay grade) today earns a range of $36,000 to $47,000, depending on one's "steps," or length of service. By contrast, a GS-9 salary ranges from $61,000 to $80,000. Source is FederalPay.org website

65 "three thousand students…" SAIS Catalogue for the 1982–1983 school year

66 "armed to the teeth…" Speech by President Ronald Reagan, May 1983

67 "Soviet-Cuban colony…" Speech by President Ronald Reagan, October 27, 1983

68 "most left-wing" professor…" *Spy Schools*. In an interview with the *Blue Wren* author in 2022, Gleijesis again said: "So I would imagine probably I am the most left wing" professor at SAIS

69 "faculty member with a soft spot for Cuba." One of the other prominent professors at SAIS during Ana's tenure was Bruce Bagley. He was an Assistant Professor of Comparative Politics and Latin American Studies and taught at least eight Latin American courses to Ana and her classmates. Bagley would go on to become "a noted expert on crime and corruption in Latin America, writing books on the topic and serving as a go-to person for journalists," the New York Times reported in late 2021. But at the same time, he "was himself involved in a bribery and corruption scheme in Venezuela." In the years after he left SAIS, federal prosecutors alleged, Bagley used bank accounts in his name to launder about $2.5 million, keeping about $200,000 for himself. The funds were "stolen from the citizens of Venezuela" and Bagley pleaded guilty in June 2020 to two counts of money laundering. He was sentenced to six months in prison. A financial fixer for Venezuelan president Nicolás Maduro also was involved in the scam, the Justice Department alleged

70 "Gwendolyn Myers was sentenced..." Public records show that Gwendolyn Myers died September 26, 2015. The Bureau of Prisons' Inmate Locator shows that she was released from prison on April 22, 2015

71 "Kendall Myers was sentenced to life..." The Bureau of Prisons' Inmate Locator shows that Myers is held at Supermax, also called Florence Admax US Prison, in Florence, CO

72 "Gleijeses is clearly sympathetic to Castro's policies..." Washington Post book review, March 31, 2002

73 "thought we were fascists..." In an article for WIRED Magazine in September 2022 titled "The Russian Spy in My Econ Class," Professor Roett was even more candid about Ana Montes. "I was told later her favorite phrase for me was FF, 'Fucking Fascist,' which I took as a point of honor," Roett said

74 "She went to parties..." True Believer

75 "finishing school for Roberto..." From public bios for Roberto Alvarez, from congressional testimony and the website of the government of the Dominican Republic

76 "for Roberto, there were other compensations..." In 2016, the author conducted an on-the-record interview with Roberto Alvarez Gil, who subsequently became the Minister of Foreign Affairs of the Dominican Republic

77 "named Minister of Foreign Affairs..." Website of the government of the Dominican Republic, and media reports

78 "FBI white paper…" FBI, "Cuban Intelligence Targeting of Academia," September 2, 2014

79 "In her graduation yearbook…" Yearbook quotes from an article in *El Nuevo Dia* newspaper, May 6, 2013

80 "made no secret of his support for the independence of Puerto Rico…" *Spy Schools.* The political leanings of Marta's father are confirmed in the *El Nuevo Dia* article from May 6, 2013

81 "protested Princeton's investments in the apartheid regime…" *Daily Princetonian* letter, April 14, 1978, edition. Letter to the Administration protesting Princeton's investments in companies doing business with South Africa

82 "Apartheid Kills!…" The photo of Velázquez at a protest may be seen in the *Princeton Alumni Weekly*, page 7 of the June 3, 1992, edition. The publication identifies Marta in the original photo from 1977 and cites, as its source, her classmate Nilsa Santiago. Santiago, who holds the sign in the photo, sent a note to the editor identifying Marta

83 "seeming disinterest" in minority students…" *Daily Princetonian*, December 1, 1977

84 "Independence and Socialism as the Only Political Alternative…" *Daily Princetonian*, March 29, 1977

85 *Daily Princetonian*, December 13, 1976

86 "senior thesis at Princeton…" Marta's senior thesis is available online through the Princeton Library's Special Collections. *Spy Schools* first reported on Marta's thesis

87 Ibid, page 23

88 "A University of Havana mathematics graduate…" *Miami Herald*, November 25, 2004, "Pain of Separation Never Fades"

89 "He wrote a white paper in Spanish…" Published by the Institute for Cuban & Cuban-American Studies (ICCAS), part of the School of International Studies at the University of Miami. January, 2002

90 "Using Cohen's insider tips…" FBI, "Cuban Intelligence Targeting of Academia," September 2, 2014

91 "Ana had already 'expressed her moral indignation'…" DOD Inspector General report

92   "Ana, I have friends who can help you..." The conversation from 1984 is inferred, based on the Justice Department's indictment of Marta dated February 6, 2004, and unsealed in April 2013

93   "They need someone to translate..." DOD Inspector General report

94   "the school had treated her unfairly..." CIA psychological report

95   "I hope our relationship continues..." Justice Department indictment of Marta Velázquez

96   "we've been over for a long time..." Letter from Ana Montes to friend Ana "Mimi" Colon, September 12, 1984

97   "Ana saw Roberto again..." Ibid

98   "six-year-old Elena Valdez fled Havana..." Author interview. "Elena" is a pseudonym chosen by the author to protect Elena's identity

99   "Cuba will not be allowed to earn hard currency..." John M. Walker, Assistant Secretary of the Treasury for Enforcement and Operations, as reported in the *New York Times* on April 20, 1982

100   "At a safe house, the Cubans handed Ana and Marta travel clothes..." Details of the trip to Madrid, Prague, and then Cuba come from the Marta Velázquez indictment, February 2004, and unsealed in 2013

101   "Just three years earlier, President Reagan..." In April 1982, President Reagan reinstated the travel ban to Cuba. In March 1982, he declared Cuba a state sponsor of terror. Council on Foreign Relations timeline

102   "they insisted on taking practice polygraphs..." DOJ indictment of Marta Velázquez

103   "The Castro regime has long targeted the United States..." Fact Sheet by the State Department's Bureau of Western Hemisphere Affairs, July 30, 2003

104   "at least eight plots involving the CIA to assassinate Castro..." CNN, "Assassination plots and schemes: Castro in the crosshairs," February 19, 2008

105   "The 702-page data dump, the CIA's so-called 'Family Jewels'..." In June 2007, the CIA declassified its 702-page "Family Jewels" report, chronicling the agency's many failed assassinations and other misdees. The non-profit National Security Archive also posted the CIA report to its website, under the title: "The CIA's Family Jewels: Agency Violated Charter for 25 Years, Wiretapped Journalists and Dissidents"

106 "She applied to the Office of Naval Intelligence…" *True Believer*

107 "I wanted something more palatable…" CIA behavioral report

108 "they even 'assisted her in preparing her application.'" DOD Inspector General report

109 "If you can get her, take her." *True Believer*

110 "After two interviews…" DOD Inspector General report

111 "The new agency proved its worth just a year later, during the Cuban Missile Crisis…" *Legacy of Ashes, Trial by Fire: The Origins of the Defense Intelligence Agency and the Cuban Missile Crisis Crucible,*" by Michael B. Petersen, DIA Historical Research Support Branch, 2011

112 "The Cold War was on its last gasps…" FBI website

113 "difference between a corporal and a colonel…" DOD Inspector General report

114 "suggested that Montes was disloyal to the United States…" DOD Inspector General report

115 "the FBI and local police arrested four men for drug trafficking…" *Miami Herald*, January 21, 1985

116 "William Sessions…" Letter from former FBI director Sessions to Lucy Montes, March 1988

117 "he had stored ten thousand pounds of marijuana…" *Mother Jones*, May 7, 2014, and the DOJ indictment of Tabraue

118 "one hundred years in prison…" Associated Press, April 13, 1989

119 "released on appeal in 2000…" *Sun Sentinel*, September 3, 2000

120 "Tabraue gained fame in Netflix's *Tiger King*…" *Deadline*, February 1, 2021

121 "She wasn't polygraphed or given psychological testing…" All details on Ana's background investigation and lack of a polygraph come from the DOD Inspector General report

122 "In reality, Ana had snorted cocaine…" DOD Inspector General report

123 "Her fiancé was Chris Mangiaracina…" Mangiaracina's artist website

124 "When you finish studying this book…" *Your Memory: How It Works & How to Improve It*, by Kenneth Higbee, 1988, Da Capo Press

125 "She presented her handlers once with a DIA phone book..." Author interview with one of her debriefers. In Ana's "proffer" to the Justice Department, she admits providing the Cubans with classified photographs and printed materials on October 3, 1996

126 "she would not leave a paper trail..." DOD Inspector General report

127 "Ana bought a book on memory techniques..." *Your Memory: How It Works & How to Improve It*

128 "high intelligence and positive attitude..." DOD Inspector General report

129 "congratulated Ana for her outstanding translating skills..." Ibid

130 "She was a phenomenal writer, extremely prolific..." Scheina as quoted in the DIA-produced documentary *The Two Faces of Ana Montes*

131 "Her reports were 'praised by policy makers'..." DOD Inspector General report

132 "Marta Velázquez has been traveling all over the world..." *Princeton Alumni Weekly*, September 14, 1988

133 "San Salvador is closer to Houston..." Speech by President Reagan, May 9, 1984

134 "In January and February 1987..." The DOD Inspector General report says Ana was in El Salvador and Guatemala in January and February 1987 for analyst orientation training

135 "They raced in with satchel charges..." *New York Times*, April 1, 1987

136 "He wanted that Green Beret..." *Philadelphia Inquirer*, April 2, 1987. "Death in El Salvador, Roots in Pennsylvania"

137 "he suspected that some of the guerrillas had 'infiltrated the army'..." *New York Times*, April 1, 1987

138 "An FMLN commander who helped attack El Paraiso..." *True Believer*

139 "a plaque celebrating her "exceptional area knowledge..." An award Ana received in December 1989 by the US Army Operational Group. See *True Believer* photo

140 "In order to defeat your enemy, you must first understand them..." Star Trek fan site quoting the episode "Face of the Enemy", from February 8, 1993

141 "There were 733 female FBI agents in 1987…" *Washington Post*, September 10, 1987, "At Revamped FBI, Morale Is High as Directorship Changes Hands"

142 "Director William Sessions announced…" *Arizona Republic*, October 1, 1988

143 "She got kudos from all over…" Quotes by Steve Smith and Marty Scheina come from the DIA documentary *The Two Faces of Ana Montes*

144 "Her unsuspecting superiors nominated her for the DIA Meritorious Civilian Service Award…" DOD Inspector General report. The mention of the medal Ana was given by the Cubans in 1989 comes from reporting and from the DOD Inspector General report

145 "the basis for her initial moral outrage…" DOD Inspector General report

146 "In February 1993, Ana was selected to run DIA's Cuba account…" DOD Inspector General report

147 "the United States might find a pretext to invade that island…" DOD Inspector General report

148 "validation, recognition, and control…" CIA behavioral report

149 "cipher the information every time you do…" FBI criminal complaint, September 2001

150 "Numbers messages were used extensively during the Second World War…" Cipher Machines & Cryptology white paper, "Cuban Agent Communications: Failure of a Perfect System," February 27, 2022, by Dirk Rijmenants

151 "There's "Swedish Rhapsody Child…" Cipher Machines & Cryptology white paper, "Numbers in the Air," by Dirk Rijmenants. In addition, for a brilliant article on the geeks who collect numbers broadcasts, read author David Segal's article in the *Washington Post* on August 3, 2004, titled "The Shortwave And the Calling." The subject of Segal's article created a bizarre collection of numbers broadcasts, called the Conet Project, which you can listen to on the SoundCloud music platform

152 "the cheat sheet for the numbers, that was all on water-soluble paper…" Author interview with FBI case agent Pete Lapp

153 "Ana passed a DIA-administered counterintelligence polygraph examination…" The March 1994 polygraph date is mentioned in *True Believer* and in the DIA documentary *The Two Faces of Ana Montes*

154 "she disclosed to the Cubans the true name of a covert US intelligence officer…" Ana's "proffer" to the Justice Department, in 2002, states that she provided the Cubans in May 1994 with the identity of a covert US intelligence officer. This happened two months after Ana's polygraph, in March 1994

155 "They understood my loneliness…" CIA report

156 "My workday typically consists of listening to recordings…" FBI website, November 18, 2005

157 "This spy ring was sent by the Cuban government…" *Miami Herald*, November 15, 1998

158 "Radio communications between the MiG-29 and the military control tower in Havana…" Transcripts of Cuban Military Radio Communications, International Civil Aviation Organization (ICAO), "Report on the shooting down of two U.S.-registered private civil aircraft by Cuban military aircraft on 24 February 1996, C WP/10441, June 20, 1996." The transcripts also appear in a report by the Inter-American Commission on Human Rights. The Clinton Administration first released the transcripts, as reported by the *New York Times* in 1996

159 "President Bill Clinton was already publicly fuming…" *New York Times*, February 25, 1996, "Exiles Say Cuba Downed 2 Planes And Clinton Expresses Outrage"

160 "According to the secondhand recollections of a coworker…" DOD Inspector General report

161 "He had heard that Ana had voiced her opposition to US policy…" DOD Inspector General report

162 "tasked the retired officers with finding ways that Washington and Havana could work together…" Ibid

163 "The DIA made it easy…" The author confirmed Ana's knowledge of the NRO program through interviews with multiple sources. The FBI criminal complaint of Ana describes her access to the classified "SAP" program but doesn't identify the US agency behind it. The complaint states: "DIA has confirmed that MONTES and a colleague with the same name as that related in the portion of the message described above were briefed into this SAP, together, on May 15, 1997." The DOD Inspector General report provides a bit more information on this SAP, and identifies the US agency behind it. It states: "In March 1997, DIA conducted a security review of Montes to support her nomination for indoctrina-

tion into a National Reconnaissance Office [phrase blacked out.] In May 1997, she was indoctrinated for [phrase blacked out.]" The DIA investigated Montes for two months and then, in May 1997, gave her access to a Special Access Program run by the NRO, the secret US satellite agency

164 "Ana once boasted to her Cuban bosses..." FBI criminal complaint of Montes

165 "the Washington Post reported that the latest generation of the MISTY satellite had almost doubled in projected cost..." *Washington Post*, December 11, 2004, by writer Dana Priest, "New Spy Satellite Debated On Hill"

166 "Because of the highly classified nature of the programs... I cannot talk about them on the floor..." Senate transcript, December 8, 2004

167 "the CIA determined that the Russians had already made it next to impossible to conceal American satellites..." April 17, 1963, CIA memo published by the National Security Archive. In the *Bulletin of the Atomic Scientists*, in May/June 2005, author Jeff Richelson explains that the author of the CIA document was James Cunningham, deputy director of the Office of Special Activities (OSA), a component of the CIA's Deputy Directorate of Research. Cunningham sent the memo, "A Covert Reconnaissance Satellite," to John Parangosky, his deputy for technology

168 "The NRO itself relies on concealment..." NRO website article on the agency's history

169 "the government didn't even acknowledge [NRO's] existence until 1992..." NRO public affairs office

170 "The 37,000-pound satellite, a pet project of the CIA and NSA..." *Aviation Week*, March 5, 1990, and January 22, 1990

171 "NASA's cost just to launch the shuttle was $115 million..." The government's cost per launch of the space shuttle was $115 million, according to the General Accounting Office (GAO) report *Military Space Programs: An Unclassified Overview of Defense Satellite Programs and Launch Activities*, published June 1990. Provided to the author by the National Security Archive

172 "The patent, for an inflatable shield..." National Security Archive, the invaluable library and archive of declassified US documents. See the US Patent application, dated September 6, 1994, for a "Satellite signature suppression shield"

173 "Amateur satellite spotters around the world are obsessed with finding spy satellites..." www.heavens-above.com website

174 "we would prefer that these things not end up on the internet…"
     WIRED Magazine, "I Spy," February 1, 2006

175 "The Soviet news agency Novosti wrote…" *Bulletin of the Atomic Scientists*, May/June 2005

176 "she had to sign a 'Sensitive Compartmented Information Nondisclosure Agreement…'" FBI's Ana Montes criminal complaint

177 "Ana was granted access to additional Special Access Programs…"
     DOD Inspector General report

178 "public records easily showed was occupied by an FBI surveillance specialist…" In March 2008, for the MSNBC blog called *Deep Background*, the author revealed that the Spy House was occupied by an FBI employee. "How do I know it's an FBI facility? A simple web search confirmed it. From my desk, I plugged the house's street address into a commercial database that NBC and many media organizations use—legally, of course—to conduct public-records searches. In about 30 seconds, and for just about $2 in fees, I learned the names of three probable residents of the house. One of the residents had helpfully provided his employer's name. There it was in black and white: 'Company: FBI.' But that's not all. Under the job-title section, this same FBI employee is described as 'Clerk Really a Spy.'" The blog is available now on the Wayback Machine internet archive

179 "the US government had constructed a secret tunnel underneath the Russian Embassy…" *New York Times*, March 4, 2001, by James Risen with Lowell Bergman, "U.S. Thinks Agent Revealed Tunnel at Soviet Embassy"

180 "mailed an unsigned letter to a DC-based KGB agent…" Robert Hanssen criminal proffer, March 1, 2001.

181 "Moscow executed…" Robert Hanssen criminal complaint, 2001

182 "Ms. Montes's strong sense of Intelligence Community responsibility…" DOD Inspector General report

183 "'*Spies Among Us*,' the Miami Herald splashed across its front page…"
     Miami Herald, September 15, 1998

184 Citation from CIA director George Tenet is from the private collection of Lucy Montes, and dated December 2, 1999

185 "fills fourteen hundred pages…" *The Guardian*, March 6, 2001

186 "She used a handwritten cipher, like a checkerboard…" FBI evidence,

and "Cuban Agent Communications: Failure of a Perfect System," by Dirk Rijmenants

187 "I was finally ready to share my life with someone but was leading a double life..." CIA behavioral report

188 "I eschew drugs..." *Psychology Today*, listing for Dr. Joseph Tarantolo

189 "We are a drug driven culture..." Email to the author, August 12, 2022

190 "he was loud, bullying, implied that I had been drugged my entire life..." ZocDoc online review

191 "She took an antidepressant for nine months..." CIA behavioral report

192 "The unclassified executive summary states that Cuba 'does not pose a significant military threat'..." "The Cuban Threat to U.S. National Security." The summary states: "This report has been prepared by the Defense Intelligence Agency in coordination with the Central Intelligence Agency, the Department of State Bureau of Intelligence and Research, the National Security Agency, and the United States Southern Command Joint Intelligence Center pursuant to Section 1228 of Public Law No. 105-85, 111 Stat. 1943-44, November 18, 1997." A version may be found online on the website of the Federation of American Scientists, irp.fas.org

193 "There is no doubt that Cuba poses a significant, dangerous, and hostile intelligence threat..." Army Lieutenant Colonel Joseph C. Myers, as told to journalist Bill Gertz in *Enemies: How America's Foes Steal Our Vital Secrets—And How We Let It Happen*, Crown Forum, 2006

194 "I remain concerned about Cuba's potential to develop and produce biological agents..." Website of the Federation of American Scientists. Archived Department of Defense news release, May 6, 1998, "Secretary Cohen Forwards Cuban Threat Assessment to Congress"

195 "Bolton has called Fulton Armstrong an 'apologist for Cuba'..." John Bolton's 2007 book, *Surrender Is Not an Option*, Threshold Editions

196 "I am proud to have you on my team..." This is a direct quote from the EIP letter that DIA director Patrick M. Hughes wrote to promotion recipient Anthony Shaffer in May 1998, one year before Ana won the same GG-14 level promotion from the same DIA director. The award may be found in congressional testimony from February 14, 2006, titled "National Security Whistleblowers in the Post-September 11th Era"

197 "I would describe Ana Montes as socially reserved..." Ana's former

colleague, Steve Smith, was interviewed for the DIA-produced documentary and training tool *The Two Faces of Ana Montes*

198 "I had her on a pedestal..." Lourdes Talbot interview with the author, September 24, 2009

199 "She was very protective of her personal life..." Ana's former colleague Lourdes Talbot was also interviewed for the documentary *The Two Faces of Ana Montes*

200 "I probably knew less about Ana..." *The Two Faces of Ana Montes*

201 "NSA first briefed the FBI on a promising Cuban UNSUB case in 1998..." The author established the date of the beginning of the FBI UNSUB case through multiple interviews with sources. In addition, the DOD Inspector General report states that the FBI and other agencies "met to discuss the unknown subject" as least as early as April 1998. The same report adds: "From 1998 to 2001, the U.S. Government continued its search for the Cuban penetration agent of the Intelligence Community. The period opens with the Intelligence Community using the profile information in its attempt to identify the Cuban penetration agent and closes with the arrest and imprisonment of Ana Montes as a Cuban spy"

202 "From 1947 to 1979, only 5 percent of all American spies caught in the US were women..." *The Expanding Spectrum of Espionage by Americans, 1947–2015*, by the Defense Personnel and Security Research Center, August 2017

203 Ibid

204 "This effort did not develop any leads..." DOD Inspector General report

205 "As everyone has said, her personality was cold..." Roger Corneretto provided written email answers to questions from the author, as part of a story the author wrote for the *Washington Post Magazine* in April 2013

206 "her supervisors handed her a $2,000 performance bonus..." *True Believer*

207 "We need your logic, expertise and ingenuity to protect the Nation..." DIA Counterintelligence recruitment brochure, 2022

208 DOD Inspector General report, page 102

209 "The dispute reflects the sore feelings that remain to this day between the FBI and DIA..." In the DOD Inspector General report, there's more evidence of the clash between the DIA and FBI. In the DIA's administrative comments on the case, it reports: "The same day that

DIA special agents learned the basic information the FBI was using to search for the unknown Cuban spy, DIA special agents identified Montes and contacted the FBI squad handling the case. The FBI summarily rejected Montes as a suspect and had to be convinced otherwise"

210 "Krzemien thanked Carmichael for his time but threw her support behind McCoy..." From reporting. Former FBI supervisor Diane Krzemien did not respond to emailed requests for comment

211 "William Doherty, the chief of the FBI's counterintelligence section..." William Doherty was identified as "the FBI's chief for counterintelligence" in a *Miami Herald* article on the Wasp Network arrests, on September 16, 1998, titled: "Alleged Spies Damage Limited." The author conducted a short interview with Doherty in July 2022, confirming his title and that he "crossed paths" with Montes prior to her becoming a suspect in the case. Doherty is retired from the FBI

212 "A young mother with a baby in a stroller..." *Spy: The Inside Story of How the FBI's Robert Hanssen Betrayed America*, by David Wise, Random House, 2002

213 "Montes left her residence and drove to the Hecht's..." Ana Montes criminal complaint, 2001

214 "The FBI began providing twice monthly briefings to the DIA director..." DOD Inspector General report

215 "They just thought of Bob as the 'The Mortician'..." Details about Hanssen's job history may be found in the Justice Department Inspector General's report on the FBI's handling of the Hanssen case. The nickname "The Mortician" comes from David Vise's book, *The Bureau and the Mole*, Grove Press, 2002; and from David Wise's *Spy*

216 "For a Russia expert who had been an FBI agent for nearly a quarter century..." Additional details about Hanssen's job at the State Department's Office of Foreign Missions come from David Wise's excellent *Spy*. Wise, who passed away in 2018, was an unparalleled expert on espionage. *Spy* is a deeply researched book that benefits from the exclusive access that Wise was given to Hanssen's psychiatrist, Dr. David Charney, who spent days interviewing the fallen FBI agent in prison

217 "The FBI censured Hanssen..." The Justice Department Inspector General's report on Hanssen

218 "Giving up on me is a mistake..." *Spy*

219 "We went back and listened to the tape again…" *Spy*

220 "Roger flew to Washington to be with Ana…" Source for Roger's travels: *True Believer*. In a 2022 interview, Roger said that he never traveled extensively with Ana, and he denied arguing with her over Christmas in 2000.

221 "the Justice Department submitted 1,005 applications to the Foreign Intelligence Surveillance Court…" Justice Department FISA report for 2001

222 "The FBI had solved the main mystery of the Blue Wren investigation…" The FBI codenamed the case "Blue Wren" without ascribing any particular meaning to the poetic, yet randomly generated phrase

223 "We feel humble, and we feel extremely proud…" *Sun Sentinel*, July 13, 2001, "FBI, Prosecutors Honored for Spy Case"

224 "On August 7, twenty unsuspecting DIA analysts got on a plane…" Reporting and *True Believer*

225 "Tucked inside Ana's wallet were the pre-paid calling cards…" Reporting and the FBI's criminal complaint of Montes

226 "As no other event in U.S. history, not even Pearl Harbor…" Details on the Pentagon attack on September 11, 2001, come from a thorough report by the Historical Office of the Office of the Secretary of Defense, dated 2007

227 "The ninety-ton airliner deliberately accelerated to 530 miles per hour…" Ibid

228 "Christine Morrison was working with about seventy of her colleagues…" Ibid

229 "The next few weeks became the most diversely challenging period of my 34-year Navy career…" Admiral Wilson's article appeared in a publication of the *Naval Intelligence Professionals*, Volume II, Number 2, Winter 2021

230 "They were acts of war…" White House archives, speech by President Bush, September 12, 2001

231 "Why would she say such a thing at that moment?…" Emilia Montes letter, February 2017

232 "I could see the Pentagon burning from my office… Dark days ahead…" The email from Ana to her friend and college roommate,

Lisa Huber, is quoted in a *Washington Post* article, "An Improbable Spy," from October 4, 2001

233 "By the zoo's pedestrian entrance on Connecticut Avenue..." After her arrest, Montes told the FBI that she had heard them over their radios on Sunday, September 16, saying something like, "She's about to make a call." If she did overhear the FBI's SSG unit as they tailed her into the Metro, it's hard to understand why she didn't flee

234 "Ana got an instant promotion to branch chief..." Reporting and *True Believer*

235 "an angry twenty-three-page essay written in 1971 by a Harvard-educated loner..." Flynn's connection to the Unabomber case was reported by the *New York Times* on May 5, 1998, in an article titled, "FBI's 17-Year Search for Unabomber Often Seemed in Vain," and confirmed by Flynn and reported on in other media outlets

236 "I started reading it, and all of a sudden, it was 'Bing! bing! bing!...'" SFGate, May 5, 1998, "New Details Of Stakeout In Montana"

237 "Ana Montes was arrested by the FBI..." *True Believer*

238 "Ana's arrest was something that was very devastating..." *The Two Faces of Ana Montes*

239 "Ana didn't claim she was being framed..." Roger Corneretto email to author, January 2013

240 "Ana was facing a possible death sentence..." In a letter from federal prosecutors to lawyer Plato Cacheris dated February 14, 2002, the government made clear that conspiracy to commit espionage can be "punishable by death"

241 "I like the battle against the government..." Plato Cacheris obituary, *Washington Post*, September 26, 2019

242 "I don't lecture them on what they've done..." Ibid

243 "It would enable Cuba to drop its defensive measures..." Ana's statement to the court, at sentencing, comes from a verbatim transcript the author obtained from the court in 2022

244 "he rejected Ana's sugarcoated rationalizations..." DOJ Memorandum in Aid of Sentencing, filed October 10, 2002

245 "the judge had overcome hardscrabble beginnings in a Spanish Har-

lem four-story walk-up…" The background on Judge Ricardo Urbina is from an interview he conducted in 2013 with the Columbia Center for Oral History

246   "Felipe Pérez Roque, then Cuba's Minister of Foreign Affairs, wrote on a government website…" *The Miami Herald*, October 19, 2002, "Cuban Praises Jailed Spy," by the Associated Press

247   "1950s promotional travel film, 'Picturesque Sweden'…" YouTube

248   "her $96,000-a-year US government job…" The author filed a Freedom of Information Act request with USAID, which provided information of Marta's salary ($96,605/year) at the time she quit her AID job, plus a detailed breakdown of her US government postings in DC and abroad in the thirteen years she worked for the agency

249   "Marta became a Swedish citizen…" *Spy Schools*

250   "The family said they could not find her…" *Spy Schools*, quote by Roberto Aponte Toro, former professor, University of Puerto Rico School of Law, and family friend

251   "Anders Kviele, a diplomat at the Swedish Embassy in Nicaragua…" In an email from the Swedish Foreign Ministry, it lists Kviele as the "2nd Embassy Secretary" in Managua, starting in 1989. A news article from that era lists him as the embassy's "chargé d'affaires," filling in for the ambassador briefly

252   "Velázquez and Kviele fell in love in Managua and married in 1996…" *Spy Schools*

253   "Marta moved from Managua to Washington…" USAID employment records for Marta show her detailed to "GC/ANE," the General Counsel's Office for the Asia Near East Bureau, from October 1994 to May 1998

254   "She supervised lawyers in DC and abroad…" *Spy Schools*; her promotion also was listed in the *Front Lines* USAID employee newsletter, page 11, in March 1997

255   "With the help of a Swedish investigative journalist…" Note: Author Daniel Golden has an excellent section on Marta Velázquez in *Spy Schools*, published in 2017. Golden was the first American reporter to track down Marta's home outside Stockholm and report on her teaching career; she refused his emailed interview requests. Golden and his Swedish researcher never got the opportunity to confront Marta in person

256 "The couple bought their yellow two-story home…" Swedish prop-
     erty records show that Marta and Anders bought their home in 2013
     for 4,550,000 Swedish Krona, or about $432,000 US

257 "In 2009, she even worked for the British Council…" Marta's teach-
     ing career is outlined in her résumé, provided to the author by local
     government officials in Sweden

258 "The population of the Administrative Housing Unit includes inmates
     on death row…" District of Columbia Corrections Information Coun-
     cil report on FMC Carswell, July 6, 2018

259 "a SuperMax for 'female inmates with histories of escapes'…" Carswell
     prison's Psychology Internship description, July 2017

260 "five to seven years behind bars…" Ibid

261 "Carswell has been the recurring subject of disturbing allegations…"
     Star Telegram, "Ex-correctional officer pleads guilty to sexually abus-
     ing women at Fort Worth prison," May 18, 2022

262 "In a 2022 Prison Rape Elimination Act audit…" Bureau of Prisons
     "Prison Rape Elimination Act (PREA) Audit Report," April 6, 2022

263 "eight inmates have died of COVID at Carswell…" *Star Telegram*,
     "Woman's death from COVID-19 at Fort Worth prison sparks fear of
     virus resurgence," October 5, 2021

264 "She was placed in quarantine…" *Star Telegram*, "Fort Worth prison re-
     sponsible for new mother's COVID death, family says in $20M claim,"
     March 22, 2022

265 "house of horror…" *Star Telegram*, "Women at 'house of horror' Fort Worth
     prison say they face COVID, rotten food, abuse," September 3, 2020

266 "Accusations of gross medical neglect, rape by prison guards…" *Fort
     Worth Weekly*, "Hospital of Horrors," October 19, 2005

267 "The unit is frequently and unpredictably locked down for hours…"
     Campaign to Close Carswell website

268 "I act like I'm neutral like Sweden or a rock in the corner…" Note:
     In Spanish, Ana writes that she acts like "el sueco," or a neutral party
     much like Sweden

269 "Her lawyers argued at trial that she was mentally ill…" Associated
     Press, "A closer look at the case of Aafia Siddiqui, jailed in Texas," Jan-

uary 15, 2022; and *New York Times*, "Pakistani Sentenced to 86 Years for Attack," September 23, 2010

270 "a 'shell of a human being'..." CBS News, "Killer Nurse Gets Life," March 26, 2001; and *Boston Globe*, "Caregiver or killer?", October 8, 2000

271 "Ana's only prison friend was fifty two years old..." *New York Times*, "U.S. Executes Lisa Montgomery for 2004 Murder," January 13, 2021

272 "Ana Belén, you were misguided..." Letter from Emilia to Ana, March 26, 2002, days after Ana pleaded guilty

273 "I am a person who is extremely rigid..." Ana Montes letter to friend Mimi Colon, August 29, 2013

274 "But mostly the letter is a disjointed justification of Ana's criminality..." Ana Montes letter to her nephew Matthew, February 24, 2010

275 "She mocked the *Washington Post Magazine* cover story I wrote about her..." *Washington Post Magazine*, April 18, 2013, "A Most Dangerous Spy"

276 Backiel has written a half dozen pieces for *Monthly Review*, which describes itself as "An Independent Socialist Magazine."https://monthlyreview.org/author/lindabackiel/

277 *New York Times*, Letter to the Editor by Linda Backiel, Oct. 27, 2014. https://www.nytimes.com/2014/10/31/opinion/mending-us-relations-with-cuba.html?searchResultPosition=5

278 Backiel wrote "An Analysis of the Case of the Cuban Five" for the National Committee to Free the Cuban Five, in 2003. http://www.freethefive.org/legalFront/LFAnalysis2003.htm

279 A *New York Times* article from March 18, 1984, states that Backiel is "representing Kathy Boudin." https://www.nytimes.com/1984/03/18/nyregion/reporter-s-notebook-jurors-take-stand.html

280 *Law and Disorder Radio* transcript, September 2014. https://lawanddisorder.org/wp-content/uploads/CJAtalk-final-w-trans.pdf

281 *New York Times,* Feb. 15, 1991. https://www.nytimes.com/1991/02/15/us/defense-lawyer-is-jailed-over-client-confidentiality.html?searchResultPosition=4

282 Miriam Montes Mock, Ana Montes's cousin, shared a thank-you letter from Ana on Facebook. https://www.facebook.com/groups/1323209251182586/search/?q=belen

INDEX